How to write Dissertations & Project Reports

Kathleen McMillan and
Jonathan Weyers

Prentice Hall
is an imprint of

Harlow, England • London • New York • Boston • San Francisco • Toronto
Sydney • Tokyo • Singapore • Hong Kong • Seoul • Taipei • New Delhi
Cape Town • Madrid • Mexico City • Amsterdam • Munich • Paris • Milan

Pearson Education Limited
Edinburgh Gate
Harlow
Essex CM20 2JE
England

and Associated Companies throughout the world

Visit us on the World Wide Web at:
www.pearsoned.co.uk

First published 2007
Rejacketed edition published 2010

ISBN: 978-0-273-72693-7

British Library Cataloguing-in-Publication Data
A catalogue record for this book is available from the British Library

10 9 8 7 6 5 4 3 2 1
13 12 11 10 09

Typeset in 9.5/13pt Interstate by 35
Printed and bound in Great Britain by Ashford Colour Press Ltd., Gosport

The Publisher's policy is to use paper manufactured from sustainable forests.

Smarter Study Guides

Instant answers to your most pressing university skills problems.

Are there any secrets to successful study?

The simple answer is no - but there are some essential skills, tips and techniques that can help you to improve your performance and success in all areas of your university studies.

These handy, easy-to-use guides to the most common areas where most students need help (even if you don't realise it!) provide accessible, straightforward practical tips and instant solutions that provide you with the tools and techniques that will enable you to improve your performance and get better results - and better grades.

Each book in the series allows you to assess and address a particular set of skills and strategies, in crucial areas such as exam preparation and performance, researching and writing dissertations and research projects, and planning and crafting academic essays. Each book then delivers practical no-nonsense tips, techniques and strategies that will enable you to significantly improve your abilities and performance in time to make a difference.

The books in the series are

- *How to succeed in Exams and Assessments*
- *How to write Essays and Assignments*
- *How to write Dissertations and Project Reports*

Or for a complete handbook covering all of the study skills that you will need throughout your years at university:

- *The Smarter Student: Study Skills and Strategies for Success at University*

Get smart, get a head start!

The Smarter Student series is available at all good bookshops or online at **www.pearson-books.co.uk/studyskills**.

Contents

Preface and acknowledgements ix
How to use this book xi

Introduction

1 **Tackling a dissertation or project report** - how to make the best possible start 3

2 **Choosing a dissertation or research topic** - how to decide on a theme for your investigation 10

Planning your research

3 **Writing a proposal** - how to structure a successful dissertation or research proposal 21

4 **Time management** - how to write your dissertation or project while balancing family, work and leisure 29

5 **Planning for dissertations** - how to begin your research and evolve a model for your writing 40

6 **Planning for experimental projects** - how to organise your efforts effectively 51

Finding and filtering information

7 **Information literacy** - how to make best use of the library resources 61

8 **Effective academic reading** - how to read efficiently and with understanding 71

9 **Analysing and evaluating source material** - how to filter and select relevant material as part of the research process 85

10 **Note-making from source material** - how to create effective notes to support your dissertation and project research 94

Applying research techniques

11 **Principles of quantitative research** - how to obtain and analyse numerical information 109

12 **Principles of qualitative research** - how to obtain and analyse descriptive information 123

13 **Experimental research and field visits** - how to develop and apply your skills 135

14 **Thinking critically** - how to develop a logical approach to analysis and problem-solving 143

Working with data and numbers

15 **Number crunching** - how to solve problems in arithmetic and algebra 157

16 **Interpreting and presenting data** - how to understand and produce graphs, tables and basic statistics 170

Addressing issues of plagiarism, referencing and ethics

17 **Plagiarism and copyright infringement** - how to avoid being accused of 'stealing' the ideas and work of others 185

18 **Citing and listing references** - how to refer appropriately to the work of others 194

19 **Ethics in researching and reporting** - how to follow good research practice 211

Writing a first draft

20 **Structuring a dissertation** - how to organise your writing within a standard framework 221

21 **Structuring a project report** - how to select and shape your content appropriately 227

22 **Academic writing style** - how to adopt the appropriate language conventions 235

Editing, revising and presenting

23 **Reviewing, editing and proof-reading** - how to make sure your writing is concise and correct 249

24 **Exploiting feedback** - how to understand and learn from what your supervisor writes on your work 258

25 **Presentation of dissertations and reports** - how to follow the appropriate academic conventions 264

References and further reading 277
Glossary 278

Preface and acknowledgements

Welcome to *How to Write Dissertations and Project Reports*. We're pleased to you have chosen this book and hope it will help you compose and present high-quality work that reveals your academic skills in the best possible light. Our aim has been to provide practical tips to guide you from planning to submission, so that your work is well developed and meets academic requirements. We've tried to remain faithful to the philosophy of our earlier book, *The Smarter Student*, by creating a quickly accessible resource that you can dip into in time of need. We had many kinds of students in mind when we decided to write this text and we hope that it will meet your personal needs - regardless of your experience and background.

We would like to offer sincere thanks to many people who have influenced us and contributed to the development and production of this book. Countless students over the years have helped us to test our ideas, especially those whose writing we have supervised or guided. We are grateful to following colleagues and collaborators who have helped us directly or indirectly: Margaret Adamson, John Berridge, Margaret Forrest, Alan Grant, Neale Laker, Fiona O'Donnell, Neil Paterson and Anne Scott. Also, we acknowledge those at other universities who have helped frame our thoughts, particularly our good friends Rob Reed, Nicki Hedge and Esther Daborn. We owe a special debt to the senior colleagues who encouraged various projects that contributed to this book, and who allowed us the freedom to pursue this avenue of scholarship, especially Robin Adamson, Ian Francis, Rod Herbert and David Swinfen. At Pearson Education, we have had excellent advice and support from Steve Temblett, Georgina Clark-Mazo and Joan Dale Lace. Finally, we would like to say thanks to our long-suffering but nevertheless enthusiastic families: Derek, Keith and Fiona; and Mary, Paul and James, all of whom helped in various capacities.

We'd be delighted to hear your opinion of the book and receive any suggestions you have for additions and improvements.

Kathleen McMillan and Jonathan Weyers
University of Dundee
April 2007

How to use this book

How to Write Dissertations and Project Reports has been organised and designed to be as user-friendly as possible. Each chapter is self-contained and deals with a particular aspect of planning, researching and writing. You can therefore read the book through from end to end, or in sections, or dip into specific chapters as and when you think you need them.

At the start of each chapter you'll find a brief paragraph and a **Key topics** list, which lets you know what's included. There is also a list of *Key terms* at this point, and, should you be uncertain about the meaning of any of these, you will find definitions in the glossary (pp. 278–86).

Within each chapter, the text is laid out to help you absorb the key concepts easily, using headings and bulleted lists to help you find what you need as efficiently as possible. Relevant examples are contained in figures, tables and boxes, which can be consulted independently, if necessary. The inset boxes are of three types:

Smart tip boxes emphasise key advice to ensure you adopt a successful approach.

Information boxes provide additional information, such as useful definitions or examples.

Query boxes raise questions for you to consider about your personal approach to the topic.

At the end of each chapter, there's a **Practical tips** section with additional tips. You should regard this as a menu from which to select the ideas that appeal to you and your learning personality.

Finally, the **And now** box provides three suggestions that you could consider as ideas to take further.

Introduction

1 Tackling a dissertation or project report

How to make the best possible start

Dissertations and project reports are extensive exercises in writing and they usually contribute significantly to module and degree classification grades. It makes sense, therefore, to tackle them professionally and with energy. This chapter offers strategies that will help you to start off well and achieve your full potential.

Key topics:

→ Starting off well
→ Making sure you work efficiently and effectively
→ Avoiding the common pitfalls

Key terms

Effectiveness Efficiency Learning objective Learning outcome Perfectionism

Looking proudly at the finished version of your dissertation or project report will probably be one of the highlights of your undergraduate academic career. In most cases, its production will be the result of many months of serious work. The final document will represent the pinnacle of your achievements at university and provide concrete evidence of your advanced academic skills in your discipline.

In carrying out the necessary research, thinking, writing and presentation, you will be delving deep into the subject material of your chosen discipline and stretching yourself in the production of a piece of original work. In some cases, the skills involved may be very closely allied to those you will use in the workplace: employers will be interested in seeing your work because it represents your full potential in the working environment. Your university tutors will demonstrate the perceived importance of dissertations and reports by allocating a high proportion of marks from them towards your final grade.

These are all good reasons for trying to produce the best possible product and, to do well, you will need to be focussed from the start and disciplined in your effort.

Taking account of the task you have been set

While there are many similarities in the production of dissertations and project reports, there are also some key differences. Throughout this book, we have tried to provide generic material wherever possible, but have also written chapters and sections that focus on tasks and outcomes relevant to specific types of document. You should select the material of relevance both to your personal needs and the approach required in your discipline.

→ Starting off well

In this chapter, the emphasis is on starting as you mean to go on, and establishing good working habits. Many students drift aimlessly at the start of their project or research-based studies, so one of the most important things you can do is to become focussed on the task right from the beginning. To ensure this happens you should:

- **Make sure you understand precisely what you are being asked to produce, and how.** You can do this by reading the supporting material in the course handbook or regulations (particularly the learning objectives or outcomes), or by speaking to your supervisor or a potential supervisor.
- **Try to make the initial connection with your research or source material.** Sometimes this will appear bewildering in its breadth, obscure in its jargon or genuinely difficult to master. The only way you will overcome this is to immerse yourself in the topic, read background material and ask questions. The sooner you take this step, the better.
- **Try not to luxuriate in the comfort of having a deadline many months away.** Graduates will tell you that every part of the process took longer than they estimated, and that, if they had to do it all again, they would try to organise themselves better.

The time will quickly evaporate, and the earlier you start the more likely you will be to avoid stress near to the end. Details of the component elements of any extensive writing task, and advice for good timetabling and project management, are provided in **Ch 4** and **Ch 6**.

- **Do something active.** Appropriate actions will depend on your subject, but will probably include taking notes of your background reading, or creating a plan of action or timetable. In some research projects it will involve making initial observations or setting up a pilot experiment; in others getting your hands on the right textbooks and references.

How motivated are you?

Getting started and maintaining momentum depend on your motivation to succeed. It may be assumed by friends, family and tutors that you are highly motivated. If this is indeed true, use this feeling to energise your start to work, and tap into your motivation whenever things get difficult. If you feel that you lack motivation, you should speak to someone about this: some supervisors are excellent at motivating students; staff in support services such as counselling and the careers service will also be able to help. Sometimes all it takes to rekindle an interest in a subject is to immerse yourself in it. Recognise this fact and use it to push yourself over any initial barriers.

Starting off well also means understanding what constitutes good working practice and avoiding common pitfalls. There follows a quick summary of these aspects, as they apply to the research and writing phases of your dissertation or project.

→ Making sure you work efficiently and effectively

Efficient working means using your time well. If you can do this, it will mean you have more time available for thinking and relaxing, creating a virtuous cycle that will result in a better end product. The keys to working efficiently are:

- thinking and planning ahead for each day or part of a day;
- understanding what you are trying to achieve during each day or part of a day;
- getting down to work as quickly as possible;
- prioritising tasks appropriately;
- avoiding distractions;
- keeping your papers and workplace well organised; and
- taking breaks when you need to rest.

smart tip

Efficient working in a nutshell

This involves means cutting out wasteful or unproductive effort, and focussing on using your time to maximise productivity.

Effective working is effort that results in meaningful results. It involves having a continual focus on the end product and making sure that for each subsidiary task undertaken you keep this in mind. The keys to working effectively are:

- getting started;
- focussing on the end product;
- minimising unproductive work;
- identifying things that are barriers to progress;
- finding ways to overcome obstacles to progress; and
- making sure you complete each component, even if this means some loss of quality.

Effective working in a nutshell

This involves smart working, rather than putting in extra effort. This means identifying **SMART** goals, that is, those that are:

Specific (What am I aiming to achieve in this work episode?)

Measurable (What milestones can I set myself for this period?)

Attainable (What can I achieve in the time available?)

Realistic (Have I created a goal that is achievable?)

Tangible (Will I be able to see the progress I'm making?)

→ Avoiding the common pitfalls

Your dissertation or project report will probably be the most extensive piece of writing you will have to complete on your course. In addition, it will require and test some demanding skills, in relation to both research and presentation. Because of this, you should be aware of potential risks, so that you can take steps to avoid them:

- ❑ you may underestimate the time it takes to carry out the research;
- ❑ your initial reading may be aimless;
- ❑ your writing skills may be rusty;
- ❑ you will need to organise large amounts of information;
- ❑ you will need to keep records of research sources so you can cite them properly;
- ❑ you may need to carry out advanced forms of data analysis;
- ❑ you may need to adopt a professional approach to data presentation;
- ❑ you may underestimate the time it takes to write, or suffer from writer's block;
- ❑ you will need to be aware of copyright infringement and plagiarism; and employ strategies to avoid them;
- ❑ you may need to allow time for your supervisor to provide feedback;
- ❑ you may need to allow time to take your supervisor's feedback into account; or
- ❑ for longer pieces of work, you will need to allow time for your dissertation or report to be typed, or, if you need this service, for graphics to be produced or printed, and for binding, if this is required by your department.

Suggestions on how to avoid most of the common problem areas are provided in subsequent chapters.

smart tip

Try not to be a perfectionist

Many projects never get started, stall or fail to be completed because the people involved are aiming for perfection, when this is either impossible or impractical. Often, achieving perfection would be a waste of resources. If you identify this as a potential characteristic in yourself, try to accept that fact, and focus on minimising the larger flaws in your work and on completing the task despite any minor faults you believe are present.

Practical tips for starting your dissertation or report

Engage with the subject as soon as possible. Read a basic text to gain background; create a personal glossary of specialist terms; ask questions of your supervisor or tutors; find out about current research in your area; explore online databases to begin your literature search.

Allocate a substantial period of time to carry out initial reading around your subject. Try to distance yourself from distractions and make sure you take notes as you go. Keep a meticulous record of all material you consult because you will need this for citations in your text and for compiling your reference list.

Clear the decks. Finish other tasks that are outstanding; tidy your work area; make it clear to others that you may not be available for socialising as frequently as before; make sure you have a good stock of all your stationery and other study requirements.

Start writing. Note-making is a form of writing that ensures that your reading has a purpose. Research into academic writing has shown that the act of writing is part of the thinking process, so creating isolated paragraphs on the basis of what you have read or on what you think about what you have read can help you to clarify your thoughts. These short pieces of writing can form the basis for further development once you have undertaken further reading and may fit within a structure that is decided later. However, even if you are unable to use what you have written, as an exercise it will probably have contributed to your understanding of your topic, so the effort will not have been wasted. There is the added advantage of providing you with the opportunity to find your own writing 'voice', that is, where you position yourself in relation to the topic, and this signals your development as an academic author.

Work through writer's block. Some days go well; some just do not. Accept that this is simply part of the process - a feature of the human condition. As an academic author, you'll find that sometimes the words will flow almost effortlessly. At other times, every paragraph, sentence or even word is a struggle. That's all part of the thinking process and will eventually contribute to a fresh stream of high-quality writing.

Make sure that you are keeping on track. Review each day as it passes. Ask yourself:

- What have I achieved?
- What went well?
- What could have gone better?
- Am I keeping up with my timetable?
- What do I need to do next?
- What do I need to do to ensure the next session is better?

GO And now . . .

1.1 Reflect on your experience in writing of a similar nature. What limited your progress and ability to start and to complete the task? Were these factors under your control or the outcome of other influences? What were the good and bad aspects of your work or study practices? What aspects of your approach would you change? Try to continue good practice and reduce or eliminate poor approaches.

1.2 Make lists. There are two important lists: those things you need to do before you can start properly and those things that can safely be put to one side to tackle once the project is finished. Focus all your efforts on making sure that the preliminary tasks are achieved and be self-disciplined about not undertaking the post-project tasks as a displacement activity that distracts you from working on the project.

1.3 Make an appointment to meet with your allocated supervisor or a potential supervisor. Discuss what might be achievable goals for your work, and what might be profitable avenues to pursue. You might also want to consider, with your supervisor, the order in which you should do things and also ask for guidance about the first directions.

2 Choosing a dissertation or research topic

How to decide on a theme for your investigation

The correct choice of dissertation topic or research project will improve the chances of a successful outcome. This chapter outlines the issues that you need to think about as you weigh up the possibilities.

Key topics:

→ Taking account of the options open to you
→ Deciding on your personal interests
→ Other factors to take into account

Key terms

Action research Dissertation Qualitative research Quantitative research Supervisor

The topic you choose to research has a great influence on how well you succeed in carrying out the investigation and in writing up your work. A crucial factor is whether you have a genuine interest in the subject matter, as this will motivate you to complete the task to the best possible standard. In addition, many practical matters need to be taken into account, such as the availability of relevant resources, or the feasibility of the intended investigation.

→ Taking account of the options open to you

In many cases, you may find that the dissertation or project topics are prescribed or restricted. The decision is not so much one of what you would like to research, but more which topic you will choose from a list of options provided by academic staff. A variation on this closed option list is the semi-closed list, where academics provide a list of broad topics but leave the student to choose the detailed perspective that they wish to pursue.

Constraints such as these may feel restrictive, especially at first when you do not know the details of the topics outlined. However, they are generally designed to provide you with a degree of freedom within parameters controlled by those who will need to supervise and assess the finished work, and who will have carefully considered the practicalities of each option and the chances of obtaining a successful outcome.

Your own topic

If you have a specific topic in mind that is not on a prescribed list of dissertation or research project options, you could try approaching a potential supervisor and asking whether it might be considered. If you do this, be prepared to answer searching questions about its viability as a research theme.

A less restricted approach to the selection of dissertation topic or research project is also found. In this case, no list is provided and you are asked to choose not only the topic but the specific research question to be addressed. In this open-choice case, you will be expected to make a selection largely on the basis of your personal interests within the discipline. These might have developed from your personal experience or from previous detailed consideration of related topics arising from your course of study, for example, from reading carried out when studying for coursework.

Where approval on the topic or perspective is required, you may need to present a written proposal that outlines the question and the method of approach to be adopted (**Ch 3**). This may involve presenting a reasoned argument justifying the research topic and approach. This then goes to the supervising academic or a panel of academics for consideration and approval.

Make your decisions with speed but not haste

If a list of dissertation or research options is presented, find out about it as quickly as possible, as there may be competition for specific topics or for particular supervisors. However, make sure you take all relevant factors into account in a deliberate decision-making process, rather than hastily choosing under pressure. You should give the matter high priority and allocate time and attention to activities that may help you make a decision, such as library or internet searches and discussions with potential supervisors.

→ Deciding on your personal research interests

It is essential that you find your study area interesting and that there is enough about the topic that is novel and challenging for you. If this is the case, then your levels of motivation will be high and may sustain you through any problems you encounter. If not, you will be liable to become bored or disillusioned, and this will hinder your ability to complete and write up your work.

By the time that you're considering a potential research topic, you will almost certainly have an above-average interest in the broader field of study. However, you may never have thought rigorously about your true underlying interests. Now, when you are forced into making a decision, this will need to be considered quite deeply. For some, stating a primary interest might be easy, but for many, it will be quite difficult to commit their efforts to one highly focussed subject, or to settle on which option on a list interests them most. There may be a range of possibilities, each with a balance of attractions and negative aspects.

smart tip

Rewind your past experiences

Remind yourself about the issues that arose in debate in the lectures, tutorials, seminars or practicals. Reflect on those areas of your course where you found your curiosity and interest being fired. This may give you some direction in selecting a topic.

What, then, is the best way to arrive at a decision? This may depend on your personality, the discipline and the degree of choice you have been given:

- If you have an open choice, then one approach might be to brainstorm possible topics and sub-topics within your subject, then to rank these in order of your interest. You could do this in phases, moving sequentially from broader subject fields to more closely specified research areas, until a clear favourite emerges or you can narrow down the choices.
- If your choice is restricted or from a menu of options, consider each option in turn. Do not reject any possibility out of hand until

you know more about it. Obtain background information where necessary and, if a reading list is offered, consult this. Rank the options according to how they appeal to you.

With luck, you will now have created a shortlist of potential topics. The next phase, potentially of equal importance, is to think further about the practical matters that should influence your decision.

smart tip

A simple way of ranking your choices

Consider each option in turn, and award it a mark out of 10. When you have completed a scan of all the options, look again at the ones which scored highly and reject the ones that scored weakly. Try explaining the reasons for your scores to someone else. This may force you to put into words how you feel, and thereby become more confident in your decision.

→ Other factors to take into account

Many factors will influence your ability to complete your studies to a high standard, and they should all be borne in mind as you arrive at a decision. You should also think about how useful the experience and end product might be. Again, it will be beneficial to score these aspects in relation to the specific topics in your shortlist. You may wish to take into account the following:

Potential research approaches

While you may have distinct preferences for specific areas of study, you should still consider the options at a finer level before making a final decision. Is it possible for you to identify the approach that might be required? Is there a question to be answered, a problem to be solved or an issue to be debated? How will you restrict the potential areas to cover? How exactly will you set about researching the topic? You may alter this 'research angle' through time, but refining your thoughts might aid the decision-making process. Also, bear in mind that if you have a distinct direction to your work from the start, this will increase your chances of success.

smart tip

Finding out more about a research option

If the answers to questions about the practicalities or relevance of a topic are not immediately evident, ask around. Discuss options with a potential supervisor or other academic contact. Sometimes it is useful to get more than one perspective on the issue, so try to find several people who can give you an opinion.

Time aspects

In selecting a topic, it is particularly important to guard against being over-ambitious. Ensure that you will have enough time to be able to demonstrate, through your written work, that you have completed the task required. You need to factor in not only the time that you will need to read, analyse or present the material, but also the sometimes considerable period that it may take simply to obtain the material or data you need. You should also bear in mind that if you spend too much time on project work and/or writing this may adversely affect your performance in other coursework.

In some cases, approval for your work will be required from an ethics committee, and this may also take time (see **Ch 19**). Remember too that the writing phase for a dissertation or a project report requires a lot of time. Where you can anticipate that simply identifying and obtaining the material, let alone reading and digesting it, is going to take an inordinate amount of time, then you may need to eliminate some of your first-choice possibilities.

Availability of resources or experimental material

Some dissertations or research projects run into difficulties because it is not possible to obtain the material required to carry out the work.

- **Obtaining printed material.** You will need to evidence your work by reference to the literature (**Ch 7**, **Ch 17**, **Ch 18** and **Ch 22**). Thus, access to printed material is critical to the research process. You need to review the materials relevant to each potential topic that:
  - are available locally in hard copy in book and journal format within your own institution's library;
  - can be accessed electronically through your library's subscription to online journals;

- can be obtained through inter-library loan (taking into account any cost implications; and
- may require you to visit another library site for on-site access.

How can I find out about what sources are available?

The best people to consult are the subject librarians in your library. They will know about:

- the resources already present in your library, including stored materials;
- the main routes for obtaining information, including advanced online searches;
- alternative approaches that you may not have thought about;
- obscure resources and how to access these;
- contacts at other institutions who can help; and
- professional organisations that may have exclusive databanks that you might be able to access through your department.

- **Obtaining data.** You need to take into account the most realistic method of garnering data, recording and interpreting the findings within the time-frame that you have to do the work. If you need to analyse quantitative data, then you should also consider what statistical analysis software packages you may need to master. Where your data are qualitative in nature, then you should also consider with your supervisor the most appropriate methods for gathering and interpreting the information. For example, an action research approach might require different techniques to a questionnaire-based approach (**Ch 12**).

Using new primary sources

Research topics may focus on contemporary events and you may have to use recently published primary sources as the basis for your study. For example, you might consult material such as a recently produced *Royal Commission Report*, a new piece of legislation, or a newly published item of literature. Since the novelty of the topic would make it unlikely that there would be very little, if any, critical appraisal of such things in the public domain, then your research task would be to place your own interpretation on this material. If you encounter difficulty, then from your supervisor.

Depth

Your dissertation or research topic will need to offer sufficient depth to allow you to show off your skills. These may depend on your discipline, but might include the ability to think critically through analysis and evaluation, or the ability to design an experiment or survey and report it professionally. Avoid choosing a well-worked area or even one that you feel is likely to provide easy results, if it will not allow you to demonstrate advanced skills.

Extent of support and supervision

At all levels of study, the writing of the dissertation or project report is a major task and you will not be expected to do this alone. Incorporated into the process will be a level of support provided by an assigned supervisor. However, you need to be clear at the outset about what you can expect in terms of this support. In some institutions, supervision is mapped onto the research/writing process with regular student-supervisor meetings. In others, arrangements are agreed by the partners for meetings as required. Generally, the supervision will enable you to ask questions, seek guidance and debate some key issues. Be sure, however, that you reach an understanding with your supervisor about the extent to which you can expect them to review and provide feedback on your written work. Often this will not extend to reading the whole dissertation, nor to proof-reading the text, as this is regarded as being the responsibility of the student.

smart tip

Choosing a supervisor

If you have a choice, bear in mind that this should be a member of staff you feel comfortable talking to, who you feel will offer support and guidance, and inspire you to work hard and complete on time. Ask past students if you want the 'inside track' on different tutors, and, where appropriate, the environment where you will be expected to work.

Impact on your CV and career options

Although this is rarely the primary aspect to consider, it is a factor to bear in mind. It may already be that your subject interests are very closely aligned to your ideas for your future career. You may also wish to take into account specific skills you might gain that will be of interest to an employer. If you are an undergraduate interested in further studies, your choice of topic may be valuable in giving you experience to take to a potential postgraduate supervisor.

smart tip

Weigh up the pros and cons of your options

If you remain undecided after considering both your interest in potential topics and the practical aspects, try laying out your thoughts about the options in a set of simple tables with columns for advantages and disadvantages. This process may help order your thoughts and clarify the factors that are important to you.

Practical tips for choosing your dissertation or research topic

Make sure that you are making an informed choice. Do the necessary background reading. Discuss the topics with your course director or assigned supervisor so you avoid taking on a topic that is risky and understand fully the challenges of the topic area.

Speak to students who have already completed this kind of study. Postgraduates in your department might be useful contacts to ask. Discuss with them any aspects in the process that they felt were important to them when they were researching and writing their dissertations or project reports.

Look at past work. Dissertations and reports produced by students in previous years will help you gain a sense of the style and standard required. They will also enable you to look at a variety of approaches relevant to your discipline. But don't be put off by apparently sophisticated structure and style in these completed examples. Remember that achieving this standard did not happen spontaneously. Your starting point may not be at this level, but the learning process will very likely result in a similarly high standard of report.

Plan out a dissertation or report as part of the decision-making process. Sketch out the structure at the macro-level and then, later, for selected options, think about a more detailed plan. In practice, you may not stick rigidly to the plan you create, but the process of planning will help you to sort out the ideas and decide how appealing and feasible they are.

Think for yourself. When choosing a topic, try not to be influenced by other students' opinions. This is, and should be, a highly personal decision. Some of your peers may have their own reasons for liking or disliking certain topics or supervisors; you will need to distance yourself from their thoughts when considering your own options.

Finding a topic for yourself. If you are given the option to choose your own topic, but have difficulty identifying a theme, then you might find it stimulating to refer to some of the generic periodicals - such as *Nature*, *New Scientist*, *Time*, *The Economist*, or *The Spectator* - to identify emergent issues, new strands of research or possible controversies arising from contemporary developments in your field.

GO And now . . .

2.1 Set aside time to make your decision. As indicated throughout this chapter, you should consider your options very carefully and carry out the necessary research to ensure your decision is informed. This will take time, but you must act quickly, or others may choose an option before you. Therefore, as soon as information is available, lay aside the necessary time to focus your attention on this issue.

2.2 Go back to basics. If the choices are bewildering, it may pay to revisit your old lecture notes and general texts to gain an overview of potential research areas. It may also be valuable to avoid the constraints of the booklists, if provided, and look at material that might be available online, for example, from writers and publishers in other countries. This can sometimes introduce a refreshingly different angle to a subject that might help you decide.

2.3 Visit your library and its website. Browse journals and books within your discipline shelving areas to obtain ideas; consult library staff or the online catalogue to find out about the availability of resources relevant to potential study areas.

Planning your research

3 Writing a proposal

How to structure a successful dissertation or research proposal

A dissertation or project proposal may be required by your department before you start studying in depth or writing seriously. In some cases, your choice of topic may influence the selection or allocation of the person who will act as your supervisor. However, you should not regard your proposal solely as an administrative exercise; it will help you organise your preliminary thoughts, plan your approach and complete your work on time.

Key topics:

→ Benefits of writing a proposal
→ What will be taken into account in assessing your proposal
→ Writing your proposal

Key terms
Aims Objectives Proposal

The procedures for writing a dissertation or project report may involve constructing a proposal. This document will outline the scope and methods of the research you intend to carry out and, in some cases, will indicate how you plan to organise your writing. At an early stage in the process you will probably be allocated a supervisor and your proposal may need to be referred to the appropriate ethics committee within your institution (see **Ch 19**). You may also be offered feedback on your proposal and advice on how to proceed. Once approval is given, you may be given the go-ahead to proceed with your studies under the guidance of your supervisor.

→ Benefits of writing a proposal

The discipline of composing a proposal is a valuable exercise and you should approach this task in positive frame of mind. The benefits include:

- ensuring your research has aims and objectives that are achievable in the time allocated;
- compelling you to read and review some of the relevant background material to orientate your thoughts;
- checking that you have a realistic notion of the research methods you could and should use;
- making sure you think about resources you may require at an early stage;
- verifying that you have considered safety and ethical issues relating to your research;
- assisting you to create an outline structure for your dissertation or report;
- helping you to create a viable timetable for your work; and
- matching your interests and needs to an appropriate supervisor.

smart tip

Your relationship with your supervisor

A supervisor may be a lecturer or other member of staff. They will usually be experienced in conducting research and in mentoring students, so their views are worth taking seriously. Supervisors have a notional amount of time for advising dissertation students and this time is therefore precious. Thus, it is important that you attend all meetings promptly, come well prepared and communicate effectively with your supervisor. Making a list beforehand of questions or issues you want to raise at these meetings will save time and lend structure to them, and your organisation will commend you to your supervisor as someone who is taking on the responsibility of autonomous research. Responding appropriately to your supervisor's feedback will almost certainly improve the quality of your dissertation. Remember, too, that your supervisor will be a potential referee when you apply for professional employment.

→ What will be taken into account in assessing your proposal

The person or group reading your proposal will be considering it from several viewpoints. They will expect to be able to answer 'yes' to the following questions:

- ❑ Do you have an up-to-date and accurate view of the research field?
- ❑ Have you outlined the focus of your studies (in some disciplines, the hypothesis you intend to test) in sufficient detail?
- ❑ Is the scope of your proposed study realistic in the time allocated?
- ❑ Is your proposed research study sufficiently original?
- ❑ Is your proposed research sufficiently challenging?
- ❑ Will the research allow you to demonstrate your academic ability?
- ❑ Will the research give you the chance to refine your skills?
- ❑ Are the proposed methods appropriate and are you aware of their limitations?
- ❑ Are you likely to gain access to all the resources you need?
- ❑ Are you planning to deal with safety and ethical issues appropriately?
- ❑ Is the proposed structure of your dissertation or project and the underlying research evident?
- ❑ Will your proposed dissertation and the underlying scholarship meet the requirements of the department or university regulations?
- ❑ Have you carried out appropriate background reading?

Finally, and in summary:

- ❑ Is your dissertation or project report likely to meet the required standard?

A key element that will be assessed is the 'core hypothesis' or idea underlying your dissertation or project report, so you should try to express this clearly. Essentially, this involves framing a question or topic that you will be seeking to address. The word 'address' is used deliberately here rather than 'answer', because a clear-cut answer or conclusion is rarely possible, and, in fact, you will gain credit by considering the evidence from all sides of an argument or case, arriving at a clearly stated viewpoint, and giving reasons for adopting this position.

Topics that will be looked on favourably are those that are novel, take an unusual perspective on a research area, and are relevant within the research field as it stands at the time of writing. A mistake commonly made is to try to cover too 'large' a problem or area of discussion, rather than one capable of adequate analysis given the resources likely to be at hand.

smart tip

Example of refining a subject area

Let's say you are interested in bi-cameral systems of government. Clearly you cannot expect to write a dissertation on this topic in its entirety. Suppose you had been enthused by a lecturer (a potential supervisor?) who talked about the checks and balances that arise from having two chambers of government. However, you are interested in contrasting the idea of an elected second chamber with one that is dependent on patronage and selection. Perhaps you are interested in exploring arguments for changes in the composition of the UK House of Lords as the non-elected second chamber in the UK. This might help you define a topic related to the implications of replacing the existing system with a method where the Members of the Lords might be elected rather than selected by birth or by patronage. This might lead you into examining the current composition of the Lords and examining the levels of participation and contribution to the governmental process made by selected members in contrast to the activities of elected Members of the Commons. This might be translated to a dissertation title such as: *Representative Second Chambers: the House of Lords as a case study.*

→ Writing your proposal

In many cases, a form may be provided for your dissertation or project proposal. This will normally include some or all of the components shown in Table 3.1, so that the person or committee evaluating your proposal can answer the questions noted in the previous section.

Present your proposal neatly. It should be word-processed and should stick very closely to any word limits. Regardless of any length constraints, try to make your proposal succinct and to the point. There will be ample time to expand your thoughts when writing the real dissertation or project report. The proposal committee will be trying to arrive at a quick decision and this will be made easier if your proposal is 'short and sweet'.

Table 3.1 Typical components of a dissertation or project proposal. A selection of these categories will be used in individual cases. The choice of elements used in a proposal will depend on the discipline and level of study.

Component	Content and aspects to consider
Personal details	Required so that you can be identified and contacted
Details of your degree course or programme	There may be subtle differences according to your precise degree
Proposed title	This should be relatively short; a two-part title style can be useful
Description of the subject area/Summary/Background/Brief review/Statement of the problem or issue to be addressed	A brief outline that provides context such as: a synopsis of past work; a description of the 'gap' to be filled or new area to be explored; a summary of current ideas and, where relevant, hypotheses
Aim of research	General description of the overall purpose; a statement of intent
Objectives	Listing of specific outcomes you expect to fulfil in order to achieve the aim
Literature to be examined	Sources you intend to consult during your researches
Research methods or critical approach	How you propose to carry out your investigation
Preliminary bibliography	Details (in appropriate format) of the key sources you have already consulted
(Special) resources required	Information sources, samples, instruments, people, etc. necessary to carry out your investigation
Outline plan of the dissertation or project report	For example, the likely section or chapter headings and subheadings
Indication of whether discussions have already been held with a nominated supervisor/indication of a potential supervisor	Valid only in cases where there is an element of choice of supervisor
Indication of whether discussions have already been held with the programme or course director in case of a project report	Valid only in cases where this is an administrative requirement
Names of possible supervisors	Your chance to influence this aspect
Timetable/plan	A realistic breakdown of the stages of your dissertation, ideally with appropriate milestones
Statement or declaration that you understand and will comply with safety and/or ethical rules	The committee's guarantee that you have considered these; details may be required in certain cases (see **Ch 19**)

Try not to prepare your proposal in a rush - if possible, write out a near-final draft and leave it for a few days before coming back to it again with a critical mind, then make suitable modifications before your final submission.

smart tip

Choosing a title

The point at which you write your proposal may be the first time you have concrete thoughts about your title. Consider adopting a two-part title - an attention-grabbing statement, followed by a colon or a dash and a secondary title that defines the content more closely. It is also worth noting that the title given at the proposal stage should be seen as provisional, for the nature of the study and the outcomes may dictate a change at the end of the process.

Practical tips for producing a successful proposal

Carry out an appropriate amount of background reading beforehand, selecting the sources carefully. You don't need to read all of the papers at the start, as this will take up too much of your study time, but you do need to gain an up-to-date appreciation of key topics and trends in your chosen field. Choose recently published reviews of the area, especially those likely to prompt ideas about key aspects that need to be looked at in more detail.

Try to formulate a key hypothesis or idea to investigate. Your dissertation needs a focus and this will come from trying to answer a specific question; investigate a key issue or highlight a specific topic. Use brainstorming techniques as you read sources to help you develop your ideas and potential topics.

Remember that your proposal is only a proposal. You do not need to write the complete work at this stage. You merely need to establish, for the benefit of the reviewing group, that you have chosen a reasonable topic and are likely to succeed in producing a dissertation or project report that meets the regulations or learning outcomes of your course.

Discuss your proposal with staff beforehand. At an early stage, try to arrange an appointment with a staff member for a brief discussion about possible directions. If you have been allocated a supervisor, then consult them; if not, think about who you would like to be a supervisor and ask them.

Get feedback from your peers. Show an early draft to a friend or family member, or swap proposals with a classmate. Ask for comments and respond to them. This kind of feedback is especially valuable to ensure that the logic of your proposal is transparent to readers.

Use appropriate language. Your proposal should be clear to the non-specialist, but include appropriate terminology to show that you understand key concepts and jargon.

Set yourself realistic aims and objectives, bearing in mind the need for originality in your work. The group considering your proposal will be aware that a major reason for students having problems with dissertations and project choices is that they were over-ambitious at the start.

The difference between aims and objectives (goals)

The distinction between these can be confusing. Widely accepted definitions generally suggest that *aims* are statements of intent or purpose that are broad in nature, and hence defined in general terms perhaps relating to an overall outcome, while *objectives* (goals) are outlined in more specific terms and tend to relate to individual, achievable outcomes that are required to achieve the ultimate aim. For example, the aim of a dissertation might be to 'summarise viewpoints within a particular research field' while an objective might be to 'compare the various research methods in use to measure a particular variable'. Ideally objectives will state 'what', 'how', 'where' and 'when' (as appropriate). Some people favour **SMART** objectives that are: **S**pecific, **M**easurable, **A**chievable, **R**ealistic and **T**angible (see p. 6).

GO And now . . .

3.1 Imagine you are assessing your own proposal. Having completed a draft, answer all the questions in the checklist on p. 23 for any answers that might be problematic, go back to the proposal and see if you could improve on it, or provide evidence to back up your case.

3.2 List potential dissertation or project report titles. Consult other dissertations and project reports completed recently to gain a feel for the modern style in your discipline. Write down a few options for your own work and ask your supervisor or fellow students what they think of them.

3.3 Create a detailed timetable for your research and writing. Consult **Ch 4** for advice on managing time and remember to factor in some slippage time. Include suitable milestones, for example, 'finish first draft'.

4 Time management

How to write your dissertation or project while balancing family, work and leisure

Managing your time effectively is an important key to completing a dissertation or project report. This chapter provides ideas for organising your activities and tips to help you maintain focus on the key tasks in the research and writing process.

Key topics:

→ Diaries, timetables and planners
→ Listing and prioritising
→ Routines and good work habits
→ What to do if you can't get started on a task or can't complete it

Key terms

Perfectionism Prioritising Writer's block

Successful people tend to have the ability to focus on the right tasks at the right time, the capacity to work quickly to meet their targets, and the knack of seeing each job through to a conclusion. In short, they possess good time-management skills.

As a student preparing to undertake dissertation or project report writing, you will need to balance the time you devote to study, family, work and social activities. Although you probably have more freedom over these choices than many others, making the necessary decisions is still a challenge. Table 4.1 illustrates why good time management is especially important at this level. However, time management is a skill that can be developed like any other. Here are some simple routines and tips that can help you improve your organisation, prioritisation and time-keeping. Weigh up the following ideas and try to adopt those most suited to your needs and personality.

Table 4.1 Some of the ways in which students demonstrate poor time management. Examples of 'last-minute' strategies that don't work well for large pieces of writing like dissertations or project reports.

Personality type	Typical working ways . . . and the problems that may result
The late-nighter	Luke likes to work into the small hours. He's got a draft chapter to finish with a deadline tomorrow morning, but just couldn't get down to doing it earlier on. It's 2.00 a.m. and now he's panicking. Because the library's shut, he can't find a reference to support one of his points; he's so tired he won't be able to review his writing and correct the punctuation and grammatical errors; and he feels so shattered that he'll probably sleep in and miss the 9.00 a.m. deadline . . .
The extension-seeker	Elaine always rationalises being late with her draft submissions. She always has good reasons for being late, and it's never her fault. This time her printer packed up just before submission, last time she had tonsillitis and the time before she had to visit her granny in hospital. This is beginning to wear rather thin with her supervisor . . .
The last-minuter	Lorna is a last-minute person and she can only get motivated when things get close to the wire. She produces her best work close to deadlines when the adrenaline is flowing. However, her final-year dissertation is supposed to be a massive 10,000 words, there's only two weeks to go and she hasn't felt nervous enough to get started until now . . .
The know-it-all	Kevin has it all under control. He thinks that the literature is all on the Internet or in e-journals, so there's no need to get worked up about this project. He'll catch up on his sleep and his social life; he'll run off the report over the weekend. Trouble is that his university doesn't subscribe to the journals he'll need and that means that he can only read the abstracts or summaries, not the full text . . . at the weekend the library will be closed and so he'll not be able to get hold of any of the books . . .
The perfectionist	Pat wants to do really well at uni. She signed up for a vocational degree and has plans to land a plum job on graduation to start her climb up the career tree. She did really well in her assignments and it's vital that the project report that she's working on starts with a cracking first sentence. Just can't phrase it right though – she's tried 15 different ways and crossed them all out. Time is running out now, and the quality of the analytical section and conclusion is bound to suffer . . .

→ Diaries, timetables and planners

Organising your activities more carefully is an obvious way to gain productive time.

Diaries

Use a diary to keep track of your day-to-day schedule (for example, meetings, lectures, sports activities) and to note submission deadlines for university work including that for your dissertation or project report.

- Work your way back from key dates, creating milestones such as 'finish library work for research' or 'prepare first draft of section 1'.
- Refer to the diary frequently to keep yourself on track and to plan out each day and week. Try to get into the habit of looking at the next day's activities the night before and the next week's work at the end of the week. A diary with the 'week-to-view' type of layout will enable you to plan over the longer term.
- Number the weeks, so you can sense how time is progressing over longer periods, such as a term or semester.

Choosing a diary

Some universities and many bookshops sell academic diaries that cover the year from September to August. This format helps you keep track of the numbered weeks in each semester or term, and to highlight draft or final submission dates for your written work.

Timetables

Create a detailed timetable of work to make sure you take into account all aspects of the work you have to complete by:

- breaking the task down into smaller parts;
- spacing these out appropriately;
- scheduling important work for when you generally feel most intellectually active (e.g. mid-morning).

One advantage of a timetable is that you can see the progress you are making if you cross out each mini-task as it is completed.

Wall planners

These are another way of charting out your activities, with the advantage that you can see all your commitments and deadlines at a glance.

smart tip

Advantages of being organised

If you organise your time well, you will:

- keep on schedule and meet your submission deadline;
- complete work with less pressure and fulfil your potential;
- build your confidence about your ability to cope;
- avoid overlapping commitments and having to juggle more than one piece of work at a time.

Being organised is especially important for large or long-term tasks because it seems easier to put things off when deadlines seem distant.

→ Listing and prioritising

At times you may run into problems because you have a number of different tasks that need to be done. It is much better to write these tasks down in a list each day, rather than risk forgetting them. You will then have a good picture of what needs to be done and will be better able to prioritise the tasks.

Once you've created a list, rank the tasks by numbering them 1, 2, 3 and so on, in order from 'important and urgent' to 'neither important nor urgent' (see Figure 4.1). Your 'important' criteria will depend on many factors: for example, your own goals and submission dates.

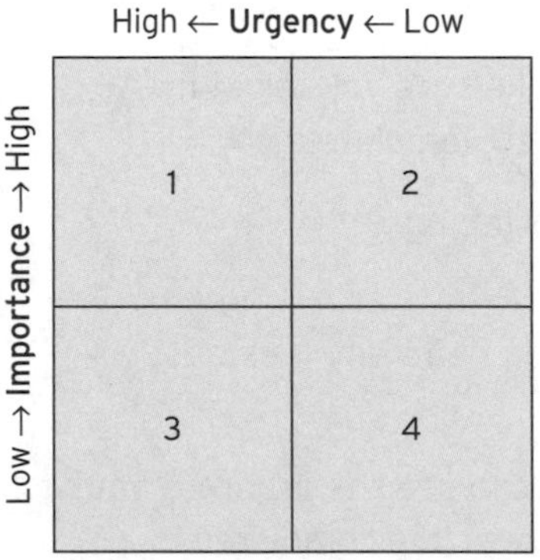

High ← **Urgency** ← Low

Low → **Importance** → High		
	1	2
	3	4

Figure 4.1 The urgent-important approach to prioritising. Place each activity somewhere on the axes in relation to its importance and urgency. Do all the activities in sector 1 first, then 2 or 3, and last 4.

How can you decide on your priorities?

This involves distinguishing between important and urgent activities.

- **Importance** implies some assessment of the benefits of completing a task against the loss if the task is not finished.
- **Urgency** relates to the length of time before the task must be completed.

For example, in normal circumstances, doing your laundry will be neither terribly important nor particularly urgent, but if you start to run out of clean underwear, you may decide otherwise. Hence, priorities are not static and need to be reassessed frequently.

Each day, you should try to complete as many of the listed tasks as you can, starting with number one. If you keep each day's list achievable, the process of striking out each task as it is completed provides a feeling of progress being made, which turns into one of satisfaction if the list has virtually disappeared by the evening. Also, you will become less stressed once high-priority tasks are tackled.

Carry over any uncompleted tasks to the next day, add new ones to your list and start again - but try to complete yesterday's unfinished jobs before starting new ones of similar priority, or they will end up being delayed for too long.

This technique works well for practical aspects of researching. Once you get to the writing-up phase of your dissertation or project report, it becomes less easy to apply list-making on the writing task itself. However, keeping lists of non-writing things you need to do helps you to deal with this items separately and so keep your mind free to focus on the writing in progress.

→ Routines and good work habits

Many people find that carrying out specific tasks at special periods of the day or times of the week helps them get things done on time. You may already adopt this approach with routine tasks like doing your shopping every Tuesday morning or visiting a relative on Sunday afternoons. You may find it helps to add work-related activities to your list of routines - for example, by making Monday evening a time for library study.

Good working habits can help with time management:

- **Do important work when you are at your most productive.** Most of us can state when we work best (Figure 4.2). When you have worked this out for yourself, timetable your activities to suit: academic work when you are 'most awake' and routine activities when you are less alert.
- **Make the most of small scraps of time.** Use otherwise unproductive time, such as when commuting or before going to sleep, to jot down ideas, edit work or make plans. Keep a notebook with you to write down your thoughts.
- **Keep your documents organised.** If your papers are well filed, then you won't waste time looking for something required for the next step.
- **Make sure you always have a plan.** Often, the reason projects don't go well is because there is no scheme to work to. Laying out a plan for any academic writing helps you to clarify the likely structure behind your efforts. Writing out a fairly detailed plan will save you time in the long run. It is also an aid to firming up your thinking.
- **Extend your working day.** If you can deal with early rising, you may find that setting your alarm earlier than normal provides a few extra hours to help you achieve a short-term goal.

Time period	Alertness rating
 am	
 pm	
 pm	
 pm/am	

Figure 4.2 Are you a morning, afternoon or night person? Rate yourself (marks out of 10) according to when you find yourself most able to study productively.

→ What to do if you can't get started on a task or can't complete it

People agree that one of the hardest parts of time management is getting started on tasks. Putting things off - procrastination - is all too easy, and can involve the following:

- convincing yourself that other low-priority work is more important or preferable;
- switching frequently among tasks, and not making much progress in any of them;
- talking about your work rather than doing it;
- planning for too long rather than working;
- having difficulty starting a piece of writing (having 'writer's block');
- spending too long on presentational elements (e.g. the cover page or a diagram), rather than the 'meat' of the project;
- finding mundane TV programmes fascinating or being easily persuaded to go out socialising.

If you admit to any of these symptoms, you may be subconsciously procrastinating. Becoming more aware of how you might be falling into this trap is the first stage in consciously avoiding it.

Definition: procrastination

This is simply putting off a task. As the poet Edward Young wrote: 'Procrastination is the thief of time'.

Delaying completion of a task, in itself a form of procrastination, is another aspect of time management that many find difficult. Procrastination is a special problem for perfectionists (see **Ch 1**). Good time managers recognise when to finish tasks, even if the task is not in a 'perfect' state. At university, doing this can mean that the sum of results from multiple assignments is better, because your attention is divided more appropriately, rather than focussing on a single task.

Tips for getting started on tasks and completing them on time are provided in Table 4.2.

Table 4.2 Ten tips for getting started on academic tasks and meeting deadlines

1 **Improve your study environment**. Your focus and concentration will depend on this. • Create a tidy workplace. Although tidying up can be a symptom of procrastination, in general, it is easier to start studying at an empty desk and in an uncluttered room. • Reduce noise. Some people like background music, while others don't - but it's generally other people's noise that really interrupts your train of thought. A solution might be to go to a quiet place like a library. • Escape. Why not take all you need to a different location where there will be a minimum of interruptions? Your focus will be enhanced if the task you need to do is the only thing you can do, so take with you only the notes and papers you require.
2 **Avoid distractions.** If you are easily tempted away from study by your friends, you'll have to learn to decline their invitations politely. Hang up a 'do not disturb' sign, and explain why to your friends; disappear off to a quiet location without telling anyone where you will be; or switch off your phone, TV or email. One strategy might be to say to friends 'I can't come just now, but how about having a short break in half an hour?'
3 **Work in short bursts while your concentration is at a maximum.** After this, give yourself a brief break, perhaps a short walk, and then start back again.
4 **Find a way to start.** Breaking initial barriers is vital. When writing, this is a very common problem because of the perceived need to begin with a 'high impact' sentence that reads impressively. This is unnecessary, and starting with a simple definition or restatement of the issue or problem is perfectly acceptable. If you lack the motivation to begin work, try thinking briefly about the bigger picture: your degree and career, and how the current task is a small but essential step to achieving your goals.
5 **Focus on the positive.** You may be so anxious about the end point of your task that this affects your ability to start it. For example, many students are so nervous about the apparent difficulty, or prospect, of writing a dissertation or project report that they freeze in their preparation and put the whole thing off. One way to counter this would be to think about the aspects of the work ahead that excite you - doing the research, experiments or field work. Once you become immersed in your research topic the writing will become less daunting.
6 **In written tasks, don't feel you have to tackle the writing in a linear fashion.** Word-processing software allows you work out of sequence, which can help get you going. So, for a large report, it might help to start on a part that is 'mechanical', such as a reference list or results section. Sometimes it's a good idea to draft the summary, abstract or contents list first, because this will give you a plan to work to.

Table 4.2 continued

7	**Cut up large tasks.** If you feel overwhelmed by the size of the job and this prevents you from starting it, break the task down to manageable, achievable chunks. Then, try to complete something every day. Maintaining momentum in this way will allow you to whittle away the job in small pieces.
8	**Work alongside others.** If you arrange to work alongside others, you can spur each other on with sympathy, humour and the promise of a drink or coffee after each study period.
9	**Ask for help.** You may feel that you lack a particular skill to attempt some component of the task (e.g. the ability to use a statistics program) and that this is holding you back. Don't be afraid to ask for help, rather than suffering in isolation: consult a fellow student, lecturer, or skills adviser; or visit one of the many websites that offer assistance.
10	**Don't be a too much of a perfectionist.** We all want to do well, but doing your very best takes time - a commodity that should be carefully rationed so that all tasks are given their fair share. Perfectionism can prevent or delay you getting started if you feel your initial efforts need to be faultless (see point 4 above). Also, achieving fault-free work requires progressively more effort, with less return as you get nearer to perfection. The time you need to spend to attain the highest standards will probably be better used on the next task.

Practical tips for managing your time

Invest in items to support your time management. Helpful items could include a diary, wall planner, personal digital assistant (PDA), mobile phone with diary facility and alarm clock.

Investigate how you really use your time. Time-management experts often ask clients to write down what they do for every minute of several days and thereby work out where the productive time disappears to. If you are unsure whether you are optimising time you might like to keep a detailed record for a short period, using a suitable coding for your activities. When you have identified any time that has been less productive you could try analysing how this has happened. Those of a more numerical bent might wish to construct a spreadsheet to do this and work out percentages spent on different activities. Once you have completed your timesheet, appraise it to see whether you spend excessive amounts of time on any one activity or may not have the balance right. As you think about this, remember that universities assume you will be carrying out academic-related activities for roughly 40 hours per week.

Create an artificial deadline. Set yourself a finishing date that is ahead of the formal submission deadline for your dissertation or project report. That way you will have the luxury of time to review your work, correct errors and improve the quality of presentation.

Build flexibility into your planning. We often end up rushing things because the unexpected has interrupted a timetable that is too tightly scheduled. To avoid this, deliberately introduce empty slots into your plans to allow for these contingencies.

Try to prioritise the items on your 'to do' list. If you produce a daily list of tasks, then spend some time thinking about how you wish to prioritise and order them through the day. You might adopt a numerical system or one using stars, for example.

Ask yourself whether your lifestyle needs radical surgery. You may find that little in this chapter seems relevant because your time is dominated by a single activity. This might be socialising, caring for others, outside employment or travelling, for example. In these cases, you may need to make fundamental changes to your lifestyle to place greater emphasis on your studies. In some cases a student counsellor might be able to help you decide what needs to be done.

GO And now . . .

6.1 Analyse your time-management personality. Can you recognise any character traits that are preventing you from organising your time effectively? Might any of the 'Practical tips' help you become better at time management? How could you adapt them to your own situation?

6.2 Experiment with listing and prioritising. If you haven't used this strategy before, test it out for a week or so. Make a list of all your current and future tasks, academic commitments, appointments and social events. Rearrange the list in order of priority. Take special care to take account of events that depend on other jobs being completed. Now try to complete the different components, ticking them off the list as you go. After your trial period, decide how effective the method was in organising your activities and helping you to ensure that tasks were done on time.

6.3 Declutter and reorganise your life. If you reckon that disorganisation is a reason for lack of progress (Table 4.2), make a determined effort to tidy things up. Start with your room and study environment, and, if necessary, invest in files and boxes to help you organise things. Keep out only that which is relevant to current activities and carefully store the rest. Decide how you can better arrange your affairs to keep on top of routine tasks. Now you should be in a better mental and physical position to get on with your dissertation or project work.

5 Planning for dissertations

How to begin your research and evolve a model for your writing

At all stages in the production of a dissertation, the author must exert control over both the content and the way in which it is organised. Different approaches are possible to the same subject, and you will therefore need to choose a specific topic, decide on an intellectual approach to this, and select a structural model which suits your intended approach. This chapter outlines the initial reading and planning that is required for this, then explores some of the options available for structuring and planning your writing.

Key topics:

→ Identifying the key themes in your text
→ Realistic time planning
→ Exploring the topic
→ Finding and selecting relevant source material
→ Selecting a structural model

Key terms

Brainstorm Regulations

Writing a dissertation is an opportunity to demonstrate:

- your knowledge and understanding of the topic area;
- your ability to research a specific aspect within that area;
- your capacity to think critically about the information, views and conclusions reached by others; and
- your ability to organise supporting information and evidence within a well-structured text that follows academic conventions relevant to your discipline.

In these extensive pieces of writing it is worth planning your work carefully and ensuring that you select a way of explaining your viewpoint that demonstrates your analytical abilities.

People and their thought processes are different and so individual approaches to planning an outline for a piece of writing will vary. For some people, this can be a highly detailed process; for others, it may be a minimal exercise. Too much detail in a plan can be restricting, while too little can fail to provide enough direction. Therefore, a reasonably detailed plan should give some guidance while leaving you the flexibility to alter the finer elements as you write.

→ Identifying the key themes in your text

Starting points for your planning will include your initial research proposal (**Ch 2**), discussions with your supervisor, and any initial thoughts of your own.

In thinking about potential structures for your writing, it is important to recognise that university work needs more than simple reproduction of facts (**Ch 14**). You need to be able to construct an argument and to support this with evidence. This means that you need to draw on the literature that you have read in order to support your position. In some instances, dependent on the topic and discipline, it may be appropriate to present differing viewpoints and evaluate arguments one over the others, and, if appropriate, address counter-arguments to these. What is important is to present a tight, well-argued case for the view you present or conclusion you have reached.

Once you have evolved your own response to the task you have been set, you then need to place this within a framework that presents your response in a way that is well structured. Writing that follows a sequence of sound logic and argument will improve your final submission.

Lower- or higher-order thinking?

Dissertations are opportunities to demonstrate advanced thought processes (**Ch 14**). Often, written assignments require some initial description of context or process to outline the background to the topic. This is then followed by in-depth consideration of the topic, using more analytical or critical approaches.

→ Realistic time planning

Good planning ensures that you can realistically complete the work before the submission date. It also allows you to balance the time spent on different components and devote sufficient time to aspects such as editing and proof-reading.

Value of planning

Time spent deconstructing the task and planning your response will enable you to save time in the long run and, as with most jobs, the quality of the preparation will be reflected in the quality of the end product. It is well worth the time ensuring that you break down the task into its different elements.

Consult the course regulations for the assignment submission date. Work out how long you have between the starting point and due date, and then work out how much of that time you can devote to completion of the work. Remember to take into account things you may need to do, for example, to attend lectures, tutorials or practicals, and any part-time work commitments (see **Ch 4**).

Next, divide the available time into convenient working periods and decide how much time you wish to allocate to each aspect of the task (Table 5.1). Map these time allowances onto the available time.

Table 5.1 Stages in producing a large writing task with their estimated timing. A possible method of organising your time when planning a lengthy written assignment.

Aspect of task	Time required	When I plan to do this
Analysing the topic		
Doing preliminary reading		
Planning your analysis of the topic		
Doing supplementary reading		
Writing the first draft		
Reviewing the first draft		
Editing/proof-reading the final copy		
Printing/writing out the final copy		
Time margin for the unexpected		

→ Exploring the topic

You can start the process of exploring your topic by creating a brainstorm 'map' (**Ch 2**). At this stage, include as many related aspects as you can within a free-flowing diagram (see Figure 10.5 as an example). If you have already produced a proposal (**Ch 3**), your map will be strongly influenced by this, but your aim at this early stage should be to lay down some initial personal thoughts before you are influenced by any reading material. If you already have a title, try to consider all aspects of the subject as suggested; if not, take as wide a view as possible of the broad area you intend to work on. It is important to exercise your critical thinking skills (**Ch 14**) as you analyse the topic and think about potential content and approaches - you need to decide for yourself what you think is important about the topic, and why. Your initial 'map' will develop as you move into the reading and research phase which follows.

smart tip

Brainstorming techniques

To create an effective brainstorm 'map', use a single sheet of A4 in the landscape position. This gives more space for lateral thinking and creativity. It also leaves more space for additions to be made at later stages.

→ Finding and selecting relevant source material

You will find it useful to obtain some general background information about the topic and you may or may not be given a reading list to direct your initial research. Generally, reading lists are extensive to give some choice; they often list basic texts and then sources that go into greater depth. It is not usually expected that you read everything on these lists. In some subjects, you may only be expected to look at one or two recommended texts. In some other subjects, book lists are lengthy and the volume of reading may seem daunting, but the task will be more manageable if you approach it systematically. However, for advanced academic tasks such as dissertation writing you do not need to stick to a prescribed list alone; in fact, you will be expected to locate other sources (**Ch 7**).

Sources of background information

Handouts/PowerPoint slides: should outline key issues and ideas, pose problems and provide solutions related to your topic.

Lecture notes: easy to locate in your file if you've noted lecturer, topic and date.

General or subject encyclopaedias: provide a thumb-nail sketch of useful background information; give key points to direct your reading in more detailed texts. Electronic versions may be available through your university library.

ebrary: readily accessible, and reliable in its validity.

E-journals: specialist material that is reliable in its provenance.

Library resources: the electronic catalogue will enable you to locate many resources in addition to those listed above. For specific help, consult the readers' adviser or liaison librarian who can advise you on specialist material and sources. However, you may also find things serendipitously by browsing in the relevant zone of shelving in the library, where it is possible to find books and journals that may not necessarily come up from the search headings you have selected when consulting the catalogue.

Time is precious when you are researching, so it is sensible to be as efficient as possible in identifying the material you need (**Ch 8**). Use the contents page and the index in partnership to identify which sections are relevant to your topic. Some authors put key pages in bold type in the index and this will help you to focus your reading rather than cover every mention. At this stage also, preliminary encyclopaedia reading will help you to identify sections in a book resource that are more relevant to the present task.

Begin by doing the necessary reading and note-making. This has to be focussed and you need to be reading with discrimination (**Ch 10**). As you move from basic texts to more specialist books or journal articles that give more detailed analysis, your understanding of the topic will deepen. This may mean, for example that you begin to build up a more informed picture of events, implications of a procedure or the possible solutions to a problem. What are you looking for? This could be, for instance, facts, examples, information to support a particular viewpoint, or counter-arguments to provide balance to your analysis of the topic.

smart tip

The reporter's questions

Sometimes it is difficult to distinguish the important from the unimportant, the relevant from the irrelevant. A well-tried strategy, for many subjects, is to ask yourself the questions that trainee journalists are advised to use:

- **Who?** Who is involved in relation to this topic, for example, people/organisations?
- **What?** What are the problems/issues involved?
- **When?** What is the time-frame to be considered?
- **Where?** Where did it occur?
- **Why?** What reasons are relevant to this issue/topic?
- **How?** How has this situation been reached?

As you become more familiar with the issues, the easier it will be to think critically about what you are reading and consequently build your response to the task you have been set. Continue to add to your initial brainstorm.

→ Selecting a structural model

Knowing what information to put aside and what to retain requires a more disciplined appraisal than the more wide-ranging approach you will have followed in your initial reading. Certain questions may help you to focus on what is important to your topic. For example:

- Who are the key actors in a sequence of events?
- What are the necessary criteria that explain particular situations?
- What explanations support a particular view?
- What patterns can be identified, for example short-, medium- and long-term factors?
- What themes can be identified in different treatments of the same issue?

Having thought about these matters, you should start to decide which structural models you would like to use to organise your writing. Table 5.2 lists seven classic structural types you can consider.

Table 5.2 The seven most common structural models for academic writing

1 Chronological	Description of a process or sequence
2 Classification	Categorising objects or ideas
3 Common denominator	Identifying a common characteristic or theme
4 Phased	Identifying short-/medium-/long-term aspects
5 Analytical	Examining an issue in depth (situation - problem - solution - evaluation - recommendation)
6 Thematic	Commenting on a theme in each aspect
7 Comparative/contrastive	Comparing and contrasting (often within a theme or themes)

The basic structure of a dissertation is discussed in **Ch 20**, but within this format, your detailed intellectual analysis may need to follow a range of approaches suited to the specifics of the subject material. By adopting one of the models described in Table 5.2, you will be creating a structure within which your thinking and writing will be organised, logical and coherent. Moreover, approaching a topic in this way may help you to balance your discussion of relevant issues. These qualities in your writing will become apparent to the reader and should result in higher marks for your work. You may need to adapt your approach in different sections, or 'nest' models, by incorporating one within another. For example, within the common denominator approach it may be necessary to include some chronological dimension to the discussion. Examples of the different approaches are provided below.

Chronological approach

An example of the chronological approach would be describing a developmental process, such as outlining the historical development of the European Union. This kind of writing is most likely to be entirely descriptive.

Classification approach

An example of this approach could be to discuss transport by subdividing your text into land, sea and air modes of travel. Each of these could be further divided into commercial, military and personal modes of transport. These categories could be further subdivided on the basis of how they are powered. Such classifications are, to some extent, subjective, but the approach provides a means of describing each category at each level in a way that allows some contrast. This approach is particularly useful in scientific disciplines. The rationale also is sympathetic to the approach of starting from broad generalisation to the more specific.

Common denominator approach

This approach is useful in contexts where a single element can be identified as a common factor in the analysis of a situation. For example, in considering levels of high infant mortality in developing countries the common denominator is lack or deficiency. Thus, the topic could be approached by considering each of the following elements in turn:

- Lack of primary health care
- Lack of health education
- Lack of literacy.

Phased approach

An example of adopting a phased approach to a topic might be research into the impact of water shortage on flora and fauna along river banks.

- **Short-term factors** might be that drying out of the river bed occurs and annual plants fail to thrive.
- **Medium-term factors** might include damage to oxygenating plant life and reduction in wildlife numbers.
- **Long-term factors** might include the effect on the water table and falling numbers of certain amphibious species.

Analytical approach

This conventional approach might be used for complex issues. An example of a research topic that you could tackle in this way might be potential solutions to the problem of 'identity theft'. You could perhaps adopt the following plan:

- Define identity theft, and perhaps give an example.
- Explain why identity theft is difficult to control.
- Outline legal and practical solutions to identity theft.
- Weigh up the advantages and disadvantages of each.
- State which solution(s) you would favour and why.

smart tip

A useful strategy for analysis

The 'SPSER method' is particularly helpful in the construction of dissertations, projects and case studies. It is also useful whenever you feel that you cannot identify themes or trends. This approach helps you to 'deconstruct' or 'unpack' the topic. There are five elements:

- **Situation:** describe the context and brief history.
- **Problem:** describe or define the problem.
- **Solution:** describe and explain the possible solution(s).
- **Evaluation:** identify the positive and negative features for each solution by giving evidence/reasons to support your viewpoint.
- **Recommendation:** identify the best option in your opinion, giving the basis of your reasoning for this. This element is optional, as it may not always be a requirement of your task.

Thematic approach

This approach is similar to the phased approach, but in this case themes are the identifying characteristics. Precise details would depend on the nature of the topic, but possible examples could be:

- social, economic or political factors;
- age, income and health considerations;
- gas, electricity, oil, water and wind power.

Comparative/contrastive approach

This is a derivative of the themed approach. For example, consider a task that instructs: 'Discuss the arguments for and against the introduction of car-free city centres'. You might approach this by creating a 'grid', as in Table 5.3, which notes positive and negative aspects for the major stakeholders.

There are two potential methods of constructing text in this comparative/contrastive approach:

- **Method 1.** Introduce the topic, then follow Column A in a vertical fashion, then similarly follow Column B and conclude by making a concluding statement about the merits and demerits of one over the other. In relation to the grid, this would result in the structure: introductory statement, then A1 + A2 + A3 + A4 + A5, then B1 + B2 + B3 + B4 + B5, followed by concluding statement.

Table 5.3 Model grid for planning comparison-type answers

		Column A	Column B
	Stakeholders	Positive aspects	Negative aspects
1	Pedestrians	Greater safety, clean	Lengthy walk, poor parking
2	Drivers	Less stress; park and ride facilities	High parking fees; expensive public transport
3	Commercial enterprises	Quicker access for deliveries	Loss of trade to more accessible out-of-town shopping centres
4	Local authority	Reduces emissions	Cost of park and ride
5	Police	Easier to police	Reliance on foot patrols

- **Method 2.** Introduce the topic and then discuss the perspective of pedestrians from firstly the positive and then the negative aspects; now do the same for the viewpoints of the other stakeholders in sequence. This would result in the structure: introductory statement, then A1 + B1; A2 + B2; A3 + B3; A4 + B4; A5 + B5, followed by concluding statement.

smart tip

Comparative/contrastive structures

Each method of structuring the points has advantages and disadvantages, according to the content and the context of the assignment. For example, in an exam it might be risky to embark on method 1 in case you run out of time and never reach the discussion of column B. In this instance, method 2 would enable a balanced answer.

Practical tips for planning dissertations and projects

Conserving material. In the process of marshalling information for a writing task you will probably obtain some material that proves to be irrelevant to the current writing task. It is well worth keeping this in your filing system because this topic may come up again at a later date in a subtle way. In exam revision, this personal cache of information could be useful in revitalising your knowledge and understanding of this topic.

Spending time reading. This is a vital part of the planning and writing process, but recognise the dangers of prolonging the reading phase beyond your scheduled deadline. This is an avoidance strategy that is quite common. Students may delay getting down to planning the structure and moving on to the writing phase because they are uncomfortable with writing. Facing up to these next phases and getting on with them is usually much less formidable once you get started, so it's best to stick to your time plan for this assignment and move on to the next phase in the planned sequence.

Keeping records of sources. Identify the requirements of the referencing system favoured in your discipline and ensure that you get into the habit of noting all the necessary detail required by that system (**Ch 18**). This will make citation and referencing much easier and less time-consuming.

Explaining your approach. Although the models outlined in this chapter are fairly standard approaches to tackling academic issues, it is still necessary to identify for your reader which approach you intend to adopt in the piece of text. Your reader should learn at an early point in your writing of the route you intend to follow. In most cases this would be included in your introduction.

GO And now . . .

5.1 Compare textual patterns. Look at a chapter in a basic textbook and analyse the structural approach the author has taken. Identify the proportion of space allocated to 'scene-setting' using description, and to the analysis/argument/evaluation components of the text.

5.2 Identify structural models. Look at some past dissertations or other types of extensive writing and try to work out what structural approach has been taken, either overall or in each component part.

5.3 Create your own project plan. Go back to **Ch 4** (Time management) and consider how, with reference to Table 5.2, you will plan out the process of conducting the research and writing up of your dissertation or project report.

6 Planning for experimental projects

How to organise your efforts effectively

Experimental project work is an important component of many science degrees. With limited time and resources, it is essential to make the most of your time and effort in the lab or field. This chapter outlines aspects to consider in a plan of action, ways in which you can work productively, and how to prepare for writing up your thesis or report.

Key topics:

→ Adopting a flexible approach
→ Focussing on the end product from the start
→ Creating a plan of action
→ Working efficiently in the lab or field
→ Organising information and results ready for writing up

Key terms

Confounding variable   Control   Hypothesis   Thesis   Work placement

Scientific method involves observation and experimentation. Learning how to create hypotheses and design experiments that allow you to test them is a vital element of scientific training. Related skills include gathering and analysing data, presenting results, and drawing conclusions. The experience of carrying out a research project gives you a chance to develop these abilities and, even if you choose not to take up research as a career, this provides you with an insight into how science works and how scientific knowledge is obtained.

For these reasons, project work is included in most science degrees, and the weighting given to related assessments is high. A typical research project mark might account for 25 per cent of a final degree grade, and therefore it deserves considerable attention and effort.

The honours project

Most project work is carried out in the final year, by which time you will have chosen the subject(s) you wish to study in depth, and have gained knowledge and skills that will allow you to make the most of the opportunity. However, in some courses, short projects may be carried out in earlier years to allow you to gain experience and develop your skills. Similar principles apply to these.

→ Adopting a flexible approach

As discussed in **Ch 2**, there are several ways in which you can arrive at a project topic. You may have been allocated a project, made a choice from a list of options, or negotiated a topic with a potential supervisor.

Your initial discussions with your supervisor will probably identify a starting point for your research, for example, a 'simple' set of observations, an uncomplicated experiment, or a test of a key instrument or technique. However, whatever the initial direction, it is important to realise that the precise area of study may change significantly as you proceed with your research, and to be aware of the need to be adaptable in the way you plan your work. For example, if one line of investigation fails to yield results, you should be ready to change tactics, perhaps by using different methods, conditions or experimental subjects.

A good supervisor will guide you not only in the initial approach, but also in the interpretation of results and any modifications you need to make to your initial plan. Others in your supervisor's research team may also be able to help, so ask their advice as well, particularly if your supervisor is a very busy person who prefers to timetable meetings in advance – try not let problems build up and delay your work.

In many cases, telling the story of the progression of your research will be an important part of your project report. This will demonstrate the scientific method in practice. You will be given credit for taking a logical approach in relation to the results you obtain, and in particular for an insightful view of what your results told you and how you responded to them in terms of experimental design and drawing appropriate conclusions.

smart tip

Learning from unexpected results

So-called 'negative results' should not dispirit you - they are a vital part of scientific progress and your personal development as a scientist, so turn them to your advantage by explaining what happened and why, and, where possible, by altering the design of your next experiment appropriately.

→ Focussing on the end product from the start

One of the main keys to success in project work is working with the end product in mind throughout. In most cases this will be a thesis, report or dissertation. Having a concrete idea of what you are expected to produce will help you to plan better; gather the right information; analyse your data appropriately; and think more clearly about ways of presenting your results. You can find out more about this by:

- **Examining the course handbook or regulations.** These will include, for example, 'fine print' about expected length and presentation; relevant learning objectives and marking criteria; and the due date for submission.
- **Looking over project reports produced by past students.** These may be available in a supervisor's lab or from the students themselves if they have moved on to postgraduate study. Submitted theses, projects or dissertations will give you an idea of the style, content and quality of presentation that is expected.
- **Talking to staff or postgraduate students.** These people may be able to supply extra information and advice related to your subject speciality.

Definition: thesis (plural theses)

This literally implies a 'position' in debate or discussion, but has come to mean a (substantial) written paper or report on a specific topic. This term is frequently used to describe an honours project report.

→ Creating a plan of action

In most cases, experimental project work will be carried out over at least one term/semester. Many students start off with the feeling that they have plenty of time to work out what to do and to put their ideas into practice. In fact, the reverse is true. Lab and fieldwork is very time-consuming and your opportunities to do either will be limited, perhaps to one or two sessions per week. Also, research rarely goes smoothly. As a result, many projects are rushed at the end. This not only affects the quality of any write-up, but may adversely affect the energy and time you can devote to other aspects of assessments such as final exams.

What should your plan take into account?

- **Preparatory work.** This includes reading, surveying, ordering equipment or chemicals, making up solutions, and so on. Do any work like this as quickly as possible, so that you are ready to gain useful results.
- **Preliminary observations or experiments.** These may pave the way for later work, but as noted above may also form a vital part of your dissertation or project. Doing a 'quick and dirty' experiment can allow you to practise technique and point out imperfections in your approach.
- **The set of observations or experiments that test your central hypothesis.** This is the core of your report. You should leave time for unexpected interruptions or the need to repeat work, and you should be prepared to move to 'plan B' if necessary. Make sure you design experiments that include suitable controls for all confounding variables.

smart tip

Compromise is vital in experimentation

No experiment is perfect and it is better to obtain some results from an imperfect design rather than delay until you can do the best experiment possible. Your first task is to make sure you have some results to present and discuss. Even if things do not turn out as expected, you can gain marks by pointing out the imperfections in your own work. Remember that some of the best learning comes out of things that do not go well.

- **Time to analyse and present data.** This phase can be very time-consuming and is best done as you go along: the analysis may reveal aspects that cause you to alter your later approach.
- **A period to write up and proof-read your work.** This part always takes much longer than you think, so you should consider writing up as much as you can as you go along. For example, there is no reason why a draft introduction cannot be produced at an early stage, and there are benefits from writing up the materials and methods section while you are working so that you get the details correct. Always leave some time for editing and proof-reading.

Definition: confounding variables

Whenever you alter a particular variable in an experiment (for example, the pH, or acidity, of a bathing medium for cells) you will also alter other things (perhaps, in this example, the concentration of a cation like K^+). These are confounding variables. Controls, where you alter the confounding variable but not the original one, allow you to test which variable actually caused the results you have observed.

→ Working efficiently in the lab or in the field

Since your time will be scarce, you must use it well by making sure you are well organised.

- Prepare for each day by having a plan of action. For example, create a checklist of things you hope to accomplish and prioritise your activities (see p. 32).
- Do any background work that might allow you to progress more quickly. Read up about any techniques or equipment you will be using, so that you have useful background knowledge. Lay out tables in your lab notebook ready to receive results.

Safety issues in the lab

By the time you reach the stage of carrying out a project of your own, you will have been well trained in lab safety. You will carry a certain amount of responsibility for your own safety and should bear this in mind at all times.

- Come prepared. Bring the right equipment and clothing. If you need to discuss results with your supervisor, make sure you have produced graphs and tables to the necessary standards, and have ideas about what they show and what you might do next.
- Maintain your focus and don't be distracted by those working to a different timetable.
- Prepare for your next working day. Tidy up your bench space, fume hood or cupboard. Label specimens or solutions and store them appropriately. Start a new list of things to be done.

→ Organising information and results ready for writing up

This is an important way in which you can save time. Keep a lab notebook to record all relevant details of what you are doing. Take copies of lab schedules and protocols that apply to your work - you can waste a lot of time hunting these down later on.

Every project report requires an introduction and this is something you can draft from an early stage. Your supervisor will probably point you in the direction of a few relevant research papers or reviews, and from there you can expand your knowledge of the relevant literature.

Likewise, as you carry out observations and experiments and analyse your data (see above), it's a good idea to use spare time to create graphs to the requisite standard and to jot down notes for your results and discussions sections.

Ch 20 covers the structure of scientific project reports.

smart tip

Compiling references

A good time-saving tip is to research the format for citing and listing references in your discipline or department and then record the details for each reference in this format within a word-processed file, ready for including in the 'literature cited' section of your thesis. It's far better to break up this tedious and time-consuming task than to do it all in one session. Note that there are some software packages for creating reference lists, but it takes time to learn how to use these (see **Ch 18**, p. 196).

Practical tips for planning project work

Always think ahead. You can waste a lot of time if you haven't prepared well, and you may miss a window of opportunity if you aren't ready to take advantage of something like a booking for a key instrument.

Write up as you go along. This has been emphasised at several points in this chapter, but is worth saying again as it saves so much time. Experimental work often involves long pauses and you can use these to good effect to carry out some of the mundane tasks of writing up.

Communicate with your supervisor. Be ready to show and discuss any preliminary results you have obtained. These discussions will help you think about what your results mean (take notes) and may help orientate the next phase of your work. If things seem to be going wrong, discuss this as soon as possible so that corrective action can be taken.

Keep back-up files of your work. Your project mark is vital to your degree classification and it is common sense to protect it from loss.

Leave plenty of spare time near to the submission date. Students always underestimate how long it takes to write up. Also, you need to allow for the unexpected, such as a printer malfunction, so 'going to the wire' is not a good idea.

And now . . .

6.1 Find out about the expected report format. Knowing what you will be expected to include will help you produce an appropriate plan of action. **Ch 21** describes the layout of a standard experimental research project report, which follows the design of a standard research paper. Precise details for your discipline will be found in your course handbook or regulations.

6.2 Create appropriate filing systems for your experimental project work. This includes files for hard-copy resources, such as methods protocols and safety sheets, electronic files both for the word-processed elements of your project report (**Ch 21**), and, where applicable, for spreadsheet-based data collection and analysis (**Ch 15** and **Ch 16**). You can then add material and organise it as your project proceeds, saving valuable time for the writing-up process.

6.3 Discuss your plans. Do not work in isolation, as others can offer valuable advice that will help you create successful plans and adapt to any setbacks. You should compare notes regularly with your fellow students, and involve other lab workers and your supervisor wherever possible.

Finding and filtering information

7 Information literacy

How to make best use of the library resources

In researching for your dissertation or project, you will generally be expected to source material for yourself. Your supervisor may suggest some resources to get you started, but after that it will be very much up to you to explore further, according to your specific project aims. Therefore, learning more about your university library from the viewpoint of a researcher is a priority. This chapter offers some suggestions and strategies for using your library effectively.

Key topics:

→ First steps for new researchers
→ Basic types of source material
→ How to access your university library's e-resources
→ Indexing and organising your resources

Key terms

Abstract Alphanumeric ATHENS Dewey decimal system Information literacy Library of Congress system Provenance Wikipedia

The library is a key resource in any research project. Modern university libraries are not just repositories of books, journals and archived material. They are information centres that co-ordinate an electronic gateway to a massive amount of online information. Accessing these resources requires a set of library information skills, sometimes called 'information literacy', that are essential to your research studies.

?

Why would I need to know more about the library?

Although you might have studied in your institution for a few years and have used the facilities quite extensively, dissertation and project research will probably mean that you need to delve into areas and facilities that you may not have had the occasion to explore or use before. Indeed, finding material at an appropriate level of detail to support your research may present a major challenge.

→ First steps for new researchers

As someone who has reached the stage of producing a dissertation or project report, you will probably have a working knowledge of how your library works. Thus, you will probably be aware of:

- How to use the electronic catalogue for your own and other libraries.
- How hard-copy resources are shelved, probably using one of the two commonly used methods: the Dewey decimal system (numerical coding) or the Library of Congress System (alphanumeric system).
- How to find a periodical or journal in hard copy or in e-journal format.
- The borrowing rules for your institution, including the borrowing periods and the system of fines that apply for different categories of borrowed resources from a librarian.

If you are unfamiliar with any of these aspects of library use, you should ask for assistance.

Library information systems are constantly changing as your library enters into agreements with new or different suppliers of online information through subscriptions to electronic media, especially e-journals, which are of particular importance in researching. Although you will probably find that your library provides an online information portal dedicated to your subject area, you may find it easier at the outset to contact the librarian with responsibility for collating links to these discipline-specific resources. Make a point of identifying this person so that you can explain your research topic and receive some guidance to get your research journey on track.

The following sections provide you with some insight into the new or not-so-new resources and techniques that you may find useful in this journey.

How can I learn more about what my library has to offer?

Apart from contacting the librarian with responsibility for your discipline, you may find that library staff run training sessions on how to use referencing packages or on the use of new or subject-specific databases. Your library's website may also carry useful tips and online access routes to databases and e-journals. Many libraries have hard-copy leaflets providing tips and guidelines for using a range of facilities and resources.

→ Basic types of source material

As noted already, you will be expected to research your topic extensively and it is worth highlighting some of the source materials that you may find useful. Some of these materials might be classed as primary sources, while others might be thought of as secondary sources (p. 87). This terminology has slightly different interpretations depending on your discipline. Typical resources obtainable through your library include:

- **Monographs:** books on a single, often narrow, subject.
- **Reference works:** useful for obtaining facts and definitions, and a concise overview of a subject. These include encyclopaedias, year books and dictionaries, and can be found in the area of the library reserved for reference material. These items usually cannot be borrowed.
- **Research papers:** very detailed 'articles' published in journals, covering specific subject areas. Proceedings of conferences where cutting-edge research had been presented would also fall into this category.
- **Reviews:** analysis of a research area, often detailed and more up to date than books.
- **Textbooks:** good for gaining an overview of the field.
- **Websites:** some are published by official bodies and should therefore be reliable in their content; however, other websites without such provenance are not wholly reliable as sources, although they may be useful for comparing viewpoints and sourcing other information.

smart tip

Using more than one source

It is fundamental to the research process that you should consult a number of sources on any given issue. These may corroborate each other, or you may find that they take different views or support different interpretations. Interrogating these different 'schools of thought' is sometimes referred to as 'reading around' a subject. This is part of the analytical processes of critical thinking (see **Ch 9** and **Ch 14**).

→ How to access your university library's e-resources

This is normally done via the library's website. Some resources are open-access, but others will require a password. You'll normally need to log on to a university network computer to initiate ATHENS username and password. Once you have obtained these, then you can log on from any Internet-connected computer. Note that different institutions will operate slightly different systems but, if in doubt, then ask a member of the library staff.

Many current items are now available online in each of the categories listed above. For example, libraries take out subscriptions to e-book repositories, e-journals, e-newspapers and online dictionaries and encyclopaedia. Your institution will have its own method of giving access to these resources, probably via the library electronic desktop.

The main advantage of this method of accessing information is that it is available 24 hours a day from any computer connected to the Internet. In some cases, more than one person can access an e-book at any time. Some e-book facilities, such as ebrary, offer additional facilities, such as searching, note-making and linked online dictionaries. One point to note is that copying/printing out from such sources is governed by copyright restrictions.

ATHENS

This is a system that provides a gateway to a number of different databases used by academic researchers. You can obtain an ATHENS password through your institutional library and this will identify you as an authorised user for as long as you are a student.

Key online research techniques

Your research skills will now need to become deeper than in your early years of study, because your dissertation or project report needs to be based on reliable, refereed evidence that is both up to date and comprehensive in relation to your topic. For example, it will not be sufficient to base your work on a few isolated references, augmented by searches of the Internet or Wikipedia. You will need to identify and access new sources.

To find sources new to you, there are three key approaches you can adopt:

1. **Database searches.** These find sources based on key words related to your research topic. The output is a listing of reference details plus abstract/summary material from a wide range of sources. From this list, you can select references that might be of particular relevance, although it may only be possible to judge how significant they are when you read the full paper.
2. **Citation-based searches.** With this kind of search, you start with an article and its reference list. From this list, you backtrack through selected references making judgements about their relevance and value and, potentially, in turn looking at items cited in their reference lists. This enables you to gain a perspective on the literature of your subject area, working backwards from the starting point of your most recent source, but it does not enable you to identify more recent research.
3. **Searches using citation indices.** These searches rely on the availability of databases (for example, the *Science Citation Index* or *British Humanities Index*) which give details of publications that have cited a given reference. In other words, they allow you to work forward in time towards more current research. This can be very useful if your original sources are slightly dated.

Access to the sources identified by any of the above methods is not guaranteed. They may be published in journals to which your library does not subscribe. However, some materials are obtainable via a system of inter-library loans that can be arranged through your own library site by a specialist inter-library loan librarian, although there are cost implications in this process (usually, the cost is borne by the borrower).

Shared library resources

Most libraries share resources with those of neighbouring institutions and all are linked to the British Library, the national library of the UK. This receives a copy of every publication produced in the UK and Ireland, and its massive collection of over 150 million items increases by 3 million items each year. Some university libraries are designated as European Documentation Centres holding key documents of the European Union (**http://ec.europa.eu/europedirect/visit_us/edc/index_en.htm**).

Should I use a source that I've found by chance on the Internet?

'Browsing' your topic using one of the major search engines will probably produce a wealth of links. This approach can produce good material that has been provided for open access. However, be sure that the sites you enter are authoritative sources and do not contain unsubstantiated and possibly erroneous information. As a ground rule, if the material appears to be useful, then try to triangulate it with references from within recognised academic publications, whether online or in hard copy.

Keeping tabs on web sources

The nature of the Web means that it is a constantly changing environment where material is made accessible very quickly - and can, of course, be altered or even removed with similar speed. Thus, it is important to keep a detailed record of all references you have found online, and provide a 'last accessed' date (see **Ch 18**).

Accessing 'raw' data

Electronic databases make it easier to access information from public bodies, and much of that kind of information is also now more readily available online. For example, statistical population details are available through the National Statistics website (**www.statistics.gov.uk**), while papers and publications produced by the Houses of Parliament can also be accessed electronically (**www.parliament.uk**). Clearly, the types of data in this category that you may wish to access will depend on your research topic.

→ Indexing and organising your resources and notes

Dissertation or project research has the potential to generate a considerable quantity of source material either in hard copy or in printouts/photocopies, in addition to e-sourced material read online. This presents three related problems:

1. How to file and organise the hard copies you have obtained (usually by photocopying, but sometimes directly from the author(s)).
2. How to cross-reference your notes on the material, so you refer to the right references in the right places.
3. How to create a database that allows you to create a reference list of all the references you cite.

Hard-copy approaches

One simple 'low-tech' method for storing hard copy and related reference information involves creating a record card for each item. Each hard copy document is given an 'accession' number in sequence (1, 2, 3 . . .) and is stored sequentially in boxes or files. Each document is matched by an index card of the same number. On the card you note essential bibliographical information and any comments you want particularly to note. You then store the cards in alphabetical order by author. Thus, if you recall that an article written by E. Burke (2003) is relevant, you can find the card, identify the accession number and immediately retrieve the relevant document from your filing system. The accession numbers or the record cards themselves can be used to group references in different topic areas, and the cards can be re-ordered alphabetically when writing up your reference list. This system is labour-intensive in creation and has the disadvantage that the final list will probably have to be typed up as a single exercise; nevertheless it might suit some learning styles better than the computer-based and database models described below.

Personalised computer-based approaches

Following the 'accession number' approach in the hard-copy model, an alternative, computer-based system involves creating a file folder in which you insert sub-folders arranged by themes or aspects within your work. In each sub-folder (theme) you create a word processor file that contains a simple table in which you list bibliographical references of each source in order of 'accession number' and record alongside notes of your thoughts about the content and findings in relation to your own study. Some people find that a spreadsheet rather than a Word table is more suited to this purpose. Within the same folder, you might wish to keep any detailed quotes that you have taken directly from source material; any downloaded materials on that theme; and any pieces of ongoing written work. When creating a reference list, the reference information can then be cut and pasted into a word processor file and sorted alphabetically, eliminating any duplication. This method has the advantage of allowing on-screen manipulation of bibliographical data and interpretations.

Both the hard-copy and computer-based methods have the disadvantage of requiring extensive cross-checking and proof-reading of the final list to ensure that all the conventions of the referencing method are applied consistently.

Using commercial bibliographic software

Using commercial bibliographic database software is another possibility, as these systems offer great potential for organising citations within your text and for preparing your reference list. In order to use the systems, appropriate bibliographic data must first be entered into fields within a database (some versions assist you to search online databases and upload data from these). The database can then be searched and customised in the style of your choice to create a consistent reference list for your dissertation or project. The advantage is that the database system will avoid punctuation inaccuracies in the final version. In addition, most packages offer the functions of inserting citations according to different referencing methods and output can be altered to suit different requirements for different publication contexts. However, on the negative side, you have to consider whether the effort taken to learn how to use whichever package is available to you (for example, *EndNote*, *Reference Manager* or *ProCite*), is worthwhile in a research project that may have relatively few references.

Practical tips for making the most of library resources

Register for any courses introducing new information handling packages. Librarians often run specific training sessions to introduce more complex software related to information management. Time spent undertaking such training may pay considerable dividends in the longer term.

Take advantage of reciprocal library arrangements. Your university library may have agreements with others in your area, including national libraries. In some instances, you may be able to borrow books from the partner libraries.

Find and join the local authority library. If you have not already done this, you may find that a local public library offers material not held by the university library. Where there is duplication, you may find that the demand is not so heavy as in the university library and that you might be able to borrow the resource for longer.

Define your catalogue and database searches carefully. Remember that there are often several ways to spell surnames, for example, Brown/Browne or Nichol/Nicol/Nicoll. To find a resource using the author's name that you may only have heard mentioned (as opposed to having seen in print), you may have to try various permutations to find the correct author. Be aware also of surnames for which the pronunciation is totally unlike the spelling, for example, St. John ('*Sinjun*'), Manwaring ('*Mannering*') or Marjoribanks ('*Marchbanks*'). Selecting appropriate terms for database searches is an art in itself, not dissimilar from effective web browsing. Seek advice if you feel your searches are missing potentially important sources.

Ask for advice if you can't access a seemingly vital reference source. You may be able to identify from the title, authors, abstract or from the way the work has been cited by others, that a specific title will be essential for writing up your dissertation or project. If standard approaches to accessing the paper fail to produce results, consult a subject librarian. They may be able to use advanced methods or resources that you do not know about. If it proves impossible to obtain the reference, you may need to use a secondary referencing technique (**Ch 18**).

Keep your cross-referencing system as simple as you can. There is no 'best' way to organise this material as this depends on your personal thought processes which, in turn, relate to the nature of the research and the area being covered. At this level, it is as well to remember that creating a fully functional database or a beautifully colour-coded cross-referencing system may be too time-consuming and labour-intensive given the tight parameters limiting your study.

GO And now . . .

7.1 Spend some time becoming thoroughly acquainted with the electronic library resources available to you. Look, in particular, at any subject-specific resources that are provided on the catalogue system or via the library website.

7.2 Explore the shelves covering your subject area. Identify this area from the library catalogue and the information in the shelving isles. 'Browsing' the books on foot may reveal interesting resources you might not find by other searching methods.

7.3 Find out about alternative library facilities. In some cases, there may be satellite libraries on different campuses or in different buildings. Some of these may be departmental libraries, containing specialist resources. These can contain duplicate holdings of books in the main library. Importantly, you may find they represent convenient or preferable study areas. Even if they do not cover your subject area, you may find their atmosphere more suited to your mood, learning style or personality.

8 Effective academic reading

How to read efficiently and with understanding

Whatever your discipline, you will find that you are required to do a lot of reading when researching. This chapter explains how to develop the speed-reading skills that will help you to deal more effectively with academic text.

Key topics:

→ Surveying the overall organisation of a source
→ How to examine the structure of the writing itself
→ Speed-reading techniques

Key terms

Blurb   Finger tracing   Gist   Terminator paragraph   Topic paragraph   Topic sentence

Much of the material you will read as part of your research will be journals, books, chapters, research papers and reviews written following traditional academic style, and may appear, at first glance, to be heavy going. However, by analysing the way printed academic resources are organised and understanding how text within them is structured, you should find it easier to read the pages of print in a way that will help you gain an understanding of the content, while saving you time.

→ Surveying the overall organisation of a source

Source material may be suggested by your supervisor; alternatively, you may come across a resource in the library that looks as if it might be relevant. In either case, carry out a preliminary survey of the text to familiarise yourself with what the material contains. You can use elements of the structure to answer key questions about the content, as follows:

- **Title and author(s).** Does this text look as though it is going to be useful to your current task? Are the authors well-known authorities in the subject area?
- **Publisher's 'blurb' (book) or the abstract (journal articles).** Does this indicate that the coverage suits your needs?
- **Publication details.** What is the date of publication? Will this source provide you with up-to-date coverage? For books, is this the most recently published version?
- **Contents listing.** Does this indicate that the book or journal cover the key topic areas you need? Do the chapter or article titles suggest the coverage is detailed enough?
- **Index.** This applies only to books. Is this comprehensive and will it help you find what you want, quickly? From a quick look, can you see references to material you want?
- **References.** Does the reference list include a comprehensive listing of recently published work?
- **General impression.** Does the material look easy to read? Is the text easy to navigate via sub-headings? Is any visual material clear and explained well?

The answers to these questions will help you to decide whether to investigate further: whether you need to look at the whole source, or just selected parts; or whether the book or journal article is of limited value at the present time.

What is your reading goal?

Always decide this before you start reading.

- If you are looking for a specific point of information, then this can often be done quickly, using the index, sub-headings or chapter titles as a guide.
- If you need to take notes from the source material, then you might read more strategically (see Table 8.1 and pp. 80–2).
- If your aim is to appreciate the author's style or the aesthetics of a piece of writing, then you may read more slowly and re-read key parts. Similarly, if your purpose is to identify key numerical data or follow the rationale of a discussion, then your reading may be slower.

Sometimes, different methods may be required, for example, in English literature, 'close reading' techniques. These specialised methods will probably have been as part of your introductory studies.

smart tip

Reading and note-making

This chapter is concerned mainly with reading and comprehension as a prelude to note-making (**Ch 10**). While it is possible to read and make notes at the same time, this is not always the most effective form of studying, as your notes may end up simply as a rewrite of the source text. Notes framed after you have scanned the prescribed section of text will be better if you have a clearer idea of their context and content.

→ How to examine the structure of the writing itself

Well-structured academic text usually follows a standard pattern with an introduction, main body and conclusion in each element (**Ch 20**). Sometimes the introduction may comprise several paragraphs; sometimes it may be only one paragraph. Similarly, the conclusion may be several paragraphs or only one.

Within the structure of the text, each paragraph will be introduced by a topic sentence stating the content of the paragraph. Each paragraph performs a function. For example, some may describe, others may provide examples, while others may examine points in favour of a particular viewpoint and others points against that viewpoint.

The function of these paragraphs, and the sentences within them, is usually signalled by use of 'signpost words', which guide the reader through the logical structure of the text. For example, the word 'however' indicates that some contrast is about to be made with a point immediately before; 'therefore' or 'thus' signal that a result or effect is about to be explained.

You can use this knowledge of the structure of writing to establish the substance of a piece of text by:

- Reading the topic and terminator paragraphs, or even just their topic sentences, to gain a quick overview of that element.
- Scanning through the text for key words related to your interest. This scanning may indicate particular paragraphs worthy of detailed reading. Sometimes headings and sub-headings may be used, which will facilitate a search of this kind.
- Looking for signpost words to indicate how the text and its underlying 'argument' is organised.

smart tip

Reader as author

An understanding of the organisation of printed material and the structure of academic text are important for you as a reader or decoder of text, and they also come into play when you become an academic author and have to put your own ideas clearly - they help your reader (often 'the marker') to decode your written text.

Figure 8.1 shows a layout for a piece of text with five paragraphs, comprising an introduction and conclusion with three intervening paragraphs of varying length. Table 8.1 gives an example of an authentic text that demonstrates the structural organisation shown in Figure 8.1.

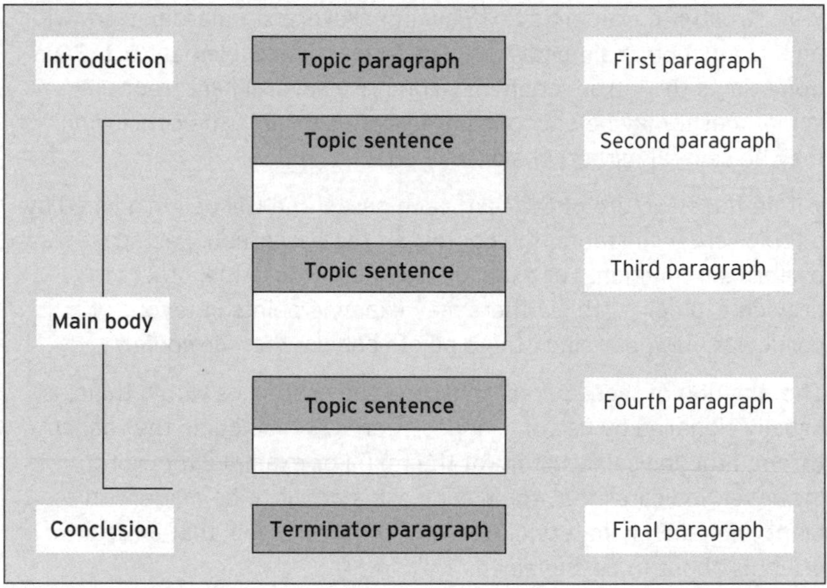

Figure 8.1 Sample textual layout. You can visualise the structure of any piece of reading material in a similar fashion.

→ Speed-reading techniques

Before describing techniques for improving reading speed, it is useful to understand how fast readers 'operate'. Instead of reading each word as a separate unit, these readers use what is called peripheral vision (what you see, while staring ahead, at the furthest extreme to the right and the left). This means that they absorb clusters of words

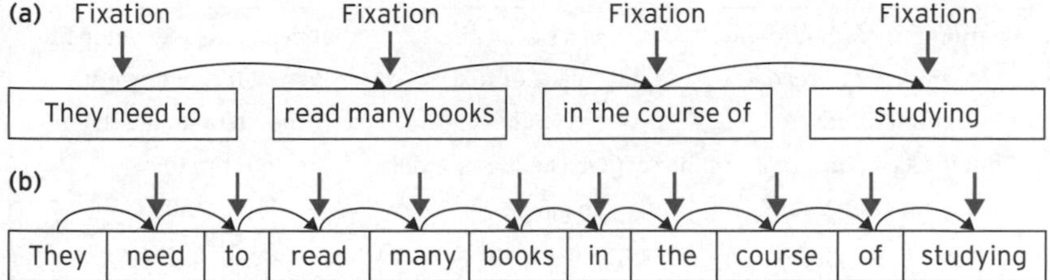

Figure 8.2 Eye movements when reading. (a) Reader who makes eye fixations on clusters of words. (b) Reader who reads every word one by one.

in one 'flash' or 'fixation' on the text, as shown in Figure 8.2(a). In this example, four fixations are required to read that single line of text.

A reader who does this is reading more efficiently than the reader who reads word by word (Figure 8.2(b)). This reader makes 12 fixations along the line, which means that their reading efficiency is low. Research has also indicated that people who read slowly in this way are less likely to absorb information quickly enough for the brain to comprehend. Therefore, reading slowly can actually hinder comprehension rather than assist it.

As a practised reader, you will probably have developed these fast-reading skills to some degree. They can be improved using techniques like the 'eye gymnastics' exercise in Figure 8.3. Other things you can do include 'finger tracing', where you run your finger below the line of text being read to follow your eyes' path across a page, starting and stopping a word or two from either side. This is said to increase your eye speed, keep your mind focussed on the words being read and prevent you from skipping back to previous sentences or jumping forward to text that follows. Some people find it helpful to use a bookmark placed horizontally along the line they are reading, because it makes a useful guide that prevents the eye jumping ahead of the text they are reading.

Origin of speed-reading

The basic techniques were developed in the 1950s by Evelyn Wood, an American educator. She set up institutes to teach students to develop an ability to read hundreds of words per minute. Those who have studied her method include businessmen and politicians, who have to learn to read lengthy papers quickly but with understanding. US Presidents Jimmy Carter and John F. Kennedy were both regarded as famous speed-reading practitioners.

Learning to read quickly	is a skill	that needs to be developed.
If you have to read	a new piece of text,	you will find it useful
first of all	to read	the first paragraph
and the last paragraph	of the section, chapter or article.	From this
you should be able	to gauge	the context
and general outline	of the topic under discussion.	While it is true
that all academic texts	should have been well edited	before publication,
it does not follow	that every text	will follow these conventions.
However,	a well-written piece	of academic writing
should follow this pattern	and, as a reader,	you should exploit
this convention	in order to help you	to understand
the overall content	before you embark	on intensive reading
of the text.		
When you are about to	take notes from texts	you should not begin
by sitting	with notepad ready	and the pen poised.
Certainly	make a note of	publication details needed
for your bibliography,	but resist the temptation	to start taking notes
at the same time as	beginning	your first reading of the text.
It is better	to read first,	reflect, recall
and then write notes	based on	what you remember.
This gives you	a framework	around which
you ought to be able	to organise your notes	after you have read
the text intensively.	People who start	by writing notes
as soon as	they open the book	will end up
copying	more and more from the text	as their tiredness increases.
In this case	very little	reflection or learning
is achieved.		

Figure 8.3 'Eye gymnastics' exercise. Try to read the text above quite quickly. Read from left to right in the normal way. The aim of the activity is to train your eyes to make more use of your peripheral vision when you are reading. In this way, you will learn to make fewer fixations on the text by forcing your eyes to focus on the centre of a group of words, which are printed in naturally occurring clusters – usually on the basis of grammatical or logical framing. It may be that you experience some discomfort behind your eyes, which indicates that they are adjusting to this less familiar pattern. If this is the case, you should keep practising using this text as a means of developing the speed of your eye movements.

smart tip

Things that can reduce your reading speed

As well as trying methods to read faster, you should be aware of circumstances that might slow you down. These include:

- distractions such as background noise of television, music or chatter;
- sub-vocalisation (sounding out each word as it is read aloud);
- reading word by word;
- over-tiredness;
- poor eyesight – if you think your eyes are not 20:20, then it might be worth going for an eye test; your eyes are too important to neglect and a pair of reading glasses may make a huge difference to your studying comfort;
- poor lighting – if you can, read using a lamp that can shine directly on to the text; reading in poor light causes eye strain and this, in turn, limits concentration and the length of reading episodes. Daylight bulbs can also help to reduce eyestrain.

Increasing your reading speed using finger tracing

Try the following method:

- Select a reading passage of about two pages in length (you could use the sample text in Table 8.1). Note your starting and finishing time and calculate your reading speed using Method B in Table 8.2.
- Take a break of 40–60 minutes.
- Return to the text and run a finger along the line of text much faster than you could possibly read it.
- Repeat, but more slowly, so that you can just read it ('finger tracing'). Again, note your starting and finishing times, and work out your reading speed. You should find that your reading speed has increased from the first reading.
- Carry out this exercise at the same time of day over a week, using texts of similar length and complexity. This should help you to increase your reading speed through time.

Table 8.1 Sample reading text, showing reading 'signposts'. This text might represent the introduction to a textbook on modern communications in electrical engineering, journalism, marketing or psychology. The light shaded areas indicate the topic sentences; darker shading indicates the signpost words. You can also use this text of 744 words to assess your speed of reading (see Table 8.2).

Introduction Topic paragraph	Technological advances and skilful marketing have meant that the mobile phone has moved from being simply an accessory to a status as an essential piece of equipment. From teenagers to grandmothers, the nation has taken to the mobile phone as a constant link for business and social purposes. As a phenomenon, the ascendancy of the mobile phone, in a multitude of ways, has had a critical impact on the way people organise their lives.	Topic sentence
	Clearly, the convenience of the mobile is attractive. It is constantly available to receive or send calls. While these are not cheap, the less expensive text-message alternative provides a similar 'constant contact' facility. At a personal and social level, this brings peace of mind to parents as teenagers can locate and be located on the press of a button. However, in business terms, while it means that employees are constantly accessible and, with more sophisticated models, can access internet communications also, there is no escape from the workplace.	Topic sentence Signpost word Signpost word
	The emergence of abbreviated text-message language has wrought a change in everyday print. For example, pupils and students have been known to submit written work using text message symbols and language. Some have declared this to mark the demise of standard English. Furthermore, the accessibility of the mobile phone has become a problem in colleges and universities where it has been known for students in examinations to use the texting facility to obtain information required.	Topic sentence Signpost word Signpost word
	The ubiquity of the mobile phone has generated changes in the way that services are offered. For instance, this means that trains, buses, and restaurants have declared 'silent zones' where the mobile is not permitted, to give others a rest from the 'I'm on the train' style mobile phone conversation.	Topic sentence Signpost words
Transition paragraph	While the marked increase in mobile phone sales indicates that many in the population have embraced this technology, by contrast, 'mobile' culture has not been without its critics. Real concerns have been expressed about the potential dangers that can be encountered through mobile phone use.	Topic sentence Signpost words

Table 8.1 continued

	One such danger is that associated with driving while speaking on a mobile. A body of case law has been accumulated to support the introduction of new legislation outlawing the use of hand-held mobile phones by drivers while driving. The enforcement of this legislation is virtually impossible to police and, thus, much is down to the common sense and responsibility of drivers. Again, technology has risen to meet the contingency with the development of 'hands-free' phones that can be used while driving and without infringing the law.	Topic sentence Signpost word
	A further danger is an unseen one, namely the impact of the radiation from mobile phones on the human brain. Research is not well advanced in this area and data related to specific absorption rates (SARs) from the use of mobile phones and its effect on brain tissue is not yet available for evaluation. Nevertheless, although this lack of evidence is acknowledged by mobile phone companies, they advise that hands-free devices reduce the SARs levels by 98 per cent.	Topic sentence Signpost word
	Mobile phone controversy is not confined only to the potential dangers related to the units alone; some people have serious concerns about the impact mobile phone masts have on the area surrounding them. The fear is that radiation from masts could induce serious illness among those living near such masts. While evidence refuting or supporting this view remains inconclusive, there appears to be much more justification for concern about emissions from television transmitters and national grid pylons, which emit far higher levels of electro-magnetic radiation. Yet, little correlation appears to have been made between this fundamental of electrical engineering and the technology of telecommunications.	Topic sentence Signpost word Signpost word
Conclusion Terminator paragraph	In summary, although it appears that there are enormous benefits to mobile phone users, it is clear that there are many unanswered questions about the impact of their use on individuals. At one level, these represent an intrusion on personal privacy, whether as a user or as a bystander obliged to listen to multiple one-sided conversations in public places. More significantly, there is the potential for unseen damage to the health of individual users as they clamp their mobiles to their ears. Whereas the individual has a choice to use or not to use a mobile phone, people have fewer choices in relation to exposure to dangerous emissions from masts. While the output from phone masts is worthy of further investigation, it is in the more general context of emissions from electro-magnetic masts of all types that serious research needs to be developed.	Topic sentence Signpost words Signpost words Signpost word Signpost word

Table 8.2 How to calculate your reading speed. These two examples show the principles of how to do this calculation.

Method A (specified reading time)		
a	Select a chapter from a textbook (this is better than a newspaper or journal because these are often printed in columns)	
b	Calculate the average number of words per line, e.g. 50 words counted over 5 lines	= 10 words per line
c	Count the number of lines per page	= 41 total lines
d	Multiply (b × c) = 10 × 41	= 410 words per page
e	Read for a specific time (to the nearest minute or half-minute) without stopping	= 4 minutes' reading
f	Number of pages read in 4 minutes	= 2.5 pages read
g	Multiply (d × f) = 410 × 2.5	= 1025 total words read
h	Divide (g ÷ e) = 1025 ÷ 4	= **256 words per minute**
Method B (specified text length)		
a	Find a piece of text of known or estimated word length (see method A)	= 744 words
b	Note the time taken to read this in seconds	= 170 seconds
c	Convert the seconds to a decimal fraction of minutes = 170 ÷ 60	= 2.8 minutes
d	Divide (a ÷ c) = 744 ÷ 2.8	= **266 words per minute**

The average reading speed is said to be 265 words per minute (wpm). Reading speed for university students may be slightly lower, as aspects like difficulty of the text, unfamiliarity with the terminology used and the complexity of the concepts being discussed in the text have the potential to slow down reading. However, as you become more familiar with the subject and the issues being covered in your course and, thus, with your supplementary reading, then your reading speed will increase.

You can assess your normal reading speed using either method described in Table 8.2. The text of Table 8.1 is a suitable piece of writing whose word length is already known, should you wish to try method B. If your reading speed seems slow, then you can work on improving it by using a similar level and length of text at the same time each day. Go through the reading speed process and, gradually, you should see your average creeping up.

There are many other strategies you can develop to read and absorb content quickly. These include:

- **Skimming.** Pick out a specific piece of information by quickly letting your eye run down a list or over a page looking for a key word or phrase, as when seeking a particular name or address in a phone book.
- **Scanning.** Let your eye run quickly over a piece of text, for example before you commit yourself to study-read the whole text. This will help you to gain an overview of the content before you start.
- **Picking out the topic sentences.** As seen above and in Figure 8.1 and Table 8.1, by reading the topic sentences you will be able to flesh out your overview of the text content. This will aid your understanding before you study-read the whole text.
- **Identifying the signpost words.** As noted above, these help guide you as the reader through the logical process that the author has mapped out for you.
- **Recognising clusters of grammatically allied words.** Subliminally, you will be grouping words in clusters according to their natural alliances. This will help you to read by making fewer fixations and this will improve your reading speed. You can improve your speed at doing this by using the eye-gymnastics exercise described earlier.
- **Taking cues from punctuation.** As you read, you will gain some understanding by interpreting the text using the cues of full stops and commas, for example to help you gain understanding of what you are reading. The importance of punctuation to comprehension is vital (a point to remember as an academic author).

To be effective, reading quickly must be matched by a good level of comprehension, while reading too slowly can mean that comprehension is hampered. Clearly, you need to incorporate tests of your understanding to check that you have understood the main points of the text. One method of reading that incorporates this is called the SQ3R method – survey, question, read, recall and review (Table 8.3). This is also a helpful strategy for exam revision as it incorporates the development of memory and learning skills simultaneously. Another test of assimilation is note-making. This is covered in **Ch 10**.

Table 8.3 Reading for remembering: the SQ3R method. The point of this method is that the reader has to engage in processing the material in the text and is not simply reading on 'autopilot' where very little is being retained.

Survey stage
• Read the first paragraph (topic paragraph) and last paragraph (terminator paragraph) of a chapter or page of notes • Read the intervening paragraph topic sentences • Focus on the headings and sub-headings, if present • Study the graphs and diagrams for key features
Question stage
• What do you know already about this topic? • What is the author likely to tell you? • What specifically do you need to find out?
Read stage
• Read the entire section *quickly* to get the gist of the piece of writing; finger-tracing techniques may be helpful at this point • Go back to the question stage and revisit your initial answers • Look especially for keywords, key statements, signpost words • Do *not* stop to look up unknown words - go for completion
Recall stage
• Turn the book or your notes over and try to recall as much as possible • Make key pattern headings/notes/diagrams/flow charts (**Ch 10**) • Turn over the book again • Check over for accuracy of recall; suggested recall periods - every 20 minutes
Review stage
• After a break, try to recall the main points

Practical tips for reading effectively and with understanding

Be selective and understand your purpose. Think about why you are reading. Look at the material you have already collected relating to the subject or topic you aim to research. For example, this may even include lecture notes, which ought to remind you of the way a particular topic was presented, the thrust of an argument or a procedure. Are you reading to obtain a general overview or is it to identify additional specific information? Use a technique and material that suits your needs.

Adjust your reading speed according to the type of text you have to read. For example, a marginally interesting article in a newspaper will probably require less intensive reading than a key chapter in an academic book or an article from an academic journal.

Grasp the general message before dealing with difficult parts. Not all academic printed material is 'reader friendly'. If you find a section of text difficult to understand, then skip over that bit; toiling over it will not increase your understanding. Continue with your reading and when you come to a natural break in the text, for example, the end of a chapter or section, then go back to the 'sticky' bit and reread it. Usually, second time round, it will make more sense because you have an overview of the context. Similarly, don't stop every time you come across a new word. Read on and try to get the gist of the meaning from the rest of the text. When you have finished, look the word up in a dictionary and add to your personal glossary.

Take regular breaks. Reading continuously over a long period of time is counterproductive. Concentration is at a peak after 20 minutes, but wanes after 40 minutes. Take regular breaks, making sure that your breaks do not become longer than your study stints.

Follow up references within your text. When you are reading, you need to be conscious of the citations to other authors that might be given in the text; not all will be relevant to your reading purpose, but it is worth quickly noting the ones that look most interesting as you come across them. You'll usually find the full publication details in the references at the end of the chapter/article or at the end of the book. This will give you sufficient information to access supplementary reading once you have finished reading the 'parent' text.

GO And now . . .

8.1 Monitor your reading speed. Choose a suitable text and calculate your speed using either method A or B in Table 8.2. If you feel your speed is relatively slow, then try out some of the methods suggested in the speed-reading section of this chapter. After a period of using these methods, and deciding which suit you, check your speed to see if you have improved.

▶

8.2 Practise surveying a text using a book from your reading list. Rather than simply opening your reading resource at the pages that appear to be most relevant, spend a few minutes surveying the whole book. Think about how the author has organised the content and why. Keep this in mind when reading the text, and reflect on whether this has improved your comprehension and assimilation of the content. As a bonus your quick survey may reveal more relevant information that you might otherwise have missed.

8.3 Become more familiar with the visual reading cues embedded within texts. Conventions of grammar, punctuation and spelling are useful in providing clues to meaning for the reader (see Table 8.1, for example). If you would like to look into these topics further, then see **Ch 22, Ch 23, Ch 24** and **Ch 25**.

9 Analysing and evaluating source material

How to filter and select relevant material as part of the research process

Access to a variety of information is now so easy, through many different media, that the evaluation of evidence, data and opinions has become a core skill. This chapter will help you understand the origin of information and ideas, the reliability of sources, and differences between fact, opinion and truth.

Key topics:

→ The origin of information and ideas
→ Assessing sources of 'facts'
→ Facts, opinions and truth
→ Backing up your own opinion or conclusion

Key terms

Citation Conjecture Objectivity Premise/premiss Primary source Provenance Secondary source Subjectivity Value judgement

When researching at the dissertation and project level, it is essential to develop the ability to evaluate information and ideas critically. This is a multifaceted skill that will differ according to the task in hand. Your analysis may centre on the accuracy or truth of the information itself, the reliability or potential bias of the source of the information, or the value of information in relation to some argument or case.

From time to time, you may come across contradictory sources of evidence or conflicting arguments based on the same information. You will need to assess their relative merits. To do any or all of these tasks, you will need to understand more about the origin and nature of information.

The nature of evaluation

In 'scientific' subjects you will need to interpret and check the reliability of data. This is essential for setting up and testing meaningful hypotheses, and therefore at the core of the scientific approach.

In 'non-scientific' subjects, ideas and concepts are important, and you may need to carry out an objective analysis of information and arguments so that you can construct your own position, backed up with evidence.

→ The origin of information and ideas

Essentially, facts and ideas originate from someone's research or scholarship. These can be descriptions, concepts, interpretations or numerical data. At some point, information or ideas must be communicated or published, otherwise no one else would know about them. Information and ideas usually appear first in the primary literature and may be modified later in the secondary literature (Table 9.1). Understanding this process is important when analysing and evaluating information and when deciding how to cite evidence or references in the text of your own work.

→ Assessing sources of 'facts'

Not all 'facts' are true. These could be misquoted, misrepresented, erroneous or based on a faulty premise. This is particularly true of web-based information because it is less likely to be refereed or edited. Logically, the closer you can get to the primary source, the more consistent the information is likely to be with the original. A lot depends on who wrote the source and under what patronage (who paid them?). Hence, another important way of assessing sources is to investigate the ownership or 'provenance' of the work (from whom and where it originated, and why).

Who should you quote?

Always try to read and cite the primary source if you can. Do not rely on a secondary source to do this for you, as you may find the author uses information selectively to support their case, or interprets it in a different way than you might. See **Ch 18** for citation methods.

Table 9.1 Characteristics and examples of primary and secondary sources of information

Primary sources: those in which ideas and data are first communicated.	• The primary literature in your subject may be published in the form of papers (articles) in journals. • The primary literature is usually refereed by experts in the authors' academic peer group. They check the accuracy and originality of the work and report their opinions back to the journal editors. This system helps to maintain reliability, but it is not perfect. • Books can also be primary sources, but this depends on the nature of the information published rather than the medium. These sources are not formally refereed, although they may be read by editors and lawyers to check for errors and unsubstantiated or libellous allegations. Note that in non-Science subjects, Government reports, company accounts or 'raw data' such as census figures or patient records are also classed as primary sources.
Secondary sources: those that quote, adapt, interpret, translate, develop or otherwise use information drawn from primary sources.	• It is the act of recycling that makes the source secondary, rather than the medium. Reviews are examples of secondary sources in the academic world, and textbooks and magazine articles are often of this type. • As people adopt, modify, translate and develop information and ideas, alterations are likely to occur, whether intentional or unintentional. Most authors of secondary sources do not deliberately set out to change the meaning of the primary source, but they may unwittingly do so. Others may consciously or unconsciously exert bias in their reporting by quoting evidence only on one side of a debate. • Modifications while creating a secondary source could involve adding valuable new ideas and content.

- **Authorship.** Can you identify who wrote the piece? In some cases it may be easy to deduce that the author is an authority in the area; if the name is unfamiliar, then putting the name in a search engine might provide information about their status or academic position.

  Of course, just because Professor X thinks something, this does not make it valid or true. However, if you know that their opinion is backed by years of research and experience, then you might take it a little more seriously than the thoughts of an unknown web author. If no author is cited, this may mean that no-one is willing to take responsibility for the content. Could there be a reason for this?

- **Provenance.** Is the author's place of work mentioned? This might tell you whether there is likely to have been an academic study behind the facts or opinions given. If the author works for a public body, there may be publication rules to follow and they may even have to submit their work to a publications committee before it is disseminated. Another question to ask is whether a company or political faction may have a vested interest behind the content or whether the author is identified by a particular 'school' of academic thought.

Table 9.2 is a checklist for assessing the reliability of information you may encounter in the process of researching your dissertation or project.

Table 9.2 A checklist for assessing the reliability of source material. These questions are based on commonly adopted criteria; the more 'yes' answers you can give, the more reliable you can assume your source to be.

Assessing authorship and the nature of the source	Evaluating the information and its analysis
❑ Can you identify the author's name?	❑ Is the source cited by others?
❑ Can you determine what relevant qualifications they hold?	❑ Is the date of the source likely to be important regarding the accuracy of the information? For example, is it contemporary to events, or is it written with the benefit of hindsight?
❑ Can you say who employs the author?	❑ Have you focussed on the substance of the information presented rather than its packaging?
❑ Do you know who paid for the work to be done?	❑ Is the information fact or opinion?
❑ Is this a primary source rather than a secondary one?	❑ Have you checked for any logical fallacies in the arguments?
❑ Has the source been refereed or edited?	❑ Does the language used indicate anything about the status of the information?
❑ Is the content original or derived?	❑ Have possible errors associated with any numbers been taken into account?
❑ Does the source cite relevant literature?	❑ Have the data been analysed using appropriate statistics?
❑ Have you checked a range of sources?	❑ If there are graphs, are they constructed fairly?

How can authorship and provenance be shown?

Authorship and publication information is easy to find in most published academic sources, and may even be presented just below the title for convenience. In the case of the Web, it may not be so easy to find what you need. However, often relevant clues can be obtained from the header, body and footer information.

→ Facts, opinions and truth

When dealing with extensive reading material and a wide diversity of viewpoints, such as you will probably find in the course of researching your dissertation or project, you can easily become confused and lose sight of the differences between fact, opinion and truth. Becoming aware of this issue is fundamental to study in many subjects, particularly in the Arts, Social Sciences and Law.

In many fields, there is often no 'right' or 'wrong' answer, simply a range of stances or viewpoints. You gain credit for constructing your own argument with evidence to substantiate your position, rather than simply following a 'line' expounded in lectures or a standard text. Even if your supervisor disagrees personally with your conclusions, they will assess your work according to the way you have argued your case.

However, in some subjects, such as History, Politics and Economics, it is very easy to stray into opinionated and biased conclusions. Sometimes these might be referred to as 'value judgements' (see p. 148). If your work includes these unsubstantiated viewpoints, you may weaken your argument.

Truth is a concept that can be problematic, because it involves a host of philosophical concepts, which may be confusing. In debate, something is only true when all sides of the argument accept it. If a particular line of argument can be shown to lack credibility or to be in some way unacceptable, this will add weight to the counter-argument.

Concepts of truth and fact involve the notions of objectivity and subjectivity:

- **objective** means based on a balanced consideration of the facts;
- **subjective** means based on one person's opinion.

Most academics aim for a detached, objective piece of writing. Nevertheless, it is important to state your own opinion at some point in the work, particularly if some of the evidence might point to a contrary view. The key is to produce valid reasons for holding your opinion.

smart tip

Fact, opinion and truth

The world record for the 100-metre sprint in athletics was 9.79 seconds at 30 September 1999. This is a *fact*. The record may change over time, but this statement will still be true. Some claim that many world records are created by athletes who have taken drugs to enhance their performance. This is an *opinion*. There is evidence to back up this position, but recent controversies have highlighted the problem of proof in these cases. Claims about drug misuse are open to conjecture, claim and counter-claim, not all of which can be *true*. Your task might be to identify the difference between fact and opinion and write with that knowledge. Do not avoid the controversy, but be clear about the facts, the truth and your opinion of the evidence.

→ Backing up your own opinion or conclusion

How your work is judged will probably depend on how convincing your argument is and how well you use the evidence to support your position. Evidence comes in many forms: for example, from statistical/numeric sources, from quotations, or from observation. You should assess all potential evidence for relevance and value, and you must make sure you cite the source of the information in your own writing, otherwise the evidence is open to accusations of plagiarism.

Above all, you should try to produce a *balanced* conclusion. This is one where you are open about counter-arguments and counter-evidence that does not, at least on the face of it, support your case. You must explain what others think or might think, then explain why you have arrived at your conclusion. Filtering material to arrive at a viewpoint is part of the broader concept of thinking critically (**Ch 14**).

Practical tips for evaluating source material

Make cross-referencing checks. This means looking at more than one source and comparing what is said in each. The sources should be as independent as possible (for example, do not compare an original source with one that is directly based on it). If you find the sources agree, you may become more certain of your position. If two sources differ, you may need to decide which viewpoint is better.

Consider the age of the source. 'Old' does not necessarily mean 'wrong', but ideas and facts may have altered between then and now. Can you trace changes through time in the sources available to you? What key events, works or changes in methods have forced any changes in the conclusions?

Look at the extent and quality of citations provided by an author. This applies particularly to articles in academic journals, where positions are usually supported by citations of others' work. These citations may indicate that a certain amount of research has been carried out beforehand, and that the ideas or results being currently reported are based on genuine scholarship. If you doubt the quality of the work, these references might be worth looking at. How up to date are they? Do they cite independent work, or is the author exclusively quoting him/herself or the work of one particular researcher?

Assess substance over presentation. Just because information is presented well, for instance in a glossy magazine or particularly well-constructed website, this does not necessarily tell you much about the quality of its content. Try to look beyond the surface.

Analyse the language used. Words and their use can be very revealing. Have subjective or objective sentence structures been employed? The former might indicate a personal opinion rather than an objective conclusion. Are there any telltale signs of propaganda? Bias might be indicated by absolute terms, such as 'everyone knows . . .'; 'I can guarantee that . . .'; or a seemingly unbalanced consideration of the evidence. How carefully has the author considered the topic? A less studious approach might be indicated by exaggeration, ambiguity, or the use of journalese and slang. Always remember, however, that content should be judged above presentation.

Try to maintain a healthy, detached scepticism. However reliable a source seems to be, it is probably a good idea to retain a degree of scepticism about the facts or ideas involved and to question the logic of arguments. Even information from primary sources may not be perfect - different approaches can give different outcomes, for reasons not necessarily understood at the time of writing. Also, try not to identify too strongly with a viewpoint, so you can be detached when assessing its merits and failings.

Try to distinguish fact from opinion. To what extent has the author supported a given viewpoint? Have relevant facts been quoted, via literature citations or the author's own researches? Are numerical data used to substantiate the points used? Are these reliable and can you verify the information, for example, by looking at a source that was cited? Might the author have a hidden reason for putting forward biased evidence to support a personal opinion?

Spot fallacious arguments and logical flaws. Concentrate on analysing the method being used to put the points over, rather than the facts themselves. Perhaps you can see one of the common fallacies in arguments that indicate a flaw in logic (**Ch 14**).

Look closely at any data and graphs that are presented and the way they have been analysed. If the information is numerical in form, have the errors of any data been taken into consideration, and, where appropriate, quantified? If so, does this help you arrive at a conclusion about how genuine the differences are between important values? Have the appropriate statistical methods been used to analyse the data? Are the underlying hypotheses the right ones? Have the results of any tests been interpreted correctly in arriving at the conclusion? Look closely at any graphs. These may have been constructed in such a way as to emphasise a particular viewpoint, for example, by careful selection of axis starting points (see **Ch 16**).

Don't be blinded by statistics. Leaving aside the issue that statistical methods don't actually deal with proof, only probability, it is generally possible to analyse and present data in such a way that they support one chosen argument or hypothesis rather than another ('you can prove anything with statistics'). To deal with these matters, you will need at least a basic understanding of the 'statistical approach' and of the techniques in common use.

Look at who else has cited the author's work, and how. In many scientific subjects you can use the citation indices (p. 65) to find out how often an article or author has been cited and by whom. You may then be able to consult these sources to see how others have viewed the original findings. Works that review the same area of study, published after your source, may also provide useful comments.

GO And now . . .

9.1 Use the checklist in Table 9.2 to assess a source about which you are uncertain. If you are unable to establish its reliability, you should research further around the topic.

9.2 Analyse the nature of your sources. Each time you encounter what seems to be a relevant piece of information, decide whether it should be considered as primary or secondary, and why (see Table 9.1). If secondary, does it quote any of the primary sources? Try to get a copy of one of the primary sources, if available, and see if this reveals anything to you about the nature of knowledge, how it arises and how it is modified during translation. This will assist you to cite work appropriately in your dissertation or project report (**Ch 18**).

9.3 Find out how articles in your subject area come to be published. Next time you are looking at a journal in the primary literature, look out for the 'information for authors' section. This appears every three months or so in current (unbound) volumes, or on specific web pages for e-journals. This will provide valuable insights and background information about the submission, refereeing and editing process for contributions to the primary literature.

10 Note-making from source material

How to create effective notes to support your dissertation and project research

Keeping a record of the content of your reading is essential when researching at dissertation and report levels. There is simply too much information to remember and retain. This chapter outlines practical ways in which you can keep a record of what you read in appropriate note form so that it is meaningful to you at a later date.

Key topics:

→ Why are you taking notes?
→ What do you need to record?
→ How are you going to lay out your notes?

Key terms

Annotate Citation Citing Landscape orientation Mnemonic Portrait orientation

Your dissertation or project research will involve reading a broad and varied range of material. Depending on your subject, this may include textbooks, journal articles and web-based materials. You may be given specific references; but, as noted elsewhere, at other times you will have to find the relevant material in the text for yourself. The techniques described in **Ch 8** will help you identify the most relevant parts of the text quickly and provide the material for your note-making.

You will have developed note-making skills throughout your studies. It takes time and experimentation to achieve a method that suits you, but the larger project you now need to complete may mean that you need to modify your strategy. This chapter suggests a range of techniques you can choose from in order to abstract and write down the key points from your sources in ways that are efficient and retrievable. This is important because the way you organise your notes may help you to organise your own thinking about the research topic.

smart tip

Note-making formats

Sometimes notes may be better suited to being laid out on paper in the landscape rather than the portrait position. This clearly suits methods such as mind maps (modelled in Figure 10.5). Similarly, you can take advantage of the landscape format when making matrix (grid) notes (Figure 10.6) by creating columns across the page.

→ Why are you taking notes?

Some texts will simply be 'dip in and out', while some will require intensive reading. You need to decide what your purpose is in making the notes. For example, it may be to:

- frame an overview of the subject;
- record a sequence or process;
- enable you to analyse a problem;
- extract the logic of an argument;
- compare different viewpoints;
- borrow quotes (with suitable citation - see **Ch 18**);
- add your own commentary on the text, perhaps by linking key points with what has been discussed in a lecture or tutorial.

This will influence the style, detail and depth of your notes.

→ What do you need to record?

One of the pitfalls of making notes is that people often start off with a blank sheet, pen in hand, and then begin to note 'important' points as they read. Within a short time, they are rewriting the original in its entirety. To avoid this, the trick is to:

- identify your purpose;
- scan the section to be read;
- establish the writer's intention, for example to provide:
  - a narrative of events or process
  - a statement of facts
  - an explanation of reasoning or presentation of a logical argument
  - an analysis of an issue, problem or situation
  - a critique of an argument;

- work out their 'take' on the subject, and how this relates to your purpose;
- decide on the most appropriate note-making style and layout for the task; and
- ensure you paraphrase in your own words rather than transcribe, using quote marks and noting reference details (**Ch 17**).

smart tip

Essentials of note-making

It will save time if you develop good practice in making your notes.

- On all notes record the full details of source, that is:
  - author surname and initials
  - title in full with chapter and pages
  - date of publication
  - publisher and place of publication.

You will need this information to enable you to cite the source of information if you decide to use any of this information in your own writing.

- It's a good idea to add the date(s) you made the notes.
- Your notes have to be as meaningful in six days', weeks' or months' time. Personalise them by using:
  - underlining
  - highlighting
  - colour coding
  - numbered lists
  - bullet points
  - mnemonics
  - distinctive layout
  - boxes for important points.

→ How are you going to lay out your notes?

The reality of researching for dissertations and projects is that you may have limited access to a resource in hard copy or be time-limited in your capacity to conduct the research phase. Your notes will thus have to be accurate and include all relevant points in a form that helps you recall the meaning and detail of the original. Figures 10.1–10.7 illustrate some simplified examples of different note formats. Not all styles will be relevant to your subject, but some will. Some techniques may not seem directly suitable, but, with a little adaptation, they may work for you. Table 10.1 compares the advantages and disadvantages of each method.

Topic: DEPOPULATION OF THE COUNTRYSIDE — *Source: Ormiston, J., 2002. Rural Idylls. Glasgow: Country Press.*

Problem:	Population falling in rural areas Traditional communities disintegrate Incomer settlement – dormitory villages
Reasons:	Mechanisation of farming Creation of farming combines Bigger farms, fewer employed Decline of traditional farming & related activities
Effects:	Families dispersed – fewer children Closure of shops, post offices, schools, surgeries Transport links less viable
Solutions:	Housing subsidies to encourage families to remain Diversity economic activity, e.g. tourism/action holidays Stimulate rural economy – farm shops, farmers' markets Diversify from traditional crops – seek new markets

Figure 10.1 Example of keyword notes

Topic: OBESITY IN CHILDREN — *Source: Skinner, J., 2001. Diet and Obesity. Edinburgh: Castle Publishing.*

1. Lifestyle
   - 1.1 Television, computer-games generation
   - 1.2 Unsupervised leisure time – sedentary
2. Diet
   - 2.1 Constant 'grazing' – junk food
   - 2.2 Additives/processed foods
   - 2.3 Lack of adequate fresh food, including fruit + vegetables
3. Exercise
   - 3.1 Sport by spectating rather than participating
   - 3.2 Decline in team sports in schools
   - 3.3 Children over-protected from 'free play' outdoors
4. Family
   - 4.1 Parents overeat; children likewise
   - 4.2 Instant food
   - 4.3 Food as an incentive + reward
5. Schools
   - 5.1 School meals spurned in favour of snack bar/chip shop
   - 5.2 Health–eating programmes as part of curriculum
6. Health service
   - 6.1 Less emphasis on prevention
   - 6.2 Limited health education of parents and children

(a)

Figure 10.2 Examples of linear notes. These are drawn from three diverse disciplines where topics lend themselves to hierarchical approaches.

Topic:
GENERAL FEATURES OF ORGANIC MATERIALS

Source: Barker, J., 2001. Chemistry for University. Manchester: Midland Publishing.

1. *Solid state – molec. crystal – powder, poly. Thin films*
2. *Unique physical properties – exploit for high-tech applications*
3. *Advantages*
   - *3.1 Versatile properties – reg. by organic chemistry*
   - *3.2 Readily accessible – via organic synthesis*
   - *3.3 Low cost – cheap raw materials*
   - *3.4 Tractable – fusable, soluble: easy to fab.*
4. *Disadvantage*
   - *4.1 Relatively fragile*
5. *Important types*
   - *5.1 Conducting CT salts*
   - *5.2 Conducting poly*

(b)

Topic: OPERATIONAL AMPLIFIERS

Source: Scott, D.I., 1977. Operational Amplifiers. Coventry: Circuit Publishers.

1. *Usually an integrated circuit; can be discrete*
2. *Uses all technologies: bipolar; FET; MOS; BI-FET*
3. *Effectively a highly stable differential amplifier*
4. *Advantages*
   - *4.1 High voltage gain – typ. 100,000*
   - *4.2 High input impedance – typ. 1MΩ – can be much higher, FET, MOS*
   - *4.3 Low output impedance – typ. 600Ω*
   - *4.4 Low drift, BI-FET best*
   - *4.5 Wide voltage supply range*
5. *Disadvantages*
   - *5.1 Relatively narrow bandwidth – GBP typ. 1MHz (but operates to DC)*
   - *5.2 Very unstable in discrete versions – requires matched transistors*
6. *Common types*
   - *6.1 741 – most common*
   - *6.2 LM 380 – common AF AMP*
   - *6.3 TDA 2030 – common power amp. – 20W in to 4Ω*

(c)

Figure 10.2 continued

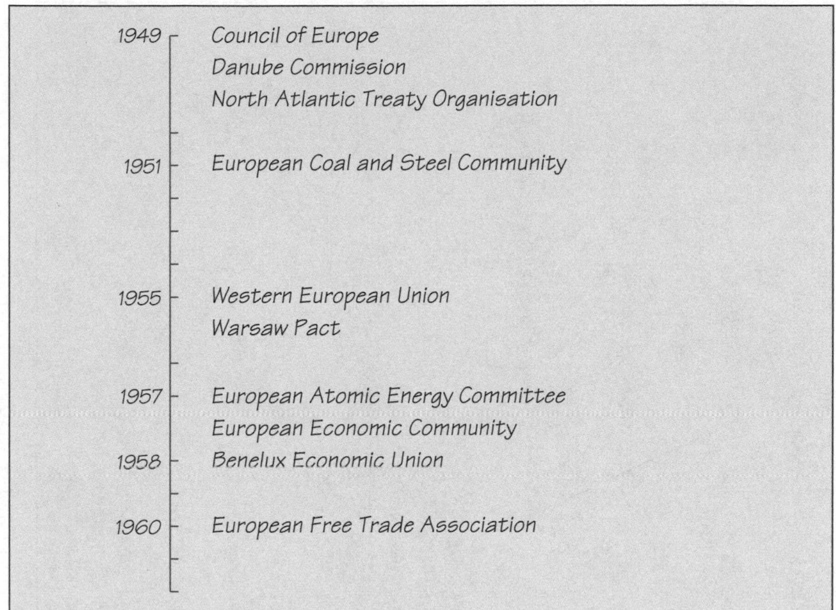

Figure 10.3 Example of time-line notes. This design is good for showing a sequence of events, in this case, the development of European organisations.

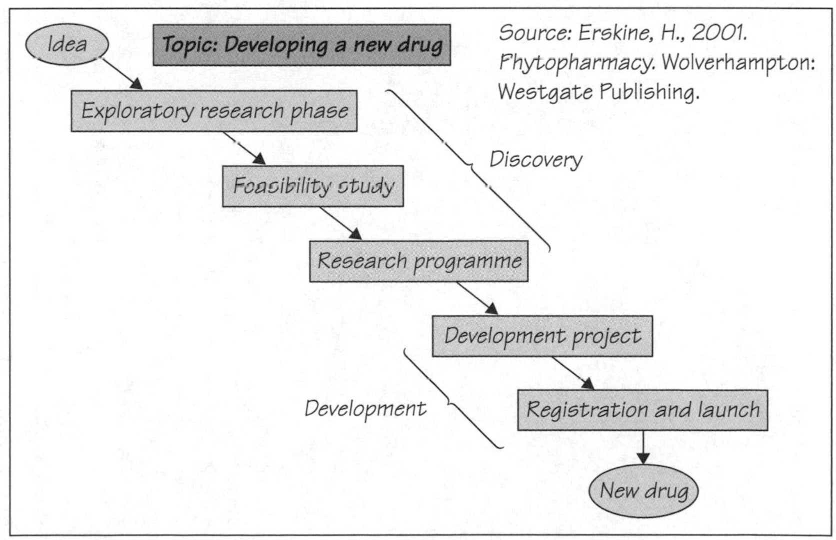

Figure 10.4 Example of flow-chart notes. These are particularly useful for describing complex processes in visual form.

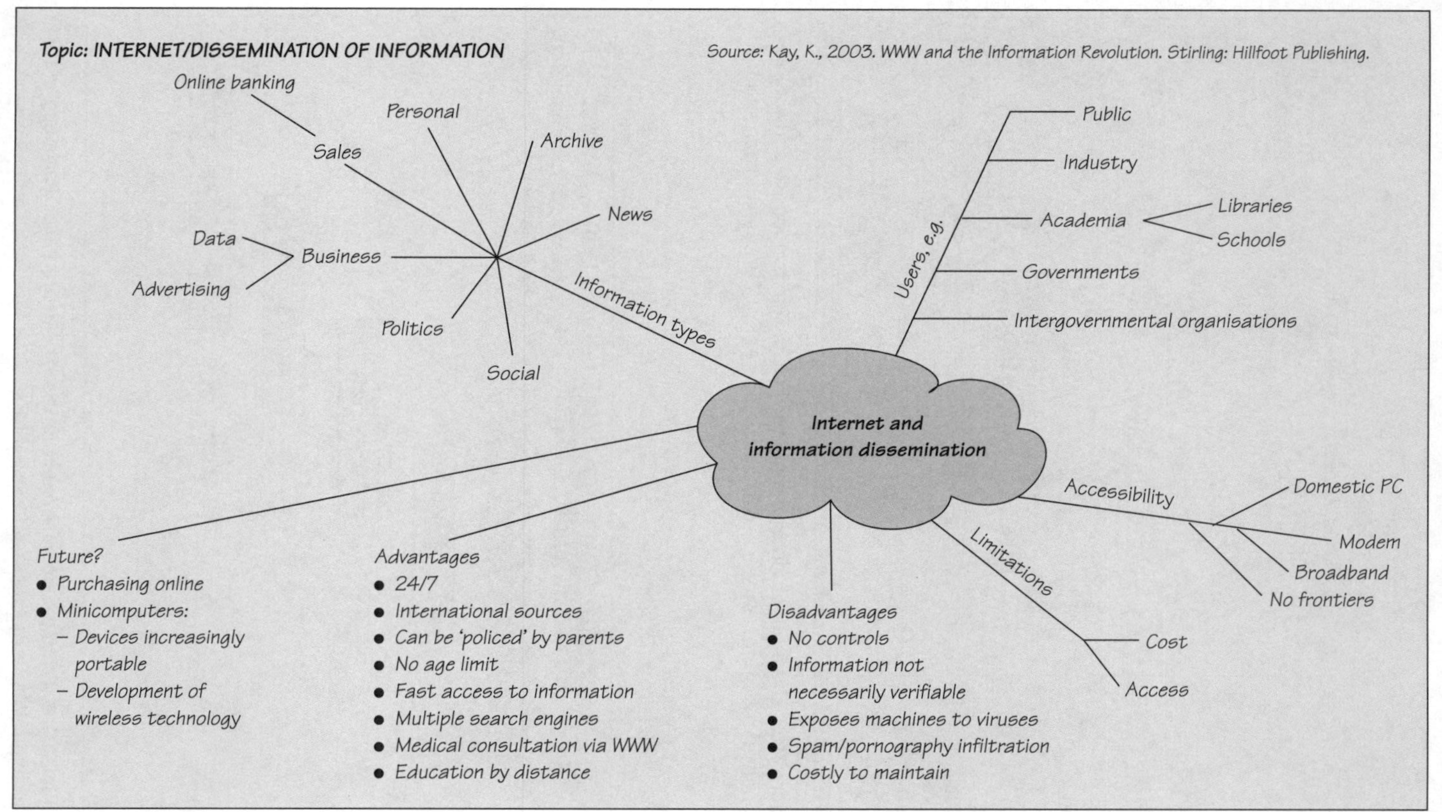

Figure 10.5 Example of a concept map. This may also be called a mind map. Suits visual-spatial/visual learners.

Topic: TRAFFIC CONGESTION		Source: Walker, I.M.A., 2005. Urban Myths and Motorists. London: Green Press.		
Solutions	**Council view**	**Police view**	**Local business view**	**Local community view**
Pedestrianisation	+ Low maintenance – Initial outlay	+ Easier to police + Less car crime + CCTV surveillance easier	+ Safer shopping and business activity – Discourages motorist customers	+ Safer shopping + Less polluted town/city environment
Park and ride schemes	+ Implements transport policy – Capital investment to initiate – Car park maintenance	+ Reduce inner-city/town traffic jams + Reduce motor accidents – Potential car park crime	– Loss of custom – Lack of convenience – Sends customers elsewhere	+ Less polluted town/city environment – Costly
Increase parking charges	+ Revenue from fines – Costly to set up	– Hostility to enforcers	– Loss of custom – Delivery unloading problematic	– Residents penalised by paying for on-street parking
Restrict car journeys, e.g. odd/even registrations on alternate days	+ Easy to administer	+ Easy to police	– Seek exemption for business vehicles	+ Encourage car-sharing for daily journeys – Inconvenience
Levy congestion charge for urban journeys	+ Revenue raised – Cost of implementing tracking system	– Traffic jams on alternative routes	– Cost of loss of custom	– Inhibit work/leisure activities – Cost

Figure 10.6 Example of matrix notes. This particular analysis lays out positive (+) and negative (–) viewpoints on an issue from a range of different perspectives.

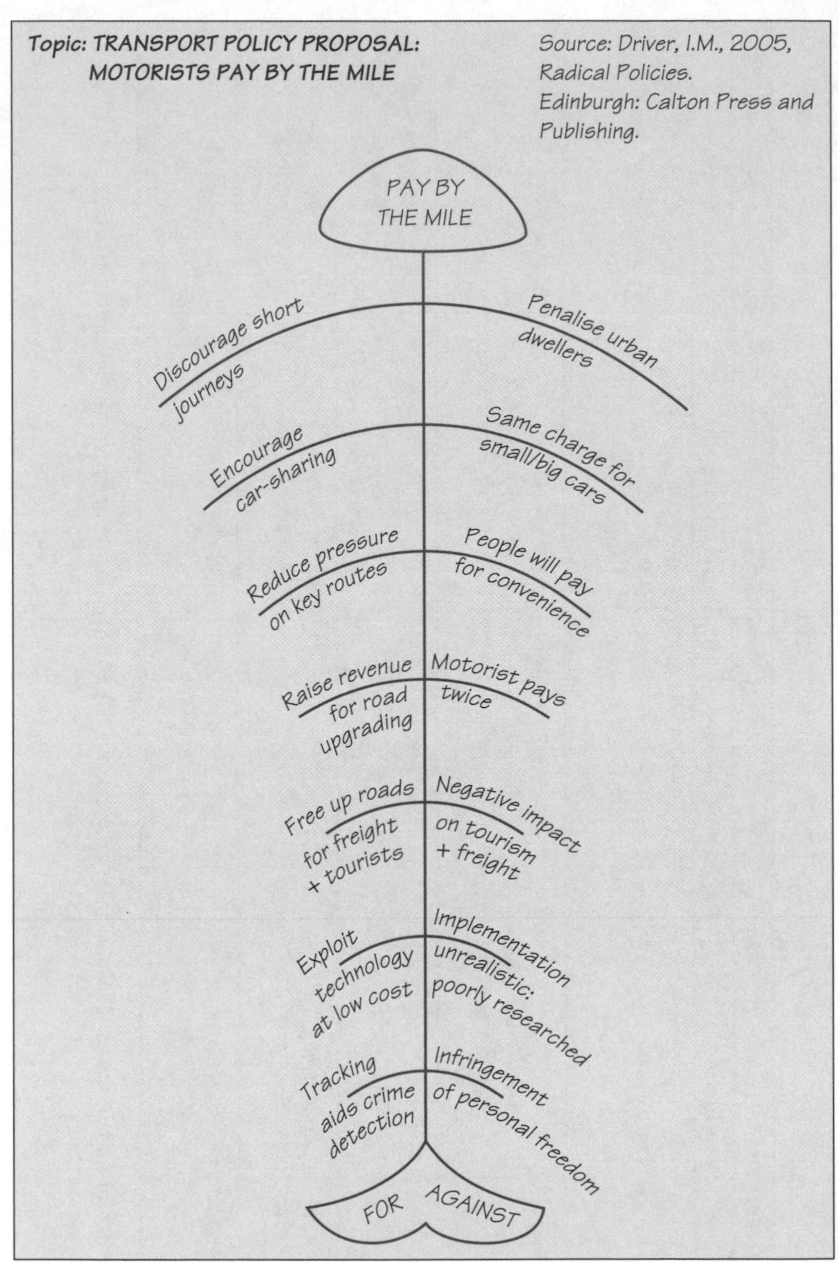

Figure 10.7 Example of a herringbone map. This design is good for showing, as in this case, two sides to an argument. May be particularly appealing to those who prefer to create visually distinct layouts.

Table 10.1 A comparison of the different methods of note-making from source material (illustrated in Figures 10.1-10.7)

Note type	Figure	Advantage	Disadvantage
Keyword notes	10.1	Good as a layout for easy access to information	Dependent on systematic structure in text
Linear notes	10.2	Numbered sequence - good for classifying ideas	Restrictive format, difficult to backtrack to insert new information
Time lines	10.3	Act as memory aid for a sequence of events; stages in a process	Limited information possible
Flow-chart notes	10.4	Allow clear path through complex options	Take up space; may be unwieldy
Concept maps/mind maps	10.5	Good for recording information on a single page	Can become messy; can be difficult to follow; not suited to all learning styles
Matrix notes/grid notes	10.6	Good layout for recording different viewpoints, approaches, applications	Space limitations on content or amount of information
Herringbone maps	10.7	Good for laying out opposing sides of an argument	Space limitations on content or amount of information

Practical tips for making personalised notes

Notes are resources, so never throw them away. The time you spend making notes is an investment. Your research may change direction and so material that seemed irrelevant may, in the longer term, become particularly important.

Use white space. Don't cram as much information as you can on to a sheet; leave white space around lists or other important points. By using the 'visual' part of your brain, you will recall information more easily. This additional space can be used if you wish to add further detail later.

Make your notes memorable. It's important to make sure that your notes are visually striking. However, spending lots of time making them look pretty will not necessarily pay dividends. Again, try to achieve a balance - visually memorable enough to trigger your recall but not so elaborate that they become a meaningless work of art without substance.

Develop your own 'shorthand'. Some subjects have their own abbreviations, for example MI (myocardial infarction) or WTO (World Trade Organisation) and, of course, there are standard abbreviations - e.g., i.e., etc. However, you will also develop your own abbreviations and symbols drawn from your own experience, for example, maths symbols, text messaging or words from other languages. As long as these are memorable and meaningful to you, then they can be useful tools in making and taking notes.

Save time by using a photocopy. Sometimes you may find that the extent of notes you require is minimal, or that a particular resource is in high demand and has been placed on short loan in the library. It may be convenient to photocopy the relevant pages, which can then be highlighted and annotated. Remember that there are copying restrictions imposed on readers due to copyright law (**Ch 19**). These apply to online as well as hard-copy material - details will be posted prominently in your library.

Take care when using material straight from a source. It is important that, if you decide to use an excerpt from a text as a direct quotation, you record the page number on which that particular piece of text appeared in the book or article you are citing. You should then insert the author, date of publication and page number alongside the quotation. More information on using quotes is given in **Ch 18** and **Ch 22**.

GO And now . . .

10.1 Find out about abbreviations. Find a general dictionary that gives a comprehensive list of abbreviations and identify ones that you might use in your notes; find a subject-specific dictionary and identify whether it provides lists of specialist abbreviations. This will help you to build your 'abbreviation' vocabulary and will mean that you'll know where to look if you come across an abbreviation that is unfamiliar to you.

10.2 Compare notes with a friend. Everyone has a different method of note-making that they have personalised to suit their own style. Compare your note-making style with that of a colleague - preferably on the same piece of text. Discuss what you have recorded and why – this may bring out some differences in reasoning, understanding and logic and encourage you to experiment with alternative and potentially more efficient note-making strategies.

10.3 Try something new. You may feel that you already have a fairly reasonable note-making strategy in place, but once you start researching for your dissertation or project, you may find that it is not quite as suitable for the type of investigation you are now carrying out. If this turns out to be the case, then try out some of the alternative styles demonstrated in this chapter to see if these are better suited to your research focus.

Applying research techniques

11 Principles of quantitative research

How to obtain and analyse numerical information

Quantitative research methods are commonplace in the sciences, but are also relevant to some arts subjects. This chapter explores the rationale for obtaining numerical data and outlines some of the main techniques used to obtain them. It also outlines the most appropriate ways of analysing and presenting these data.

Key topics:

→ Key features of quantitative research
→ Examples of quantitative research methods
→ Analysing and presenting your results
→ Practical tips for conducting quantitative research

Key terms

Bias Causality Control Correlation Demographic information Error Hypothesis Matched samples Mean Median Mode Objectivity Population Proof Quantitative research Respondent Sample Système International d'Unités (SI) Subjectivity Variable

Quantitative research methods are defined as investigative approaches resulting in numerical data, in contrast to those methods resulting in qualitative textual information. Quantitative research is especially valuable when:

- obtaining measurements (for example, in Biochemistry and Physiology);
- estimating error (for example, in Physics and Engineering);
- comparing information and opinions (for example, Sociology and Psychology); and
- testing hypotheses (for example, in most investigative science disciplines).

The ideal in this type of research is for the investigator to be detached and impartial to the results of the study.

Quantitative and qualitative research methods are not mutually exclusive and may be used in the same investigation. For example, a full description of a sampling environment may be vital to make sense of numerical data obtained within it.

→ Key features of quantitative research

Quantitative research is generally 'conclusive' in nature. It is especially important in the sciences, where its aim may be to provide a reliable value for a measurement or test a particular hypothesis. Examples include:

- Surveys and questionnaires (for example, 'Over 45 per cent of respondents agreed with this statement').
- Measurements (for example, 'The average insect wing length was 3.40 mm with a standard error of 0.14 mm, $n = 24$').
- Experiments (for example, 'Treatment A resulted in a statistically significant increase in weight gain compared with the control').

In quantitative research, your aim would usually be to base results on large unbiased samples. Large sample size is important to ensure that measurements based on the sample are representative of the population as a whole, and to improve your chances of arriving at a statistically significant conclusion.

Population and sample

Although these terms are used frequently in normal language, they have special meanings in quantitative research.

Population means the whole group of items that might be part of a study: for example, all men in the UK; all individuals of a species of bivalve mollusc on a particular beach; all Birmingham householders who use gas as a heating fuel.

Sample means a sub-set of individuals from a specific population, for example, the 28 men whose blood sugar level was measured and compared with that of 34 who had taken drug X for five weeks beforehand; the 50 bivalves collected from beach A, measured and compared with a similar sample from Beach B; the 45 householders selected for telephone interview about their satisfaction with the service provided by their energy supplier.

Obtaining numbers to describe your results reduces subjectivity and allows comparisons between data sets. The inherent objectivity of quantitative research relies, however, on an unbiased approach to data collection. Critics of the quantitative approach claim that experiments, surveys and the like are rarely entirely free of observer bias, even if this is unintentional.

Bias in quantitative research

Bias can be defined as a partial or one-sided view or description of events. Although the aim is usually to reduce bias as far as possible, it can arise because of subconscious decision(s) of the experimenter, which can mean that individuals selected for observation or experiment do not represent the population, or that values or measurements associated with them are skewed in a particular way.

Objectivity versus subjectivity

Objectivity is the ability to arrive at a detached, unprejudiced viewpoint, based on the evidence and without the influence of feelings or emotion (the object = the thing observed).

Subjectivity is the ability to arrive at a viewpoint that takes account of personal impressions, feelings and interpretations (the subject = the observer).

Numerical results can be analysed with statistical techniques (see **Ch 16**). These allow you to compare sets of observations or treatments, to test hypotheses and to allocate levels of probability (chance) of your conclusions being right or wrong. These are powerful tools and lie at the heart of much scientific scholarship.

However, just because you can measure something, or can compare data sets, this does not mean your conclusions are certain or relevant. For example, many scientists accept the conclusions of their studies on the basis that there is a 5 per cent chance of their being wrong, so, on average, this will be the case one in twenty times. Moreover, even when a hypothesis is accepted as correct, the results may apply only to the very artificial experimental or observational environment. Statistical significance should not be confused with significance in the sense of 'importance' or 'value'.

smart tip

The concept of proof

The word 'proof' should be used cautiously when applied to quantitative research – the term implies 100 per cent certainty, whereas this is very rarely justified owing to the ambiguity inherent in statistical analysis and experimental design. In reports and dissertations, 'hedging' language such as 'this indicates that . . .' are therefore preferable to phrases such as 'this proves that . . .'.

→ Examples of quantitative research methods

Surveys and questionnaires

These are valuable tools for gaining quantitative information from respondents (although it must be remembered that these tools can also provide qualitative data). Respondents can be a representative sample (for example, members of public chosen at random or using a sampling protocol) or a population (all members of Politics Class P201). Before designing a survey, you should consider what demographic information you might need to associate with other responses and how you intend to report the results (see **Ch 16**) as this may influence the questions asked and the way you write them.

Ethics and data protection

These aspects of qualitative and quantitative research are discussed in **Ch 19**. It is important that you read this material and follow local rules and the guidance on university regulations, as provided in your course handbook.

Questions fall into one of two categories, closed or open. The main types of closed answer questions are:

- **Categorical.** Here, you can only select one of the options, for example: 'Gender: M/F'; or 'Do you agree with the above statement? – Yes / No / Don't know (delete as appropriate)'. Results are best expressed as percentages of responses in each category.
- **Numerical.** These request a numerical answer, for example 'What is your age in years?' These can be summarised by appropriate statistics of location and dispersion (p. 178).

- **Multiple-choice questions (MCQs).** These are useful when there are mutually exclusive options to select. This type of question will be familiar from assessments you may have had at school and university. The answers given can be summarised easily as percentages of respondents selecting each option.
- **Multiple response questions.** These are like MCQs, only you are allowed to choose more then one answer. This type of question would be asked for a different reason than a MCQ, and the answers analysed accordingly. The answers can also be summarised as percentages selecting each option, but note that the total number of options selected may be larger than your sample size. In fact, the average number of options selected may be an interesting supplementary piece of data to report.

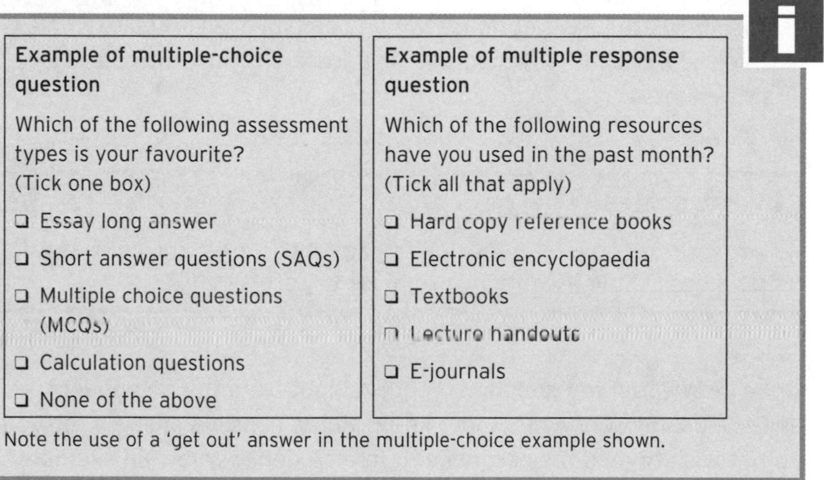
Example of multiple-choice question

Which of the following assessment types is your favourite?
(Tick one box)

- ❑ Essay long answer
- ❑ Short answer questions (SAQs)
- ❑ Multiple choice questions (MCQs)
- ❑ Calculation questions
- ❑ None of the above

Example of multiple response question

Which of the following resources have you used in the past month?
(Tick all that apply)

- ❑ Hard copy reference books
- ❑ Electronic encyclopaedia
- ❑ Textbooks
- ❑ Lecture handouts
- ❑ E-journals

Note the use of a 'get out' answer in the multiple-choice example shown.

- **Ranking (ordinal) questions.** These ask you to place possible answers in an order, for example, 'Place the items in the following list in order of preference, writing 1 for your most preferred option, 2 for the next and so on, down to 5 for your least preferred option'. You can present the results as the most common selection at each rank or as percentages of respondents choosing each rank for a specific item (perhaps as a histogram). A 'mean rank' is another possible way of expressing the data, but this should be interpreted cautiously.
- **Likert-scale questions.** These are useful for assessing people's opinions or feelings on a five-point scale. Typically, respondents are asked to react to a statement. An example would be:

'*Smoking is dangerous for your health*'. Which of the following best describes your feelings about the above statement? (Circle appropriate number.)

1. Agree strongly
2. Agree
3. Neither agree nor disagree
4. Disagree
5. Disagree strongly

Some Likert-scale designs only use four categories, missing out 'neither agree nor disagree', to force respondents to indicate a preference on one side or the other.

The results of Likert scale questions are often treated as ordinal data and non-parametric statistical tests are applied (see p. 181). Responses to Likert options may be combined, as in the example 'over 57 per cent either agreed or agreed strongly with the statement . . .'.

Likert scales

These are named after Rensis Likert, an American psychologist who first modelled the use of a five-point survey scale in 1932.

Open-answer survey questions require input from the respondent and are useful when you do not know all the possible answers, or you do not wish to lead the respondent. In a student survey, an example might be 'Why did you choose module P201?' or 'Please summarise your experience in the exam'. The text responses often provide valuable quotes for a report or case study, and this use would be classified as qualitative (**Ch 12**). It is possible, however, given a reasonably large sample, to categorise the answers and present them in a quantitative fashion, for example, in the form of a pie chart (p. 173) showing the proportion of respondents giving each type of answer.

Measurements and error determination

A measurement is an estimate of some dimension of an object as a ratio of a standard unit. It therefore consists of both a number and the symbol for the unit, for example: 0.5 metres; 1.6 litres; 39 kg.

Table 11.1 Some examples of SI units. For the prefixes normally used in association with these units, see Table 16.1.

Quantity	SI unit (and symbol)
Base units	
Length	metre (m)
Mass	kilogramme (kg)
Time	second (s)
Temperature	kelvin (K)
Amount of substance	mole (mol)
Electric current	ampere (A)
Luminous intensity	candela (cd)
Supplementary units	
Plane angle	radian (rad)
Solid angle	steradian (sr)
Some examples of compound units	
Energy	joule (J) = m^2 kg s^{-1} = N m
Force	newton (N) = m kg s^{-2} = J m^{-1}
Pressure	pascal (Pa) = kg m^{-1} s^{-2} = N m^{-2}
Power	watt (W) = m^2 kg s^{-3} = J s^{-1}
Electric charge	coulomb (C) = A s
Illumination	lux (lx) = cd sr m^{-2}

The units chosen for most scientific studies are those of the Système Internationale or SI, a metre-kilogram-second scheme with defined symbols for units and prefixes for small and large numbers that differ by multiples of 1000 (10^3). Table 11.1 provides some examples of commonly used dimensions and their official symbols, while Table 15.1 provides a list of prefixes (p. 171).

All measurements contain error, which can be of two types: accuracy or precision. In practice, measurements are often assumed to be accurate and the more important thing to estimate is the precision. There are two main ways of doing this:

- **By providing a range that relates to the observer's or instrument's ability to discriminate between readings.** For example, if measuring length with a standard ruler, you might write 104 ± 0.5 mm because you were using the scale divisions on the ruler to estimate to the nearest millimetre; that is, the dividing points between adjacent values below and above 104 are at 103.5 and 104.5 mm.

- **By providing an estimated error that is based on repeated measurements of the same quantity.** For quantifying measurement error alone, this would be obtained from several independent attempts at measurement, for example, five independent values obtained from the same weighing machine of someone's weight (mass). In many scientific studies, this error is taken to be included in the overall sampling error obtained from measurements of several replicate items.

Accuracy and precision

Accuracy is the closeness of a measured or estimated value to its true value. Example: a balance would be said to be inaccurate if, instead of giving you a value for a standard 1 kg weight as 1 kg, it consistently gave a value of 1.02 kg. All measurements of similar weights from the instrument would thus be approximately +2 per cent wrong.

Precision is the closeness of repeated measurements to each other. For example, if you weighed a specimen several times on the same balance and got very different results each time, then the instrument would be said to be imprecise. A mean of 1.000 kg might be considered to be accurate, but if the standard deviation of the measurements was 0.25 kg, this would be considered rather imprecise.

Correlation

This is a way of describing the relationship between two measured variables, for example, the number of cigarettes smoked per day and life expectancy. A variable is well correlated with another if their values alter together, either in a positive fashion, or in a negative fashion. This is illustrated in Figure 11.1. A statistic called the correlation coefficient can be used to express the strength or degree of linear correlation between two variables. This takes values between -1 and 1; the closer its value is to these extremes, the higher the degree of correlation, and the closer to zero, the lower. The sign indicates whether the correlation is positive or negative. The coefficient can be used in a statistical test to find out whether the correlation is significantly different from zero.

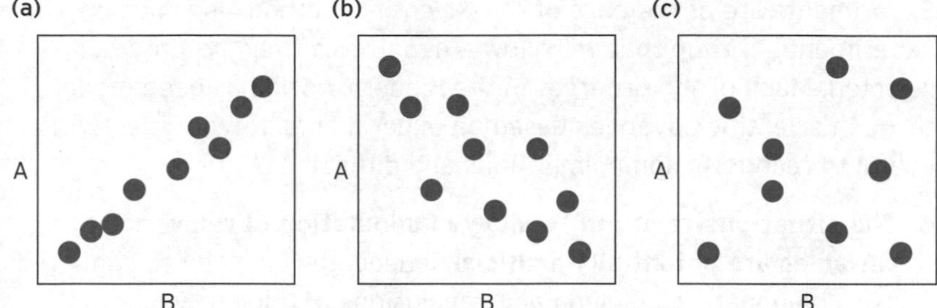

Figure 11.1 Examples of correlation. Each dot represents an experimental subject measured for variables A and B. (a) The two variables have a strong positive correlation; that is, if one variable increases, so does the other. (b) The two variables are negatively correlated; that is, if one variable increases, the other decreases, but in the case illustrated, the points are more widely scattered, so the correlation is less strong than in the first example. (c) The two variables have no strong correlation: that is, they show no discernable relationship.

smart tip

Knowing the difference between correlation and causality

Vital to an understanding of quantitative research is an awareness that correlation does not imply causality. If A is well correlated with B, this alone is not enough evidence to state that A *causes* B. It could be something related to A, or even, due to coincidence, something unrelated to A. So, if people with high blood pressure are more likely to have heart attacks, this alone does not show that high blood pressure is a cause of heart attacks, although if there were no relationship between the two, you might be inclined to rule out this possibility. The only way to become more certain is to gather more evidence.

Experiments

An experiment is a contrived or designed situation where the experimenter attempts to isolate the effects of changing one variable in the system or process, and then compares the results with the condition where no change has occurred. The aim behind many experiments is to establish causality – that is, to establish that a change in factor A causes a change in variable B. Experiments can also help elucidate in more detail *how* A causes B.

Experiments are at the core of the 'scientific method', in which an experiment is set up that will allow a hypothesis to be accepted or rejected. Much of the progress in the modern world has been made through scientific advances based on experiments. Nevertheless, it is useful to recognise some limitations and difficulties.

- **The situations required to allow manipulation of relevant variables are potentially artificial.** Indeed, they may be so contrived as to be unnatural, making any conclusions of dubious value.
- **It may be impossible to change one variable only in any treatment.** Inevitably, other aspects change simultaneously. These are known as confounding variables. For example, if you attempt to change temperature, you may also change humidity. Adding 'control' treatments are the way in which experimenters attempt to rule out the effects of confounding variables.
- **Uncertainty in conclusions.** Sampling and other errors can be taken into account in statistical analysis, but the results must always be expressed with a degree of uncertainty (see p. 179).
- **Subjectivity or bias.** There may be an unwitting element of subjectivity or bias in the choice of treatments; the choice of conditions (sometimes selected to accentuate effects of a particular treatment); and in some cases, in the recording of results.

Concept of 'the control'

A control is an additional treatment that attempts to test the effects of changing a potentially confounding variable. Suppose it is known that Drug A is acidic in nature and that the formulation available for testing also contains a synthesis by-product (impurity), Chemical B. A suitable experimental design might include the following treatments:

1. No treatment (usually involving a placebo, or pill without any added chemicals).
2. Drug A (administered as a pill).
3. Control for effects of pH (a placebo pill with the same pH or buffering capacity as the Drug A pill).
4. Control for the effect of Chemical B (a pill containing similar amounts of Chemical B as in the Drug A pill, but without any Drug A).

If the results show an effect in treatment 2, but not in 3 and 4, then the confounding variables can be ruled out; if there are also effects in 3 or 4, then the confounding variables may well be important.

→ Analysing and presenting your results

It is rare that results of observations, surveys or experiments are reported without subsequent analysis. Indeed, your ability to analyse and present your results is often allocated a high proportion of credit when your dissertation or report is being assessed.

- **Adequate description of your methods is vital, as one goal of quantitative research is to produce repeatable results from which general conclusions can be drawn.** This normally means that a 'Materials and Methods' section contains enough information to allow a competent peer to repeat your work (p. 230).
- **Descriptions should use clear unambiguous language, and qualitative terms used should be defined if possible.** For example, the colour of a specimen might be described with reference to a standard colour chart.
- **Repetition.** Simple measurements should be repeated if possible, so that a figure indicating their accuracy (dispersion, p. 178) can be provided.
- **Description.** When describing results, appropriate use should be made of figures and tables (**Ch 16**).

The results of experiments should be analysed using statistical tests (**Ch 16**).

Practical tips for conducting quantitative research

Surveys

Make sure your instructions are clear and unambiguous. Not everyone in the sample will make the same assumptions as you. For example, if you write: 'Do you agree with this statement? Yes/No', unless given clear directions, some respondents may circle the answer they agree with, others may score out the one they disagree with, and some may provide other marks that you will find are difficult to interpret. A score might look like a tick, for example. Look at the wording of others to see how they have tackled any issues that might occur.

Try out the question set with a friend or family member before using it on real subjects. This may reveal problems with the wording that you may not have appreciated, and is therefore best done with someone relatively unfamiliar with your topic, but who is willing to provide you with feedback.

Observe the following basic rules:

- Keep your survey as short as possible. Use the minimum number of questions required to obtain the information you need and only ask a question if you have a clear idea of how you will use the information obtained.
- Make sure you obtain appropriate demographic information to describe your sample and draw correlations.
- Make sure your questions are unambiguous.
- In deciding the order of questions, try to move from the general to the specific as there is then less chance of early questions influencing responses to later ones.

When explaining how your survey was conducted, supply appropriate details. These should include:

1. Sampling methods. How were the respondents contacted or chosen? What ethical procedures were followed?
2. Details of respondents. You should provide a summary of demographics (gender, age, background of those responding). This information can be derived from specific questions, often placed at the start of the survey. However, observe good research practice by ensuring that the privacy and anonymity of your respondents are protected.
3. Questionnaire design. The principles and rationale behind the design should be discussed and a copy of the questionnaire provided in an appendix.
4. Procedure. How was the survey administered?

Correct your respondents' grammar and spelling errors. When reporting responses, this is generally acceptable practice, because it is true to the spirit of what was written and helps the reader focus on the main points made. You should add a note to the 'Material and Methods' section to explain that you have done this. Clearly, however, this would be inappropriate if your study were about language and the inaccuracies in the responses were the main focus of the research.

Measurements

Focus on good technique when taking measurements. Some forms of measurement may seem simple, such as length or weight measurement. However, you should take as much care as possible, so that measurement error does not become a significant part of the overall error.

Use appropriate measures of location and dispersion to describe quantitative data. These are discussed on p. 178.

Experiments

Consider the likely method of statistical analysis at the start, as this may influence the experimental design. For example, it is possible to estimate an appropriate number of replicates to use to demonstrate a certain percentage difference between two treatments if a preliminary indication of the variability among the replicates is available. Another reason for considering statistical tests beforehand is that they may require assumptions about your data, which you can ensure by, for example, a truly random sampling procedure.

Keep your experiments simple. It is better to use a design that will provide a conclusive answer to a simple question than to over-complicate matters, run into logistical problems in setting up the experiment and collecting data, and end up with inconclusive results.

Learn from 'trial runs'. These can help you work out where there will be difficulties in procedure and layout, use of instruments, and other important limitations on your experimental design. Be aware, however, that you could spend too much time working out what to do and how to do it - remember that all experimentation involves a certain amount of compromise.

Keep safety issues in mind. Think these through before you start work and try to bear the safety of participants and researchers in mind when focussing on collecting data.

GO And now . . .

11.1 Plan out a survey or experiment, or the procedures necessary for a measurement. Aim to identify the different steps in the process and, in particular, resource constraints. In the case of a survey, these might include the respondents' time; in an experiment, the availability of test subjects or equipment; and for measurements, the number of replicate readings it is possible to carry out.

11.2 List potential forms of bias in your research. Being aware of these will help you avoid them. Discuss your list with your supervisor to see whether you have missed anything, and to explore methods of avoiding the most important sources of bias in your work.

11.3 Find out about the statistical tests that can be carried out using the specific software available to you. Will you be able to accomplish your aims using tests within a spreadsheet program like Excel, or will you need more sophisticated software? What 'learning curve' is required to understand and master these tests? To help overcome potential difficulties, try out the software functions using dummy values, before using them with real data.

12 Principles of qualitative research

How to obtain and analyse descriptive information

Qualitative research methods are commonplace in a wide range of arts disciplines and are also used in scientific project work. This chapter explores the rationale for obtaining descriptive data, outlines some of the main techniques used to obtain them, and suggests appropriate ways of analysing and presenting such data.

Key topics:

→ Key features of qualitative research
→ Examples of qualitative research methods
→ Analysing and presenting your results

Key terms

Bias Case study Demographic information Focus group Informants Moderator Population Qualitative research Question probes Question prompts Sample

Qualitative research methods are those investigative approaches that result in descriptive textual information, in contrast with quantitative methods where results are usually summarised numerically (**Ch 11**). The qualitative approach is especially useful when examining:

- opinions, feelings, and values (for example, in Political Science, Social Policy, Philosophy);
- participant interpretations and responses (for example, in Sociology, Psychology);
- behavioural patterns (for example, in Ethnography, Anthropology, Geography);
- processes and patterns (for example, in Education, Economics, Accountancy); or
- case studies including critical incidents (for example, in Nursing, Education).

In obtaining and interpreting qualitative information, there is recognition that such information is interpreted according to a set of values belonging to the researcher.

Qualitative and quantitative research methods are not mutually exclusive and may be used in the same investigation. For example, mixed types of data may be obtained as in a survey eliciting free text responses (qualitative data, p. 114) and expressions of opinion on a Likert scale (quantitative data, see p. 113).

→ Key features of qualitative research

Qualitative research is generally exploratory in nature; it may be preceded or followed by quantitative investigations. It is especially important in the social sciences, where its aim is often to understand the complex reasons for human behaviour. Examples include:

- **Case studies.** (For example, 'Student X described her experience on her first day at University as . . .').
- **Interviews.** (For example, 'Interviewee A explained that, after seeing the video, his reaction was . . . This could be interpreted as . . .').
- **Focus groups.** (For example, 'One group member stated that her experience of peer marking was . . .').

smart tip

Avoiding questions that lead or restrict the answers

If you conduct qualitative research appropriately, the participants providing information are less likely to be 'led' by the questions asked than they may be with the quantitative approach. For example, a free text question in a survey that neutrally asks for the participant's opinion of a political leader does not lead or restrict the respondent in the same way as a Likert-scale question (pp. 113–14) that asks them to grade a leader on his or her response to a specific political issue. When sequencing interview questions, care needs to be taken to ensure that an early question does not place a particular idea or concept in the respondent's mind, thereby affecting their response to a later question. Therefore, you should try to move your questions or prompts from the general to the specific; for example, by asking participants for their opinions on a wide issue without prompting, then, later, asking them to comment on specific aspects of interest to you.

Qualitative research generally involves individuals or small samples, in contrast to the large randomly selected samples favoured in quantitative research (p. 110). These small samples may be carefully selected, and they may not be representative of the population as a whole, but that is not necessarily an issue, because the value of qualitative research derives from the authentic and case-specific detail that it can encompass. The information obtained is potentially richer and deeper than that described in numbers and statistics, and can take advantage of the many subtle ways of using language to express opinions, experiences and feelings. On the other hand, these factors may mean that it is less easy to compare different cases and arrive at generalised conclusions.

smart tip

Bias in qualitative research

Qualitative research, by its very nature, implies a degree of bias. However, maintaining objectivity is as important in the conduct of the research as it is in reporting findings. It is important, therefore, to recognise the tensions that can arise between objectivity and bias. This is particularly relevant when selecting cases to study, aspects to report, and language to describe observations. Observer preconceptions, value systems and cultural influences also need to be taken into account.

→ Examples of qualitative research methods

Observation and description

This category includes a wide range of approaches where the investigator will examine an artefact, person or location and describe it in words. A narrative (outline of developments through time) might also fall into this classification. Examples of suitable topics include:

- primary source material such as that found in an historical document;
- a biological habitat;
- a patient's symptoms;
- a drawing, painting or installation; or
- acculturation process among immigrants.

The specific detailed features to be reported will depend on your discipline and research area. It is a good idea to discuss these with your supervisor before proceeding too far with your research.

Although description is sometimes categorised as a 'lower-level' academic thought process, the interpretations and generalisations that follow involve higher-level skills. For example, a detailed description you produce may be referred to when you are drawing conclusions about a wider topic.

Sometimes your purpose might involve comparing several sources of information. A useful technique when doing this is to create a grid or matrix where the columns represent the different sources and entries in the rows summarise the specific features of interest (modelled in Figure 10.6). In some cases, this table could be adapted for use in a report or dissertation, but it would also be useful when creating a written summary of the key features of the sources.

smart tip

Example of a matrix approach to comparative description

A student's dissertation might involve comparing the health systems of several countries. Having carried out background reading and scan-read through selected documents, he/she might be able to come up with a list of key aspects to compare (for example, the nature of health care provision, the source of funding, the entitlement to free health care, private health care provision, or the nature of specialist care). This list could form the basis of a matrix (grid) comparing the different aspects, following a more detailed reading of the documents. In drawing up such a grid, you should bear in mind that similarities may be just as important as differences.

Surveys and questionnaires

Often both qualitative and quantitative approaches are used in surveys and questionnaires (**Ch 11**). The main qualitative research technique is to ask an 'open' question, for example, 'What do you think about the new property valuation system?' or 'Do you have any further comments?' These questions tend to produce a variety of responses from a blank response to very detailed answers. Responses to open questions can be useful to enrich a report with authentic quotes illustrating representative points of view or opposing, polarised viewpoints. In some instances, this apparently qualitative material can be converted into quantitative information. Quantitative summaries (**Ch 11**) may be useful for establishing some of the background to research findings. Pilot studies are useful for working out what types of information might be valuable.

Value of pilot studies

In qualitative research, a pilot study is usually a preliminary study, often conducted on a small scale. This will:

1. Give you a chance to work through your approach to identify inconsistencies or weaknesses.
2. Help you decide which background demographic information will be required to correlate with participant responses.

Not only does this save time in later face-to-face interview or focus group meetings, but it can help to identify possible discussion threads for these meetings and analytical approaches to the results.

Interview-based case studies

Qualitative research often draws on individuals' experiences of events, processes and systems. These can be reported as case studies. In one ideal sense, such investigations might be carried out without preconception by allowing the participant to provide a completely unstructured and uninterrupted stream of thought, with conclusions

Action Research

Academic departments often encourage students to undertake studies grounded in 'local' issues. In such instances Action Research approaches are popular. These are particularly common in the 'caring' disciplines such as Nursing, Social Work and Teaching. The focus is directed on the context of the researcher's practice and a problem or situation within it which requires better understanding and, possibly, identification of some change to resolve or improve that situation or practice. This approach requires planning of the research approach, perhaps through data collection or observation; analysis and reflection through reference to theory; and, ultimately, a recommendation for action.

drawn following examination of the information obtained. In practice, you will use a body of prior knowledge and experience to structure an interview through a series of prompting questions. If you use a similar template for each case study, comparisons will be possible, so it is important to think this through beforehand.

Focus groups

These are small discussion groups (4–6 members is considered ideal), where participants are asked to comment on an issue or, for business purposes, a product or marketing tool. Focus groups allow you to take account of several viewpoints at a time, and to observe the outcomes of open and dynamic discussion among focus group members. Potential pitfalls include biasing any comments by leading the discussion yourself, or the tendency for focus group members to conform to a middle view if they fear exposing a minority opinion.

As focus group moderator, you would have thought through a list of discussion topics or questions related to your research interest. You would also intervene in discussion to prompt new topics or bring the discussion back to the point, because a recognised danger is that the group drifts substantially 'off message'.

Ethical and data protection dimensions for qualitative research

There are both ethical and data protection dimensions to interviews, focus groups and case studies derived from them (p. 215). It is important that you read this material and follow your university's rules and regulations carefully, as detailed in your institution's ethical guidelines. You may be required to:

- tell participants about the purpose of your study;
- obtain signed clearance from participants to use the information they provide in your research, especially where this may be reported externally;
- store participants' personal data appropriately and for a limited time only; or
- gain agreement of participants *before* recording their input and give guarantees about confidentiality and destruction of recorded audio/video material after transcription.

→ Analysing and presenting your results

In analysing and presenting qualitative data, qualitative key aim is to represent the material in a balanced and rational way. You will gain credit for this and lose marks if you do not. Do not be tempted to select only examples, answers or quotes that support your view. Consider and note the opposing evidence as well, and then arrive at a conclusion based on a careful analysis of the arguments and literature sources that have previously dealt with the topic.

A difficulty in presenting qualitative research is deciding what detail is relevant and what is not. In general, your descriptions should be 'lean' and related to the objectives of the research; however, it is not always easy to predict what details will be relevant at the outset of the research, or which information others who read your work may wish to see recorded.

In reports, case studies are sometimes presented in a self-contained box. If these are numbered, you can refer to them in the text using the same conventions as figures and tables. There are layout rules for presenting quotes from sources in an academic document (p. 198) and these should be adhered to consistently. Consult your course handbook or supervisor if uncertain.

After you have written up the interview, it is good practice to confirm the details you have recorded with the interviewee. This is less practical for focus group data.

Practical tips for carrying out qualitative research

Organising observational and descriptive data

Gather all your sources together as soon as possible. Scan-read them or carry out a quick appraisal before embarking on a detailed description or comparative exercise. However, do not use this as an excuse for delaying the start to your work.

Always note down more information than you think you will need. You can always filter extraneous material out at a later stage, but you cannot always go back to find information you missed first time round.

Where relevant, write down full referencing details as you go along. It is essential to do this as you research since this information is easily forgotten or lost, and you may be deemed guilty of plagiarism if you do not cite your sources in a report.

Base the structure of your description on other similar studies. These may be available from the literature, or your supervisor may be able to show you past examples. Postgraduate students may be a useful source of ideas and examples.

If appropriate, use photography. This might be valuable for a field study, for example, by acting as a prompt when you start to write up. Another use could be recording notes made by a focus group on a whiteboard. By using digital imaging, you can avoid great expense.

Conducting face-to-face research

Before your planned interview or focus group activity:

Ensure that conditions are suitable for the type of research activity you intend to conduct. Make sure the meeting room is in a convenient and quiet location. Offer refreshments where appropriate. For lengthy sessions, include a comfort break. Think carefully about the seating arrangements, as this could contribute significantly to the success of your interview or focus group. It is important to consider a layout where people feel comfortable with each other since this could contribute significantly to the success of your interview or focus group. Figure 12.1 illustrates a good seating arrangement for individual interviews. For focus groups, interactions among participants are said to be better if a 'closed circle' arrangement is used (Figure 12.2). In Figure 12.2(a), the scribe (S) and the moderator/researcher (M) are seated within the group whereas in Figure 12.2(b), the moderator/researcher and the scribe are positioned outside the focus group circle. It might be helpful to provide a whiteboard or flipchart so that one participant from the group can act as a recorder (R). The

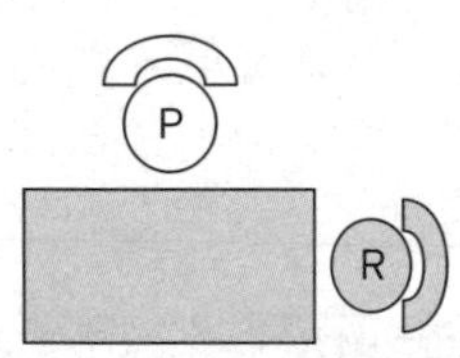

Figure 12.1 Suggested seating arrangement for one-to-one interviews. In these situations people often feel more comfortable sitting at right angles to each other rather than on opposite sides of a table or sitting side-by-side. Thus, in this example, researcher (R) sits at the shorter side of the table and participant (P) sits at the longer side.

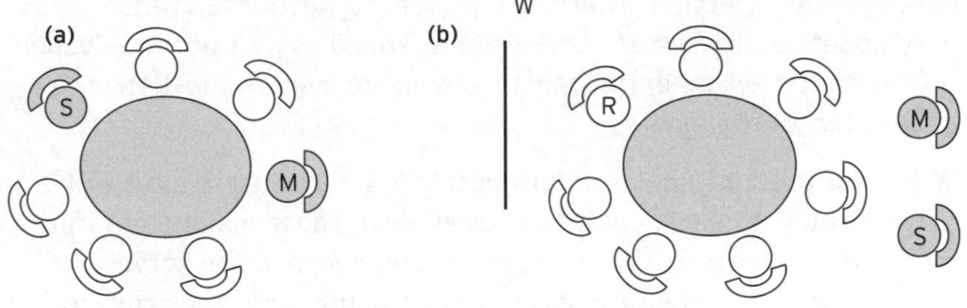

Figure 12.2 Two seating arrangements for a focus group

whiteboard addition is shown in Figure 12.2(b), but could also be offered as a facility in the layout depicted in Figure 12.2(a).

One common denominator of the circle arrangement is that all members of the group can have full view and engage the eye contact of all other participants. However, both layouts have advantages and disadvantages. One disadvantage of the Figure 12.2(a) format is that the researcher is part of the group and thus has the potential to influence group members by body language or by making interjections to the discussion. However, Krueger and Casey (2000) regard the integration of the moderator as a beneficial feature since their physical presence in the group allows them to observe the interaction, interpret body language and prompt development of the discussion by judicious use of probes while not expressing a personal viewpoint.

Where the moderator and scribe are positioned outside the focus group as in Figure 12.2(b), this allows the group to interact spontaneously without the intervention of the moderator. It is argued that this encourages the free flow of ideas and prevents domination by the moderator. A disadvantage is that it makes it less easy for the researcher to observe and interpret visual signals among the group members. Whichever layout you select, you should ensure that you create an ambience that is open and non-threatening to the group members.

Select your interviewees or focus group participants carefully. Screen participants according to a defined set of criteria, having discussed what these might be with your supervisor beforehand. For example, you might wish to interview people involved at all stages in a process (shop-floor, administrative, management, marketing and customer); or a balanced set of students of both sexes and representing the different levels of study. You will need to provide details of the selection criteria in your report. Record relevant participant details (either obtained beforehand as part of the selection process or by asking participants to complete a short questionnaire at the start of the meeting).

Write out a list of question 'prompts'. You may wish to start with a few questions to put the interviewee at ease. These might stem from responses in a pilot study, if you have done one, and can serve to produce background information to 'situate' the case. The remainder of the question set should be defined by the aims of the project, smoothly moving from general topics to the specific.

Take care of the technical aspects. With the permission of the participants, some researchers make audio or video recordings of the interview or focus group dialogue rather than take notes, preferring to stimulate a more natural discussion by simply observing the participants in the discussion. Some people do appear to relax more in these situations where there is no overt note-taking going on. If you opt to use recording methods, ensure that you:

- know how to operate the technical equipment;
- have practised using it beforehand;
- have checked it out on the day before the session begins to ensure that you will be able to hear the recording clearly on replay; and
- have sufficient battery power and memory/tape capacity for the whole period of the interview.

Consider other note-taking options. Careful note-taking and fact-checking is important in interviews, focus groups and case studies. Most people find it difficult to act as both interviewer and scribe. In any case, good secretarial skills would be required to write down every spoken word. You could ask a friend to act as scribe for you to allow you to focus exclusively on the questions and moderating the session. However, it would be useful to discuss the note-taking strategy with your scribe beforehand to ensure that the data they record is what you require. This might even involve trying a 'dry run' to clarify exactly what both scribe and moderator/researcher expect from the approach.

At the meeting

Start by introducing yourself. Explain the purpose of the event and confirm the approximate length of time that you envisage the activity will take. If appropriate, invite the participants to introduce themselves to each other.

Develop some means of identifying participants. When noting oral data, some researchers prefer to identify participants anonymously (for example, by giving them name tags or sticky label letters A, B, C, etc.), arguing that this emphasises anonymity from the outset. Other researchers feel that this approach is depersonalising and stultifies contributions. Therefore, they prefer to provide students with identifying labels or name tags on which are printed their first names. Either way, identifying contributors allows you to specify in your notes who said what and to link an individual's separate comments together.

Take notes. Either sound-record the discussion or ask a friend to act as scribe for you. Some researchers also encourage group participants to record their thoughts on a white board. If you decide to do this, you could photograph the notes as part of the record of the discussion.

Note non-verbal information. Remember that responses other than words may be of value, such as facial expressions, eye contact, voice tone and body language, and include some record of these aspects in your notes. These may be important in your interpretation and reportage of the data.

Use 'question probes' to encourage participants to develop the discussion further. For example, you might ask, 'Could you expand on that point a little further?' or 'What do you mean by x?'. One of the strengths of interactive qualitative research lies in the flexibility it offers to explore areas that might be rich in the research context but which might not have been anticipated in the question bank created by the researcher/moderator. Therefore, make sure that your programme allows participants to comment freely but within the time schedule. Otherwise, your interventions should only be made to ensure that the participant(s) do not digress significantly from the subject - be aware of the danger of 'leading' the participants. If a digression does occur, then use your question cues as a means of refocussing the discussion along the lines of your planned prompts.

Stick to the pre-arranged time. You may want to run other interpersonal research activities and if you earn a reputation for taking up more time than you stated, these or other participants may decline to be involved further in your research.

Thank the participants for their time and contributions at the end of the session. If you fail to observe the courtesy of thanking your participants, they or others in the target category may be less enthusiastic about assisting your research in future.

GO And now . . .

12.1 Seek out and try to learn from 'model' approaches to your topic. Whether you are writing a description, conducting a focus group or carrying out a case study, you should be able to find, perhaps with the help of your supervisor, a published study carried out in a similar way. Examine the approach and methods used in order to see if you can apply similar approaches to your own investigation. Look at the ways the results have been presented to see if these might be suitable to express your own findings.

12.2 Plan out a set of question 'prompts' and possible 'question probes' for interviews and focus groups. If your investigation involves either of these approaches, it will be worthwhile setting out a sequence of question prompts as the framework for your face-to-face meeting. If you also note down your reasons for asking the question, this will ensure that you garner material that is germane to your research project rather than a lot of interesting but irrelevant data.

12.3 Investigate potential methods of recording interview and focus group interaction. Think about the equipment and related facilities that might be available to you personally or ask about what you might be able to borrow from your supervisor or department. Test it so that you have a clear idea of how it should be used and can operate it competently.

13 Experimental research and field visits

How to develop and apply your skills

Many research projects, particularly in the sciences, involve laboratory work and field visits. These practical experiences provide valuable opportunities to observe specimens, carry out experiments and obtain measurements. Proper conduct and accurate data collection are both vital.

Key topics:

→ Preparing for practical research activity
→ Appropriate conduct in the lab and field
→ Carrying out instructions and noting results

Key terms

COSHH Scientific method

In many disciplines, research activity is undertaken in laboratory sessions and/or field visits, especially in the sciences, and in the non-sciences in subjects such as geography and psychology. You should treat these practical elements just as seriously as the content of the research literature.

Practical research work is given emphasis because it:

- allows you to see and interact with real examples of organisms, specimens, artefacts, processes and reactions;
- helps you to develop new skills in areas such as observation, measurement, manipulation and data analysis;
- lets you gain an appreciation of 'scientific method', by designing, carrying out and reporting original experiments carried out in your field;
- gives you 'hands-on' experience of using equipment;
- allows you to explore field locations relevant to your research;

- gives you practice in writing up your work in formats that you may later use to report your project and theses at a higher level.

Examples of skills that are developed in laboratory and field visits

- Observation
- Handling samples and organisms
- Using equipment
- Designing experiments
- Working safely
- Measuring and recording
- Creating tables and graphs
- Data analysis
- Reporting in written and spoken forms
- Teamwork

→ Preparing for practical research activity

If you want to gain the most from your practical research activity, good preparation is essential. Often lab sessions and field visits are tightly scheduled and you may be expected to be 'up and running' almost from the start. This aspect of your research may also involve new concepts and terms and if you don't understand these, then you should make it a priority to research these further via specialist resources. You should:

- read through any instructions or papers you've been given;
- make sure you have the appropriate equipment ready to take to carry out your work; and
- make sure that you identify points in the research process when you may need to reserve specialist equipment so that it is actually available when you need it.

→ Appropriate conduct in the lab and field

Any rules associated with lab or fieldwork will have your safety as their primary concern, so you must pay attention to them. You may

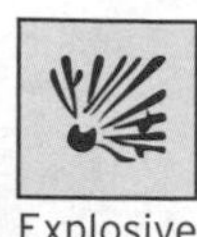

Explosive

Oxidising agent

Extremely or highly flammable

Toxic or very toxic

Corrosive

Harmful or irritant

Dangerous for the environment

Figure 13.1 Some of the main EU hazard symbols

have to work with toxic chemicals, dangerous instruments or in hazardous environments, so care is essential. It will be assumed you are familiar with basic safety measures and legislation, about the fire drill and relevant hazard symbols (Figure 13.1).

In the lab, you will be asked to wear a lab coat - which should always be buttoned up - and, if you have long hair, asked to tie it back. Eye protection goggles may be necessary for some procedures, and those who normally wear contact lenses may be subject to special rules because vapours of corrosive laboratory chemicals may be trapped between the lens and the cornea of the eye. You should never eat or smoke in a lab. You should also keep your bench space tidy and quickly dispose of specimens or sharps as instructed. All these are common sense and should be part of your normal practice. However, be sure that you keep safety as a priority and do not become slap-dash or complacent just because you've become familiar with the environment.

Where hazardous materials or procedures are involved, you will be told about the COSHH risk assessment (see below) and you have a duty to read this carefully.

Definition: COSHH

This stands for 'Control of Substances Hazardous to Health' - a UK regulation that came into force in 1999. It lays out the legal framework for risk assessment whenever hazardous chemicals, agents or procedures are used. Normally the person in charge of your lab work or field visit (your supervisor or a senior lab technician) will carry out a COSHH assessment, which should be displayed prominently and/or communicated to you.

When working with chemicals or live organisms like bacteria, take appropriate precautions:

- be aware of possible modes of ingestion, including inhalation by nose or mouth, ingestion by mouth, absorption through exposed, skin/or inoculation through skin;
- take special care with procedures such as pipetting or transferring samples between vessels;
- note where eye washes and emergency showers are located in your lab and understand the appropriate procedures when you come into contact with chemicals;
- know what to do if you spill any chemicals;
- make sure you know the location and type of fire extinguisher or fire blanket to use for the reagents being used;
- always wash your hands thoroughly after each lab session.

For field visits, you will be advised about appropriate clothing. You should take special care to use appropriate footwear and be prepared for a change of weather conditions. Try always to work with a partner, rather than alone. You should:

- take a first aid kit;
- leave full details of where you are going and when you expect to return;
- consult a weather forecast before you leave, and if working on the seashore find out about the state of the tides.

→ Carrying out instructions and noting results

Lab and field visit procedures usually contain the following components:

- **Theory, background and aims.** This is information essential to your understanding of the procedure and its interpretation, so do not be tempted to skip this and move directly to the instructions.
- **Instructions.** The language used here is generally very precise and should be followed to the letter or number. Success will often depend on, for example, the precision with which you measure out reagents, or the exact timing or temperature you use. When reading the instruction beforehand, you may wish to highlight key points so you can follow them better during the session, or lay out tables ready to record your data.

Being able to record accurately what you see and measure is a vital skill in the sciences. The following are key tips for recording your observations:

- Don't rely on your memory - write down everything.
- Never write on scraps of paper (you'll lose them) - use a proper lab book.
- Always date each page and provide full details of the specimen or experiment.
- If recording data, develop the skill of writing this information clearly - for example, ones and sevens are easily confused and you may wish to adopt the practice of crossing the latter (i.e. 7).
- If you are recording numbers, use an appropriate number of significant figures to take account of the precision (or, perhaps more strictly, the lack of precision) of your method.
- If drawing diagrams, make sure these have a descriptive title and are well labelled.
- In the field, be prepared for bad weather - buy a special wet-weather notebook or take a clear plastic bag to enclose your notebook, and use a pencil as this will write on damp paper.
- Write down any final results in the form normally used in your discipline - you may lose marks otherwise.
- Draw any graphs or tables according to the normal scientific conventions.

Table 13.1 provides a reminder of the key components of a typical scientific project report and outlines what's expected for each part. You might find it useful to revisit this formal list in order to view it through the eyes of a researcher rather than those of a novice scientist.

The language of scientific project reports

This is worth paying attention to as there are specific conventions that should be adopted. In the 'Introduction' and 'Materials and methods', the past tense, passive voice and third person are generally used (for example, 'Sturrock and Dodds (1984) were the first to show . . .' and 'the data were recorded at 5-minute intervals'). However, present tense might be used when describing figures and tables (for example, 'Table 3 shows the relationship between . . .'). Read research reports in your subject area to gain a feel for the style usually adopted.

Table 13.1 Typical components of a lab or field project report. This is one standard format used for scientific reports, but see also Table 21.2.

Section or part	Expected content
Title page	A descriptive title that indicates what was done and sometimes describes the 'headline' finding. Also the full names of the author or authors and other relevant information.
Abstract	A brief summary of the aims of the experiment or series of observations; the main outcomes (in words) and conclusions. This should allow someone to understand your main findings and what you think they mean.
Abbreviations	A list of any abbreviations for technical terms used within the text (for example, 'DNA: deoxyribonucleic acid'). These are also given within the text at the first point of use, for example '. . . deoxyribonucleic acid (DNA)'.
Introduction	An outline of the background to the project, the aims of the experiment(s) or observations and brief discussion of the techniques to be used. Your goal is to orientate the reader and explain what you have done and why.
Materials and methods	A description of what was done. You should provide sufficient detail to allow a competent person to repeat the work.
Results	A description of the data obtained, usually presented in either tabular or graphic form (never both for the same data). You should point out meaningful aspects of the data, which need not be presented in the same order in which the work was done.
Discussion (or conclusions)	A commentary on the results and an outline of the main conclusions. This could include any or all of the following: • comments on the methods used; • mention of sources of errors; • conclusions from any statistical analysis; • comparison with other findings or the 'ideal' result; • what the result means; • how you might improve the methods used; • where you would go from here, given more time and resources. Sometimes you might combine the results and discussions sections to allow a narrative to develop – to explain, for example, why one result led to the next experiment or approach. Bear in mind that a large proportion of marks may be given for your original thoughts in this section.
Acknowledgements	A list of people who helped you.
References	An alphabetical list of sources cited in the text, following one of the standard formats.

Practical tips for getting the most from laboratory work and field visits

Use lab assistants and senior researchers fully. Often, these people may be recent graduates and be sympathetic to any problems you may be facing. If in doubt, ask - it could save you lots of time. Be prepared to ask questions yourself rather than wait to be asked.

Learn how to draw up informal tables and figures quickly. Rough tables will help you to record your results neatly and quickly, while 'instant' graphs will give you an early visual indication of how the experiment is proceeding. Your tables should include a column describing what is being measured or the number or timing of the measurements, and include sufficient 'cells' in the rows for each replicate or repeated measurement you will make. When constructing graphs, you will need to assess the largest and smallest figures you are likely to obtain, so you can determine what the limits of the graph axes should be. For all tables and figures, no matter how quickly drawn up, remember to state the measured quantity and the units of measurement.

Take plentiful notes and provide detailed labels. Note down anything that might be useful at a later date - and be prepared to use most of your senses, with caution: note colours, sounds and feel, but only taste and smell when specifically instructed. Label any diagrams fully and add a time and date. As well as stating what a component is, add relevant detail such as colour and texture. All diagrams should include a scale.

Use 'dead' time effectively. During lab experiments, there may be delays between parts of your work as reactions develop, or as instruments complete a process. Use this time to look ahead to what you will be doing next, to create tables or graphs ready for recording your results, or to jot down ideas for your conclusions.

Write up your practical work when it is fresh in your mind. You may be tired after a lengthy session in the lab, but if you delay for too long you may forget useful details.

GO And now . . .

13.1 Make up a checklist of items required for each experiment or field visit. This will depend on your specific experiments or research. Refer to the list beforehand. Think ahead to ensure you don't forget anything.

13.2 Rehearse safety scenarios. Taking into account the safety information provided in the relevant lab handbooks, lab notices and your supervisor's advice, imagine what you would do in different situations, such as if there were a fire, if a lab colleague swallowed a toxic chemical, or if someone cut themselves. This will make you more aware of the dangers of the lab or field environment and might help you react faster if needed.

13.3 Purchase and organise a lab notebook. This is a vital tool for both lab and fieldwork researchers. A hardback notebook is best. Date each entry and use the notebook to record details of your experiments, observations, results and ideas. Write up each part more formally as soon as convenient in word-processed or spreadsheet format.

14 Thinking critically

How to develop a logical approach to analysis and problem-solving

The ability to think critically is probably the most transferable of the skills you will develop at university and is vital for completing a dissertation or project report successfully. Your future employers will expect you to be able use it to tackle professional challenges. This chapter introduces concepts, methods and fallacies to watch out for when trying to improve your analytical capabilities.

Key topics:

→ Thinking about thinking
→ Using method to prompt and organise your thoughts
→ Recognising fallacies and biased presentations

Key terms

Bias Critical thinking Fallacy Propaganda Value judgement

How can you apply theory and technique to help you think better? Many specialists believe that critical thinking is a skill that you can develop through practice. This is an assumption that lies behind much university teaching. Your experience of the educational system probably tells you that your grades have depended increasingly on the analysis of facts and the ability to arrive at an opinion and support it with relevant information, rather than the simple recall of fact. This is especially true when the assessed outcome is a piece of critical writing like a project report or dissertation. If you understand the underlying processes a little better, this should help you meet your tutors' expectations.

Definition: critical

People often interpret the words 'critical' and 'criticism' to mean being negative about an issue. For university work, the alternative meaning of 'making a careful judgement after balanced consideration of all aspects of a topic' is the one you should adopt.

→ Thinking about thinking

Benjamin Bloom, a noted educational psychologist, and colleagues, identified six different steps involved in learning and thinking within education:

- knowledge
- comprehension
- application
- analysis
- synthesis
- evaluation.

Bloom *et al.* (1956) showed that students naturally progressed through this scale of thought-processing during their studies (Table 14.1). Looking at this table, you may recognise that your early education mainly focussed on knowledge, comprehension and application, while learning at university requires more in terms of analysis, synthesis and evaluation.

Thus, it is important to recognise that simple description alone is not sufficient at the higher-order level of thought required in the construction of a dissertation or project report. Thinking critically means that you need to construct an analysis of different viewpoints or approaches, for example, by looking at the issue or problem from different perspectives. The matrix note-making strategy shown in Figure 10.6 shows a practical way in which to tackle this on paper. This approach can be adapted for many different sorts of analysis across a range of disciplines. By considering different positions, ideas, viewpoints or approaches, it is possible to weigh them up according to criteria that you set for yourself. In the context of the research required for dissertations or projects, these critical faculties will

Table 14.1 Bloom *et al.*'s classification of thinking processes (Bloom's taxonomy)

Thinking processes (in ascending order of difficulty)	Typical question instructions
Knowledge. If you know a fact, you have it at your disposal and can *recall* or *recognise* it. This does not mean you necessarily understand it at a higher level.	• Define • Describe • Identify
Comprehension. To comprehend a fact means that you *understand* what it means.	• Contrast • Discuss • Interpret
Application. To apply a fact means that you can *put it to use.*	• Demonstrate • Calculate • Illustrate
Analysis. To analyse information means that you are able to *break it down into parts* and show how these components *fit together.*	• Analyse • Explain • Compare
Synthesis. To synthesise, you need to be able to *extract relevant facts* from a body of knowledge and use these to *address an issue in a novel way* or *create something new.*	• Compose • Create • Integrate
Evaluation. If you evaluate information, you *arrive at a judgement*based on its importance relative to the topic being addressed.	• Recommend • Support • Draw a conclusion

enable you to examine strong and weak dimensions, identify and construct lines of argument and support these with relevant evidence drawn from the literature. Table 14.2 provides examples of the way in which different stages of thought-processing can apply in three different disciplines.

→ Using method to prompt and organise your thoughts

If you adopt a methodical approach to the analysis of problems - not only academic ones - then you will become skilled in thinking critically. The pointers below will help you arrive at a logical answer. You should regard this as a menu rather than a recipe - think about the different stages and how they might be useful for the specific research issue that you are tackling and your own style of working. Adopt or reject them as you see fit, according to your needs, and chop and change their order as appropriate.

Table 14.2 Examples of Bloom's classification of thinking processes within representative university subjects (Bloom *et al.*, 1956)

Thinking processes (in ascending order of complexity)	Examples		
	Law	Arts subjects, e.g. History or Politics	Numerical subjects
Knowledge	You might know the name and date of a case, statute or treaty without understanding its relevance	You might know that a river was an important geographical and political boundary in international relations, without being able to identify why	You might be able to write down a particular mathematical equation, without understanding what the symbols mean or where it might be applied
Comprehension	You would understand the principle of law contained in the legislation or case law, and its wider context	You would understand that the river forms a natural barrier, which can be easily identified and defended	You would understand what the symbols in an equation mean and how and when to apply it
Application	You would be able to identify situations to which the principle of law would apply	You might use this knowledge to explain the terms of a peace treaty	You would be able to use the equation to obtain a result, given background information
Analysis	You could relate the facts of a particular scenario to the principle to uncover the extent of its application, using appropriate authority	You could explain the river as a boundary being of importance to the territorial gains/losses for signatories to the peace treaty	You could explain the theoretical process involved in deriving the equation
Synthesis	By a process of reasoning and analogy, you could predict how the law might be applied under given circumstances	You could identify this fact and relate it to the recurrence of this issue in later treaties or factors governing further hostilities and subsequent implications	You would be able to take one equation, link it with another and arrive at a new mathematical relationship or conclusion
Evaluation	You might be able to advise a client based on your own judgement, after weighing up and evaluating all available options	You would be able to discuss whether the use of this boundary was an obstacle to resolving the terms of the treaty to the satisfaction of all parties	You would be able to discuss the limitations of an equation based on its derivation and the underlying assumptions behind this

Can a methodical approach inspire you creatively?

You may doubt this, and we all recognise that a solution to a problem often comes to us when we aren't even trying to think about it. However, technique can sometimes help you clarify the issues, organise the evidence and arrive at a balanced answer. This should help inspiration to follow.

- **Decide exactly the nature of the problem.** An important preliminary task is to make sure you have identified this properly. Write down a description of the problem or issue - if this is not already provided for you - taking care to be very precise with your wording. If a specific title has been given, then analyse its phrasing carefully to make sure you understand all possible aspects and meanings.
- **Organise your approach to the problem.** You might start with a 'brainstorm' to identify potential solutions or viewpoints. This can be an effective activity. In longer pieces of academic writing it might typically consist of three phases:
  - **Open thinking.** Consider the issue or question from all possible angles or positions and write down everything you come up with. Don't worry at this stage about the relevance or importance of your ideas. You may wish to use a 'spider diagram' or 'mind map' to lay out your thoughts (modelled in Figure 10.5).
  - **Organisation.** Next, you should try to arrange your ideas into categories or sub-headings, or group them as supporting or opposing a viewpoint. A new diagram, table or grid may be useful to make things clear.
  - **Analysis.** Now you need to decide about the relevance of the grouped points to the original problem. Reject trivial or irrelevant ideas and rank or prioritise those that seem relevant.
- **Get background information and check your comprehension of the facts.** It's quite likely that you will need to gather relevant information and ideas - to support your thoughts, provide examples or suggest a range of interpretations or approaches. You also need to ensure you fully understand the material you have gathered. This could be as simple as using dictionaries and technical works to find out the precise meaning of key words; it might involve discussing your ideas with your peers or your supervisor; or you could read a range of texts to see how others interpret your topic.

Sharpening your research skills

Consult the following chapters for further information and practical tips:

- **Ch 7**, for library and web searching
- **Ch 17**, for plagiarism avoidance strategies
- **Ch 18**, for collecting information that will allow you to cite sources appropriately

- **Check relevance.** You need to marshal the evidence you have collected - for example: for or against a proposition; supporting or opposing an argument or theory. You may find it useful to prepare a table or grid to organise the information - this will also help you balance your thoughts. Be ruthless in rejecting irrelevant or inconsequential material.
- **Think through your argument, and how you can support it.** Having considered relevant source material and opinions, you should arrive at a personal viewpoint, and then construct your dissertation or project around this. You must take care to avoid value judgements or other kinds of expression of opinion that are not supported by evidence or sources. This is one reason why frequent citation and referencing is demanded in academic work.

What are value judgements?

These are statements that reflect the views and values of the speaker or writer rather than the objective reality of what is being assessed or considered. For example, if the person is sympathetic to a cause they may refer to those who support it as members of a 'pressure group'; if they disagree with the cause, then its members become 'activists'; similarly, 'conservationists' versus 'tree-huggers'; 'freedom fighters' versus 'insurgents'. Value judgements often imply some sense of being pejorative (negative). For example: 'Teenagers are unreliable, unpredictable and unable to accept responsibility for their actions'.

→ Recognising fallacies and biased presentations

As you consider arguments and discussions on academic subjects, you will notice that various linguistic devices are used to promote particular points of view. Identifying these is a valuable aspect of critical thinking, allowing you to rise above the argument itself and think about the way in which it is being conducted.

Definitions

- **Fallacy:** a fault in logic or thinking that means that an argument is incorrect.
- **Bias:** information that emphasises just one viewpoint or position.
- **Propaganda:** false or incomplete information that supports a (usually) extreme political or moral view.

There are many different types of logical fallacies, and Table 14.3 lists only a few common examples. Once tuned in to this way of thinking, you should observe that faulty logic and debating tricks are frequently used in areas such as advertising and politics. Analysing the methods being used can be a useful way of practising your critical skills.

One way of avoiding bias in your own work is consciously to try to balance your discussion. Avoid 'absolutes' - be careful with words that imply that there are no exceptions, for example, *always*, *never*, *all* and *every*. These words can only be used if you are absolutely sure of facts that imply 100 per cent certainty.

Practical tips for thinking critically

Focus on the task in hand. It is very easy to become distracted when reading around a subject, or when discussing problems with others. Take care not to waste too much time on preliminaries and start relevant action as quickly as possible.

Write down your thoughts. The act of writing your thoughts is important as this forces you to clarify them. Also, since ideas are often fleeting, it makes sense to ensure you have a permanent record. Reviewing what you have written makes you more critical and can lead you on to new ideas.

Try to be analytical, not descriptive. By looking at Table 14.1, you will appreciate why analysis is regarded as a higher-level skill than description. Dissertations can be regarded as weak because the the author has simply quoted facts or statements without explaining their

Table 14.3 Common examples of logical fallacies, bias and propaganda techniques found in arguments. There are many different types of fallacious arguments (at least 70) and this is an important area of study in philosophical logic.

Type of fallacy or propaganda	Description	Example	How to counteract this approach
Ad hominem (Latin for 'to the man')	An attack is made on the character of the person putting forward an argument, rather than on the argument itself; this is particularly common in the media and politics	The President's moral behaviour is suspect, so his financial policies must also be dubious	Suggest that the person's character or circumstances are irrelevant
Ad populum (Latin for 'to the people')	The argument is supported on the basis that it is a popular viewpoint; of course, this does not make it correct in itself	The majority of people support corporal punishment for vandals, so we should introduce boot camps	Watch out for bandwagons and peer-pressure effects and ignore them when considering rights and wrongs
Anecdotal evidence	Use of unrepresentative exceptions to contradict an argument based on statistical evidence	My gran was a heavy smoker and she lived to be 95, so smoking won't harm me	Consider the overall weight of evidence rather than isolated examples
Appeal to authority	An argument is supported on the basis that an expert or authority agrees with the conclusion; used in advertisements, where celebrity endorsement and testimonials are frequent	My professor, whom I admire greatly, believes in Smith's theory, so it must be right	Point out that the experts disagree and explain how and why; focus on the key qualities of the item or argument

Appeal to ignorance	Because there's no evidence for (or against) a case, it means the case must be false (or true)	You haven't an alibi, therefore you must be guilty	Point out that a conclusion either way may not be possible in the absence of evidence
Biased evidence	Selection of examples or evidence for or against a case. A writer who quotes those who support their view, but not those against	My advisers tell me that Global Warming isn't going to happen.	Read around the subject, including those with a different view, and try to arrive at a balanced opinion.
Euphemisms and jargon	Use of phrasing to hide the true position or exaggerate an opponent's – stating things in mild or emotive language for effect; use of technical words to sound authoritative	My job as vertical transportation operative means I am used to being in a responsible position	Watch for (unnecessary) adjectives and adverbs that may affect the way you consider the evidence
Repetition	Saying the same thing over and over again until people believe it. Common in politics, war propaganda and advertising	'A vote for Bloggs is a vote for freedom' 'Your country needs you' 'Beanz means Heinz'	Look out for repeated catchphrases and lack of substantive argument
Straw man/false dichotomy	A position is misrepresented in order to create a diversionary debating point that is easily accepted or rejected, when in fact the core issue has not been addressed	Asylum seekers all want to milk the benefits system, so we should turn them all away	Point out the fallacy and focus on the core issue

importance and context, that is, without showing their understanding of what the quote means or implies.

When quoting evidence, use appropriate citations. This is important as it shows you have read relevant source material and helps you avoid plagiarism. The conventions for citation vary among subjects, so consult your regulations and follow the instructions exactly.

Draw on the ideas and opinions of your peers and academic staff. Discussions with others can be very fruitful, revealing a range of interpretations that you might not have thought about yourself. You may find it useful to bounce ideas off others. Supervisors can provide useful guidance once you have done some reading, and are usually pleased to be asked for help.

Keep an open mind. Although you may start with preconceived ideas about a topic, you should try to be receptive to the ideas of others. You may find that your initial thoughts become altered by what you are reading and discussing. If there is not enough evidence to support *any* conclusion, be prepared to suspend judgement.

Look beneath the surface. Decide whether sources are dealing with facts or opinions; examine any assumptions made, including your own; think about the motivation of writers. Rather than restating and describing your sources, focus on what they *mean* by what they write.

Avoid common pitfalls of shallow thinking. Try not to:

- rush to conclusions;
- generalise;
- oversimplify;
- personalise;
- use fallacious arguments;
- think in terms of stereotypes; or
- make value judgements.

Keep asking yourself questions. A good way to think more deeply is to ask questions, even after you feel a matter is resolved or you understand it well. All critical thinking is the result of asking questions.

Balance your arguments. If asked to arrive at a position on a subject, you should try to do this in an even-handed way, by considering all possible viewpoints and by presenting your conclusion with supporting evidence.

GO And now . . .

14.1 Practise seeing both sides of an argument. Choose a topic, perhaps one on which you have strong views (for example, a political matter, such as state support for private schooling; or an ethical one, such as the need for vivisection or abortion). Write down the supporting arguments for both sides of the issue, focussing on your least-favoured option. This will help you see both sides of a debate as a matter of course.

14.2 Look into the murky world of fallacies and biased arguments. There are some very good websites that provide lists of different types of these with examples. Investigate these by using 'fallacy' or 'logical fallacies' in a search engine. Not only are the results quite entertaining at times, but you will find the knowledge obtained improves your analytical skills.

14.3 Look now at a journal article in your subject area. Read this critically in the sense that you examine it to identify the areas where the authors have relied on the lower-order facets of thinking. Do another 'sweep' over the paper to identify areas where higher-order skills have been used. Consider the balance between those two approaches and reflect on how you will achieve a balance between lower-order and higher-order dimensions in your own dissertation or project report.

Working with data and numbers

15 Number crunching

How to solve problems in arithmetic and algebra

This chapter reviews common concepts and methods that will help you address straightforward numerical aspects of your dissertation or project. The mathematical techniques covered are relatively uncomplicated, but you may need to revisit them in order to tackle the quantitative dimensions of your research report.

Key topics:

→ Numbers and symbols
→ Manipulating equations
→ Dealing with large and small numbers
→ Presenting numbers: significant figures and rounding
→ Fractions, percentages and ratios

Key terms

Denominator   Digit   Engineering notation   Numerator   Reciprocal
Rounding   Scientific notation   Significant figure   SI system

Many research projects include elements that require skills of numeracy, especially in the later stages of study. Examples frequently occur in biology, economics, geography and psychology. If you've forgotten school maths or lack the required knowledge and technique, you may find these parts of your courses challenging. Dip into this chapter if you need to refresh your knowledge and skills.

→ Numbers and symbols

Numbers and symbols are the essence of maths. Having a good understanding of the following terms will help you work through problems confidently:

smart tip

Getting to grips with maths

If your research involves unfamiliar maths, then you will probably need to consult texts that explain the concepts and methods involved, and possibly practise carrying out analogous calculations. Your supervisor may be able to assist, or point you in the right direction for support, but will expect you to have used your own initiative first.

- **Constants.** These are unchanging values such as gravitational acceleration (g) or *pi* (π). These are often given in tables, but in some cases you will need to memorise them. In the 'straight line' equation $y = mx + c$, m and c, the quantities describing the slope and y-intercept are examples of constants. Their values stay constant in any one instance, but change for different lines.
- **Variables.** These are mathematical quantities that can take different values. For example, if x and y change according to a mathematical relationship between them, such as $y = mx + c$, then x and y would be described as variables.
- **Units and prefixes.** Constants and variables can be dimensionless, but most have units, such as metres (m), m s^{-2} ('metres per second squared'), or kg. The Système International d'Unités, or SI, provides agreed standard units and is widely adopted in the sciences (see Table 11.1). Prefixes are often used to denote very large and small numbers (Table 15.1); alternatively scientific or engineering notation may be used (see p. 162 and Table 15.2).

Definitions: sets of numbers

Whole numbers: 0, 1, 2, 3 . . .

Natural numbers: 1, 2, 3, 4 . . .

Integers: –2, –1, 0, 1, 2, 3 . . .

Real numbers: integers and anything in between, e.g. 1.54, π, e^4.

Prime numbers: natural numbers divisible only by themselves and 1.

Rational numbers: p/q, where p is integer and q is natural and they have no common factor.

Irrational numbers: real numbers with no exact value, such as π. If the final digit is repeated, it is often shown thus: 4/3 = 1.3 or 1.3r.

Table 15.1 SI prefixes. Note that after the first row, small number prefixes have the ending 'o', while large number prefixes have the ending 'a'.

Small numbers			Large numbers		
Value	Prefix	Symbol	Value	Prefix	Symbol
10^{-3}	milli	m	10^{3}	kilo	k
10^{-6}	micro	µ	10^{6}	mega	M
10^{-9}	nano	n	10^{9}	giga	G
10^{-12}	pico	p	10^{12}	tera	T
10^{-15}	femto	f	10^{15}	peta	P
10^{-18}	atto	a	10^{18}	exa	E
10^{-21}	zepto	z	10^{21}	zeta	Z
10^{-24}	yocto	y	10^{24}	yotta	Y

Table 15.2 Exponents and scientific notation: tips and examples

Tips	Examples
If you multiply a number by itself, this gives a positive power	$y \times y$ = 'y squared' = y^2 or 'y to the power 2'
Dividing a number by itself gives that number to the power 0 and is equal to 1. Continuing to divide by the number gives a negative power	$8/8 = 8^0 = 1$ $1/y = y^{-1}$, $1/z^8 = z^{-8}$ $x^{-5} = 1/x^5$ $x^{-5} = x \div x \div x \div x \div x \div x \div x$
When adding numbers expressed as powers of 10, if the exponents are the same, you can add the numerical parts, but keep the exponent the same. You may wish to change the exponent thereafter if the addition of the numerical part results in a large or small number	$(2.0 \times 10^{-3}) + (3.0 \times 10^{-3})$ $= 5.0 \times 10^{-3}$ $759 \times 10^5 + 605 \times 10^5$ $= 1364 \times 10^5$ $= 136.4 \times 10^6$
If adding numbers with different exponents, first express them to the same power before adding the numerical parts	$(7.3 \times 10^4) + (6.0 \times 10^3)$ $= (7.3 \times 10^4) + (0.6 \times 10^4)$ $= 7.9 \times 10^4$
Add the exponents when multiplying, but multiply the numerical parts	$(8 \times 10^5) \times (3 \times 10^4) = 24 \times 10^9$ note that: $x^m \times x^n = x^{m+n}$ and $x^m / x^n = x^{m-n}$
When using scientific notation to express large numbers, count digits up or down from the decimal point to work out what the exponent should be	$134.5 = 1.345 \times 10^2$ (count is two digits) $0.0029 = 2.9 \times 10^{-3}$ (count is three digits)
To work out engineering notation more easily, group digits in threes from the decimal point, using commas	$15039829 = 15{,}039{,}829 = 15.04 \times 10^6$ to four significant figures $0.000392 = 0.000{,}392$ $= 392 \times 10^{-6}$
When you are expressing numbers in either scientific or engineering notation, try to express the numeric part as a number between 0 and 1000	Rather than writing 0.1256×10^6, write 1.256×10^5 (scientific notation) or 125.6×10^3 (engineering notation)

Zeros and unity

Some basic points to remember:

- subtracting a number from itself gives zero
- multiplying a number by zero gives zero
- multiplying a number by 1 gives the number itself
- dividing a number or expression by itself gives 1
- dividing a number or expression by zero gives infinity and is mathematically meaningless

- **Operators.** These are the mathematical codes for carrying out operations with variables and constants. From day-to-day usage, you will be familiar with the basic ones, such as add (+), subtract (–), multiply (× or .) or divide (÷ or /), as well as equals (=), approximately equals (≈) and does not equal (≠). Note that a sign for 'multiply' is frequently omitted, so a term like *mx* means '*m* multiplied by *x*'. You should also know the following: greater than (>), less than (<), greater than or equal to (≥) and less than or equal to (≤). However, you may wish to refamiliarise yourself with other functions such as logs and powers if these are relevant to your studies. In complex expressions, and particularly when there are mixed operations, the order in which you carry out operations is important (see below and Table 15.3).

smart tip

Basics of maths relevant to manipulation of equations

The order in which you carry out operations is important. The mnemonic BODMAS (**b**rackets, powers **o**f, **d**ivision, **m**ultiplication, **a**ddition, **s**ubtraction) describes the order you should use, working left to right.

→ Manipulating equations

Numbers and symbols, usually letters, may be linked together in equations (formulae) or functions, such that one expression is said to equal another (or zero). The formula $y = mx + c$ is an example of an equation. These generalised expressions of the relationship between different quantities, or terms, are useful in modelling, estimation and prediction, and this branch of mathematics is called algebra.

Table 15.3 Manipulating numbers and equations: tips and examples

Tips	Examples
When working out results, carry out a bracketed calculation first, or you may obtain an incorrect result	$(ab) + c \neq a(b + c)$ $(3 \times 5) + 6 \neq 3 \times (5 + 6)$ because $15 + 6 \neq 3 \times 11$
You can remove an 'isolated' constant or variable by adding it to or subtracting it from both sides. If you change the side, you change the sign	If $x = y - z$, then $x + z = y - z + z$, so $x + z = y$, and by rearranging, $y = x + z$
You can remove a multiplying constant or variable by dividing both sides by it	If $x = yz$, then $y = x/z$ (divide both sides by z and rearrange)
Remove a dividing constant or variable by multiplying both sides by it	If $x = y/z$, then $y = xz$ (multiply both sides by z and rearrange)
Remove a power from one side by multiplying both sides by the reciprocal power or by taking logs	If $a = b^c$, then $b = a^{1/c}$ If $a = b^c$, then $\log a = c \log b$, and $c = \log a/\log b = \log(a - b)$
You can combine powers and powers of powers	$a^b + a^c = a^{(b+c)}$ and $a^b - a^c = a^{(b-c)}$ $(a^b)^c = a^{(bc)}$
It can be useful to combine expressions or express them in different ways before doing any of the above. Use parentheses (. . .) to 'isolate' parts of formulae and calculations	$ab + ac = a(b + c)$ so if you wish to find the value of a in $y = ax + az$ $y = a(x + z)$ $a = y/(x + z)$ If $xy^2 - xz = 5 - p$, find x. First, take x out as a common factor, so $x(y^2 - z) = 5 - p$. Now divide both sides by $(y^2 - z)$, so $x = (5 - p)/(y^2 - z)$

You will frequently need to rearrange equations. For example, if you wish to find a particular variable or constant in a formula, you may wish to express it in terms of other variables and constants whose values you already know. This key mathematical skill usually involves carrying out an operation on both sides of the equation so that a particular term 'disappears' from one side and reappears on the other. You may need to simplify some of the terms before doing this or express them in a different mathematical way (see Table 15.3).

→ Dealing with large and small numbers

Many calculations involve large and/or small numbers, which can be unwieldy to write down. Exponents and logarithms are useful ways of expressing these in brief.

Using powers of 10 to express very large or small numbers

This is best explained with examples:

$2000 = 2 \times 10^3$
$(= 2 \times 10 \times 10 \times 10)$

$0.0003 = 3 \times 10^{-4}$
$(= 3 \div 10 \div 10 \div 10 \div 10)$.

Exponents

In a term like x^n, *n* is known as an exponent and denotes that a number has been multiplied by itself *n* times, or is *raised to the power n*. In this type of expression, *n* may also be called the index.

Numbers are often expressed as powers of 10, such as 2.172×10^5 (= 217,200). This is called scientific notation and it makes arithmetic with large or small numbers much easier. Engineering notation is similar but uses powers of 10 in groups of three, such as 10^3 or 10^{-9}, corresponding to the SI prefixes (see Tables 15.1 and 15.3).

smart tip

Using SI prefixes

These symbols (see Table 15.1) effectively make engineering notation neater. Use them in combination with a unit to indicate very large or small numbers. For example:

5 kHz = 5000 Hz

15 μm = 0.000015 m.

Pay special attention to case, because, for example, 1.5 pg ≠ 1.5 Pg.

Logarithms ('logs')

A log to the base 10 is the power of 10 that would give that number. Thus, log (100) = 2, because $10^2 = 10 \times 10 = 100$. Natural logs (symbol ln) are powers of *e* (≈ 2.178), which is used because it is mathematically convenient in some situations.

Logs can be useful because:

$log\ (a) \times log\ (b) = log\ (a + b)$
$log\ (a) \div log\ (b) = log\ (a - b)$
$log\ (a^n) = n\ log\ (a)$

An antilog is 10^x, where x is the log value. You can convert a log value into a simple numerical value by working out its antilog. The equivalent for natural logs is e^x. These values are best obtained using a calculator.

Use of logs

Logs were exceptionally valuable tools when even complex calculations were done 'by hand'; old-fashioned mechanical calculators such as slide rules were based on them. Nowadays, digital calculators make most calculations straightforward. However, logs are still found in some formulae (for example, the degree of acidity, or pH, is calculated as $pH = -log\ [H^+]$, where $[H^+]$ is the molar hydrogen ion concentration), and it is therefore important to understand their mathematical origin.

→ Presenting numbers: significant figures and rounding

Sometimes when you carry out a calculation, and especially when using a calculator, the answer may appear with several digits, for example, 12.326024221867.

Deciding on how many digits or significant figures (s.f.) to quote in your results is important. If you do not include these in intermediate steps, your final result may be incorrect to a surprising degree; on the other hand, if you include too many in your final result, this may imply a false degree of accuracy. For example, it is incorrect to refer to a temperature of 15.34 °C if your thermometer can only be read to the nearest half degree at best.

You will often be expected to express your results to a certain number of significant figures. The number of significant figures can be worked out by counting the number of digits from the left. The first non-zero digit in a number is the first significant figure. 12.326024221867 has 14 significant figures and would be expressed as 12.326 to five s.f. and 12.33 to four s.f. (see also Table 15.4).

Table 15.4 Significant figures and rounding: tips and examples

Tips	Examples
For numbers with no leading zeros, the number of significant figures is equal to the number of digits	94.8263 has six s.f.
With leading zeros, the significant figures start after the last leading zero	0.0000465 has three s.f.
'Internal' zeros count as significant figures	0.00044304 has five s.f.
Trailing zeros are not regarded as significant figures in whole numbers	2300 has two s.f.
Trailing zeros can be significant if they come after the decimal point, as they imply a certain accuracy of measurement	10.10 cm has four s.f.
The number of decimal places is the number of digits after the decimal points. Round up or down as appropriate	56.78478 to two decimal places is 56.78 56.78478 to three decimal places is 56.785
When calculating with several values, the one with the least number of significant figures should be used to define the number of s.f. used in the answer (an exception is when using mathematical constants, which are assumed to have an infinite number of significant figures)	12.232 – 9.2 = 3.0 (*not* 3.032) 176 × 1.573 = 276 (*not* 276.848) converting 1456 m to km, this is 1.456 km, *not* 1 or 1.5 km
Always round after you have done a calculation, not before	The area in cm^2 of a rectangular piece of carpet where the sides have been measured to the nearest mm as 1286 × 1237 would be 15,908 cm^2, *not* 129 × 124 cm = 15,996 cm^2
If asked to work out an answer, but without guidance on the number of significant figures to use, consider the accuracy of your original measurements. Round up or down to the nearest whole number of your finest measurement division	The length of the piece of string measured by a ruler was 134 mm Converting millimetres to inches using the factor 0.03937, the length of the piece of string is given as 5.28 inches to three s.f. (not 5.27558 as found with a calculator)

The process of deciding what the last digit is when you do this is called rounding. In essence, you take into account the digits to the right of the last significant digit, and if they are greater than 0.5, then you round up to the next number, and if they are less then 0.5, then you round down. What you do if the remainder is exactly 0.5 depends:

to avoid bias, the usual rule is to round down if the preceding digit is even and up if it is odd. Thus, to three significant figures, 15.65 would be expressed as 15.6, while 15.75 would be rounded to 15.8. See the tip box below regarding if zeros are present.

Easier to carry out is the instruction to 'express your answer to *n* decimal places', although this may also involve rounding. Hence, if a calculator gives an answer as 60.466023 and you are asked to supply an answer to two decimal places, you should write 60.47 (see Table 15.4).

What about zeros in rounded numbers?

Significant figures (s.f.) get a little complicated if there are zeros present.

- Counting from the left, the first non-zero digit in a number is the first significant figure. Hence, 0.00012 has two s.f.
- The final zero even in a whole number is not regarded as a significant figure, because it only shows the order of magnitude of the number. Thus, 141.35 is written as 140 to two s.f.
- Zeros included after the decimal point do imply accuracy of measurement and should be regarded as significant figures. Thus 12.30 has four s.f.

See Table 15.4 for further examples.

→ Fractions, percentages and ratios

A fraction is simply one number divided by another. It does *not* have to be between zero and one. A common fraction involves two integer numbers (for example, $^3/_4$), while in a decimal fraction the denominator is always a factor of 10, such as $^3/_{10}$. Decimal fractions are often expressed using the decimal point (for example $0.34 = {}^{34}/_{100}$).

Terminology of fractions

The upper number (or the first number) is called the **numerator** and the lower number (or the second number) is called the **denominator**. When the numerator is smaller than the denominator, the fraction represents a number between 0 and 1. When the numerator is bigger than the denominator, the fraction represents a number greater than 1.

Where numerators and denominators can both be divided by a common factor, it is normal practice to express the fraction with the lowest values possible. Thus, present $^{9}/_{24}$ as $^{3}/_{8}$.

A percentage value is a fraction expressed as a number of hundredths. This is used because it is easy to comprehend. To calculate a common fraction as a percentage using a calculator, divide the numerator by the denominator and multiply the answer by 100. Thus, $^{3}/_{4}$ = 0.75 = 75 per cent = 75%. To convert a percentage into a decimal fraction, move the decimal point two places to the left.

smart tip

Common decimal fractions

You should memorise the following common fractions in terms of decimals (where *r* indicates a repeating digit):

$^{1}/_{2}$ = 0.50	$^{1}/_{3}$ = 0.33*r*	$^{1}/_{8}$ = 0.125
$^{1}/_{4}$ = 0.25	$^{1}/_{5}$ = 0.20	$^{1}/_{10}$ = 0.10

A percentage does not need to be a whole number (for example 65.34 per cent is valid), nor does it always need to be less than 100 (as in 'Jane earns 143 per cent of what John earns'), except where you are expressing a fraction of a limited total (you cannot assert that '126 per cent of dogs prefer Bonzo dog food').

A ratio expresses two or more numbers or proportions in relation to each other. The norm is to divide the larger by the smaller (or divide the others by the smallest). If you had 6 red, 12 blue and 36 orange discs, the ratio of red:blue:orange would be 1:2:6 (note the colon (:) as notation; you would say this as 'red to blue to orange'). Ratios can involve real numbers, such as 1.43:1.

Tips for manipulating fractions mathematically are provided in Table 15.5.

Table 15.5 Fractions, proportions and ratios: tips and examples

Tips	Examples
When adding fractions, you need to ensure that the denominators are the same. To do this, multiply *both sides* of one of the fractions by a number that will allow this, then add the numerator values. In complex examples, you may need to multiply both sides of the fractions by different numbers. This number will generally be the number you need to multiply the denominator by to obtain a common value (the 'lowest common denominator')	$^3/_4 + ^1/_2 = (^3/_4 + ^2/_4) = ^5/_4 = 1^1/_4 = 1.25$ (multiply both sides of the second fraction by 2 to obtain them both expressed as fourths) $^3/_8 + ^2/_3 + ^7/_9$ $= ^{27}/_{72} + ^{48}/_{72} + ^{56}/_{72}$ $= ^{131}/_{72}$
When multiplying fractions, multiply both the numerators and denominators	$^3/_4 \times ^5/_2 = ^{15}/_8$
Likewise, when dividing, divide both the numerators and denominators. Another way to do this sort of calculation is to turn the 'divided by' fraction round and multiply	$^3/_4 \div ^1/_2 = ^3/_2$ Alternatively, $^3/_4 \div ^1/_2$ $= ^3/_4 \times ^2/_1$ $= ^6/_4$ $= ^3/_2$
To work out one number as a percentage of another, simply divide the two and multiply by 100	Express 12 out of 76 as a percentage: $(12/76) \times 100 = 16\%$ (15.78947 rounded up)
To find a percentage of a number, express the percentage as a decimal fraction and multiply the number by this	75% of 320 = $0.75 \times 320 = 240$
Don't get confused by percentages less than one	0.05% is 5 in 10000 or $^5/_{10000}$
It may be convenient to express ratios as decimal numbers in relation to unity	If there are 34 girls in a class of 56, the ratio of girls to boys is 34/(56–34):1 = 1.5:1 (rounded to one decimal place)

Practical tips for solving problems in arithmetic and algebra

Get to know relevant aspects of your calculator. Features you should consider, as appropriate, include:

- what kind of notation your calculator uses (standard or reverse-Polish notation; most use standard) and what this means, in particular about how you do nested calculations;
- how the memory works;
- how to enter a constant and use it in several calculations;
- how to enter exponents; and
- how to express one number as a percentage of another.

When working with formulae, express all values in terms of base units. Nearly all scientific and engineering formulae are expressed in terms of SI base units (i.e. metres, seconds, kilograms), so if you are given a length as 10 mm, do not enter 10 into a formula, enter 10×10^{-3}, expressing the length in metres.

Check the units and scale of your results. First, make sure that you convert any data into appropriate units requested in the question, and with the appropriate number of significant figures. Second, make sure that your result is not absurdly high or low. Areas and volumes are particularly difficult to visualise. Try to relate these to 'real life' if you can - for example, imagine what the value you obtain might look like in relation to something you are familiar with, like a stamp, sheet of paper, glass of beer, and so on.

If you are unsure about the algebra using symbols, insert real numbers. The first example in Table 15.3 provides an illustration of how this might work in practice.

And now . . .

15.1 Find out which mathematical skills you will be expected to use in your research. These may be apparent from the data collection techniques you will be expected to use - and your earlier experience in practical or lab work may help you identify them. If they are not immediately obvious, then your supervisor may be able to help you identify them. Carrying out sample calculations may also reveal areas of maths that you will need to revise.

15.2 Learn and practise key mathematical skills. From the exercise carried out in point 15.1 above, pick out the aspects you feel least confident about and make a determined effort to tackle them. You should look first at the main principles and techniques in each topic, and then move on to the specifics for calculations you will need to carry out. It is worth understanding the background because if you simply rely on calculators and spreadsheets, you may make fundamental mistakes in the underlying approach.

15.3 Set up pro-forma spreadsheets for repeated calculations. These templates can save you a lot of time. They operate by having pre-formatted areas for data entry and presentation of results, with the relevant formulae already embedded in the spreadsheet. Where appropriate, pre-formatted graphical output can be created, and, even if this will not be used in your report (e.g. a calibration curve), this may be useful as a check on the way a measurement or experiment has run. Always test templates with data for which you know or can easily check the answer. You may need to brush up on your spreadsheet skills to create these templates, but the resulting saving of effort will probably be worthwhile.

16 Interpreting and presenting data

How to understand and produce graphs, tables and basic statistics

You may encounter data in many forms during your research. This may mean that you are required to understand and explain graphs, tables and statistics, or be expected to generate them from raw information. The emphasis in this chapter is to provide a 'refresher' on data interpretation, but the principles of constructing graphs and presenting tables are also covered.

Key topics:

- → How to 'read' a graph
- → How graphs can mislead
- → Creating graphs
- → Creating tables
- → Important descriptive statistics
- → Concepts of hypothesis-testing statistics

Key terms

Descriptive statistics Dispersion Error bars Extrapolation Hypothesis testing Interpolation Legend Location Qualitative Quantitative Tic mark

There are many ways of presenting data sets and the methods chosen can affect your analysis or favour certain interpretations. A healthily critical approach is therefore essential when you are examining graphs, tables and statistics. Equally, when creating these items to condense and display your own information, your primary aim should always be to do this in a manner that is simple to understand and unbiased.

smart tip

Graph types

Some common forms are illustrated throughout this chapter, but a quick way of finding out about different options is to explore the forms available in a spreadsheet program like Microsoft Excel. Look at the 'Insert > Chart > Standard Types' menu, which illustrates sub-types and provides brief descriptions. This is also a good way of exploring ways of presenting your own data.

→ How to 'read' a graph

The following elements are present in most graphs and charts (collectively known as 'figures'). Use them to work out what a specific graph means, referring to the example shown in Figure 16.1.

- **The figure title and its caption.** These should appear below the graph. Read them first to determine the overall context and gain information about what the graph shows. If the caption is detailed, you may need to revisit it later to aid your interpretation.

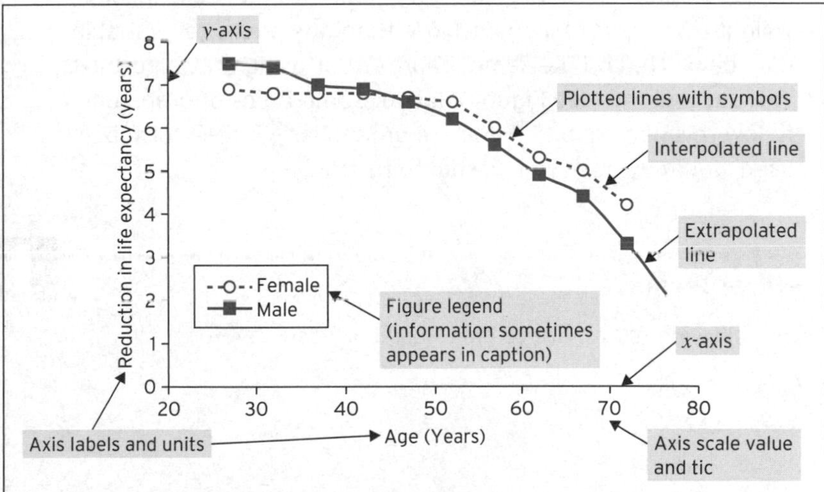

Figure 89 **A standard plotted curve.** This figure type uses x-y axes and points and lines to illustrate the relationship between two variables. *Source*: Data modified from Rogers, R.G. and Powell-Griner E., 1991. Life expectancies of cigarette smokers and non-smokers in the United States. *Soc. Sci. Med.*, 32, 1151-9.

Figure 16.1 The basic components of a graph

smart tip

Checklist for interpreting a graph

- ❑ Consider the context by reading the title, legend and main text.
- ❑ Recognise the type of graph.
- ❑ Examine what the axes show.
- ❑ Inspect the scale of the axes.
- ❑ Study the symbols and plotted curves.
- ❑ Evaluate what any error bars or statistics mean.

- **The type of figure.** With experience, you will come to recognise the basic chart types (Figure 16.2) and others common in your discipline. This will help you to orientate yourself. For example, a pie chart is usually used to show proportions of a total.
- **The axes.** Many forms of chart represent the relationship between two variables, called x and y for convenience. These are often presented between a pair of axes at right angles, with the horizontal x-axis often relating to the 'controlled' variable (for example, concentration or time) and the vertical y-axis often relating to the 'measured' variable (for example, income, weight (mass), or response). More than one measured variable may be plotted on the same graph, either using the same x-axis, or a second one (see Figure 16.2(b)). Some types of graph don't follow this pattern and if you are unfamiliar with the form being used, you may need to investigate further.

Plural terms

The following plurals are often misused or misunderstood:

Axis = singular

Axes = plural

Datum = singular

Data = plural (hence, the 'data *are* presented in Figure 14').

- **The axis scale and units.** An axis label should state what the axis means and the units being used. Each axis should show clearly the range of values it covers through a series of cross-marks (tic, or tick, marks) with associated numbers to indicate the scale. To interpret these, you'll also need to know the units. Some axes do not start from zero, or incorporate a break in the scale; others may be non-linear (for example, a logarithmic axis is sometimes used to cover particularly wide ranges of numbers). Pay attention in these cases, because this could mean that the graph exaggerates or emphasises differences between values (see Figures 16.3(a) and (b)).

- **The symbols and plotted curves.** These help you identify the different data sets being shown and the relationship between the points in each set. A legend or key may be included to make this clearer. Your interpretation may focus on differences in the relationships and, inevitably, on the plotted curves (also known as 'trend lines'). However, it is important to realise that the curves are usually hypothetical interpolations between measured values or, worse, extrapolations beyond them; and, because they may involve assumptions about trends in the data, they should be examined with care. Symbols may also include information about variability in the data collected (for example, error bars), which provide useful clues about the reliability of data and assumed trends.

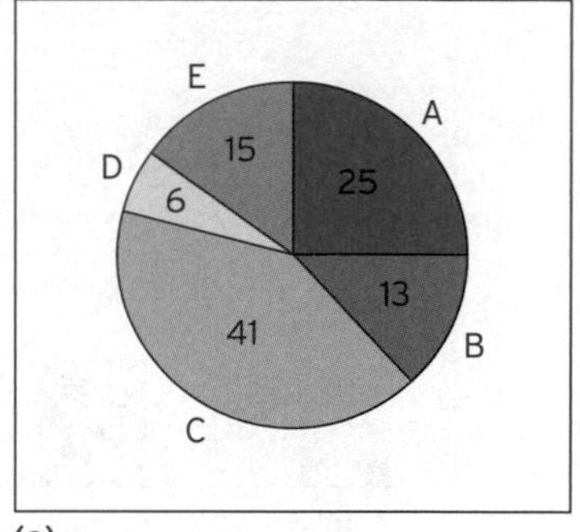

(a)

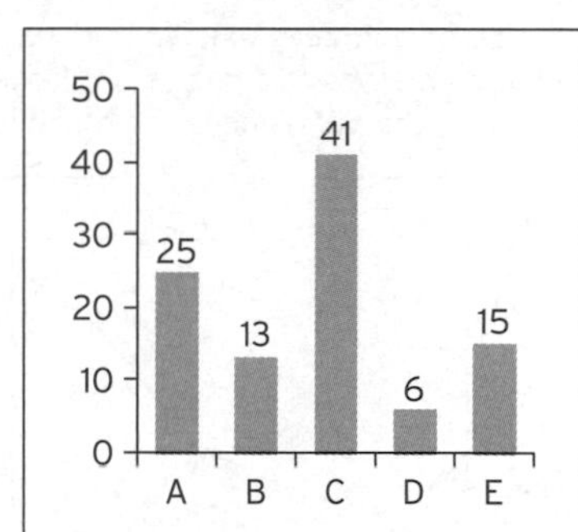

(b)

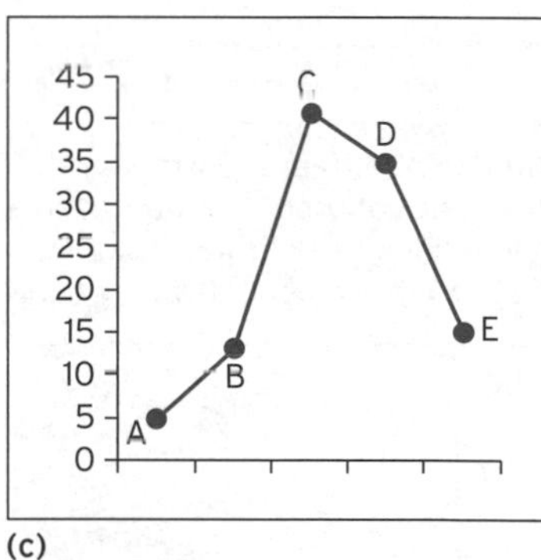

(c)

Figure 16.2 Common forms of graph. These are in addition to the standard plotted curve shown in Figure 16.1. (a) **Pie chart**, showing proportions of a total - here expressed as percentages. (b) **Histogram**, showing amounts in different categories. (c) **Frequency polygon**, showing distribution of counted data across a continuous range.

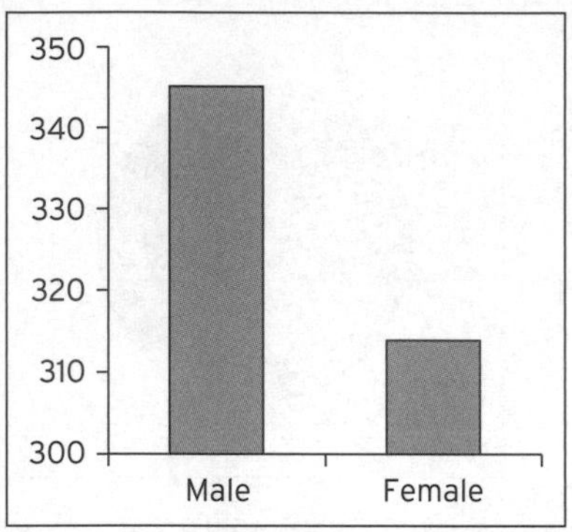

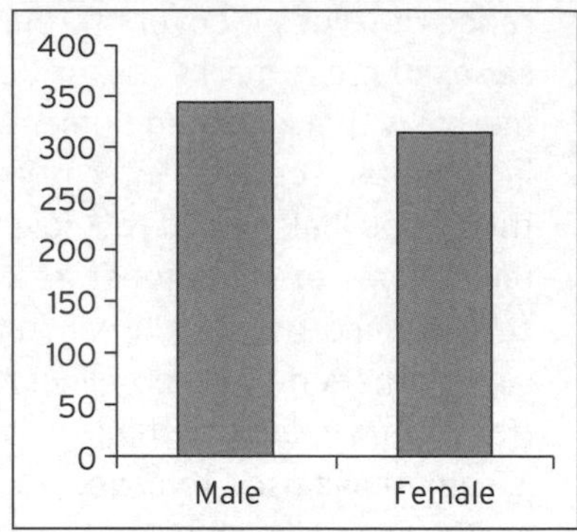

(a) Use of non-zero axis. In the chart on the left, it looks as if the differences between males and females are large; however, when the *y*-axis is zeroed, as on the right, the differences are much less noticeable.

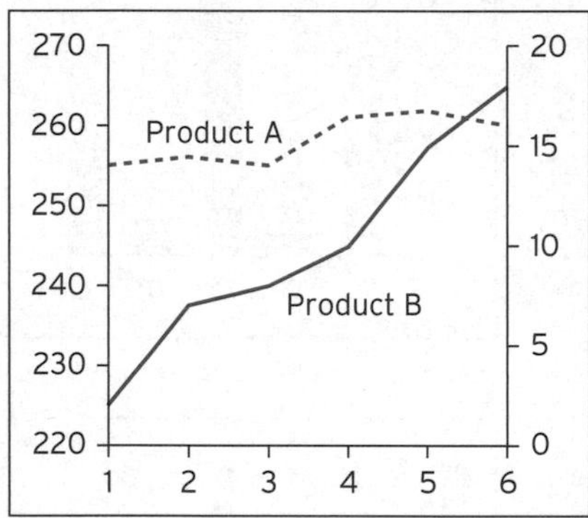

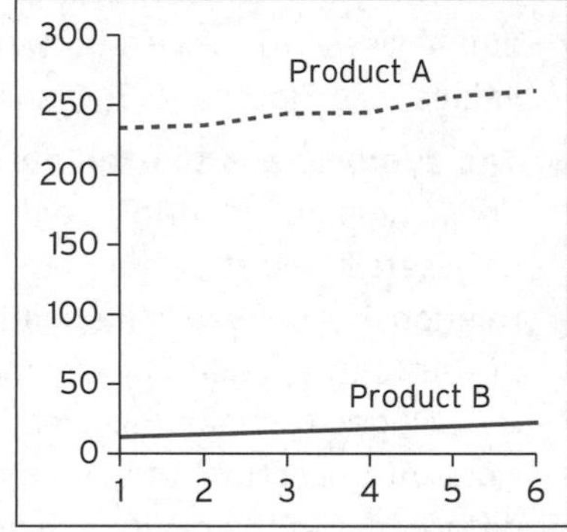

(b) Use of different *y*-axes for different curves. In the chart on the left it looks as if sales of product A (left-hand axis) are being caught up by those of product B (right-hand axis); however, when the same axis is used for both curves, then it can be seen that product B vastly outsells product A.

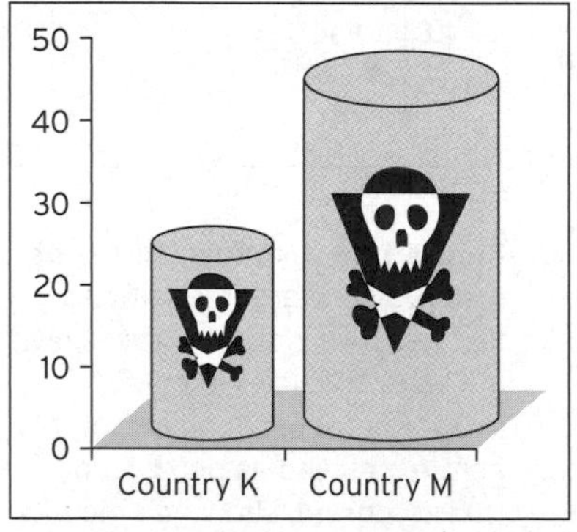

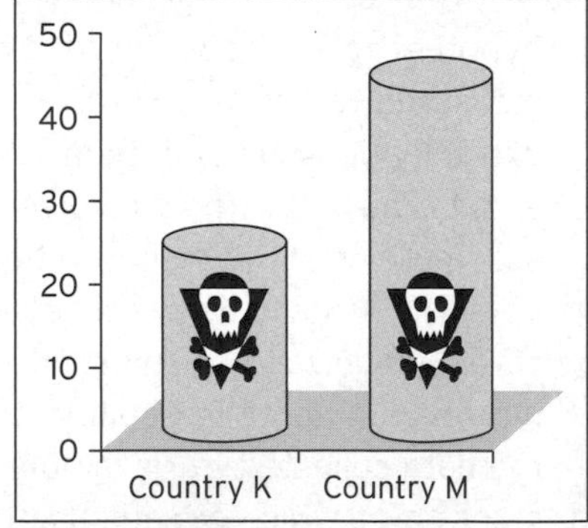

(c) Use of a two- or three-dimensional object to represent a linear scale. In the chart on the left, the barrel retains its shape in relation to the *y*-axis scale, so it makes it look as if country M produces much more toxic waste than country K. On the right, a truly linear representation is shown.

Figure 16.3 Three common examples of misleading graphs

→ How graphs can mislead

You can learn a lot about data presentation by reviewing misleading graphs and learning why they might lead to incorrect interpretations. A selection of examples is shown in Figure 16.3. You should try to avoid confusing your audience by using these forms of misrepresentation when constructing your own figures.

Definitions: graphing

Interpolation: an assumed trend or relationship *between* available data points.

Extrapolation: an assumed trend or relationship *before* or *after* (below or above) available data points. Extrapolation is risky because the assumption may be made that a trend will continue when there may be little evidence that this will happen.

→ Creating graphs

What follows is naturally a generalisation, but this sequence will suit many circumstances.

1 **Think carefully about what you want to plot and why, then choose an appropriate type of graph.** Recognising the type of data you want to present is essential for this, and reviewing the common options shown in Figures 16.1 and 16.2 may help. If you are choosing a plotted curve, then you must decide which variable will appear on the x-axis and which on the y-axis. If you have selected an unfamiliar form of graph, you may wish to sketch out how this will appear for your data set. A spreadsheet can be a valuable tool when working through this phase.

2 **Consider the range and units for the axes, where appropriate.** What are the upper and lower limits of your data? Should you start each axis at zero, and if not, will this act to distort the presentation (see Figure 16.3(a))? Will your axes be linear? Will they be in the same units as your measurements, or might you wish to work out ratios, percentages or other transformations (see **Ch 15** and below) before graphing the data? Once you have settled on these aspects, you can write the descriptive label for

the axis, which should first state what is presented and then, usually in parentheses ( ) or after a solidus (/), the units used. Other forms of graph, such as a pie chart, may require a descriptive label for each segment, or you may prefer to use a legend or key.

3 **Choose elements of presentation.** For example, if you are using a pie chart, select colours or shading for the segments. If your graph has axes, decide how frequently you wish the tics to appear: too many and the axis will seem crowded, too few and it becomes less easy to work out the approximate values of data points. Decide which symbols will be used for which data sets, and if presenting several graphs in sequence, try to be consistent on this. If measures of location (Table 16.1) are plotted, consider whether you wish to add error bars to show the variability in the data.

smart tip

Adding trend lines to graphs

If you are drawing a graph, you will need to take special care when adding a curve, because any trend line you add indicates that you have assumed an underlying relationship between the variables (see p. 173). If the points carry no (rare) or very little error, then you may be justified in drawing a straight line or curve between each point. If, however, the points do carry error, then the curve should take an 'average' line between them. Since most plotted relationships are complex, then this probably should be a smooth curve rather than a straight line.

4 **Write the figure caption.** Your aim should be to ensure that the figure is 'self-contained' and that its essence can be understood without reference to detail normally given elsewhere, such as the material and methods section of a scientific report. Items to include here are:

- the figure number;
- the figure title;
- what the symbols and error bars mean (a legend or key within the figure may or may not be acceptable - check);
- if appropriate, how the plotted curve was chosen;
- any brief details about the data (for example, differences in the treatments) that will help your reader understand the figure better without having to refer to another section.

→ Creating tables

A good table presents data in a compact, readily assimilated format. In general, you should not include the same data in a chart *and* a table. You might decide to use a table rather than a chart if:

- graphic presentation is not suitable for some or all of the data (for instance, when some are qualitative);
- there are too many data sets or variables to include in a chart;
- your audience might be interested in the precise values of some of your data;
- you wish to place large amounts of your data on record, for instance within an appendix to a report.

Think about and draw a rough design for your table before constructing a final version. Key elements include:

- **The title and caption.** Your table must have these as a guide to the content, just like a figure. Note that the numbering scheme for tables is independent from that of graphs. Titles and captions should always appear above the table.
- **Appropriate arrangement and headings.** Each vertical column should display a particular type of data, and the descriptive headings should reflect these contents, giving the units where data are quantitative. Each row might show different instances of these types of data. Rows and columns should be arranged in a way that helps the reader to compare them if this is desirable.
- **Rulings.** The default in word-processing programs such as Microsoft Word is to add boxed lines to tables; however, the modern style is to minimise these, often restricting their use to horizontal lines only.
- **Data values.** These should be presented to an appropriate number of significant figures. An indication of errors, if included, should be given in parentheses, and the heading should make it clear what statistic is being quoted.
- **Footnotes.** These can be used to explain abbreviations or give details of specific cases.

Figure 16.4 illustrates some important components of a well-designed table.

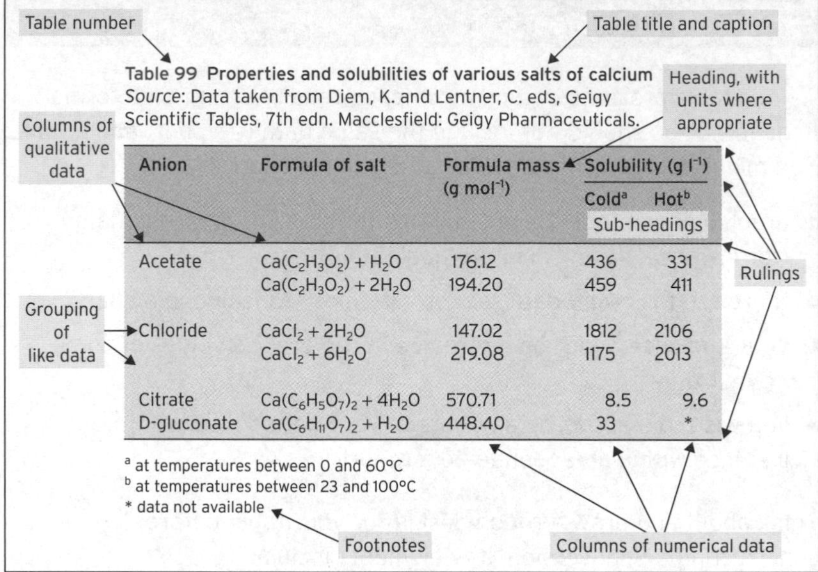
Table 99 Properties and solubilities of various salts of calcium
Source: Data taken from Diem, K. and Lentner, C. eds, Geigy Scientific Tables, 7th edn. Macclesfield: Geigy Pharmaceuticals.

Anion	Formula of salt	Formula mass ($g\ mol^{-1}$)	Solubility ($g\ l^{-1}$)	
			Cold[a]	Hot[b]
Acetate	$Ca(C_2H_3O_2) + H_2O$	176.12	436	331
	$Ca(C_2H_3O_2) + 2H_2O$	194.20	459	411
Chloride	$CaCl_2 + 2H_2O$	147.02	1812	2106
	$CaCl_2 + 6H_2O$	219.08	1175	2013
Citrate	$Ca(C_6H_5O_7)_2 + 4H_2O$	570.71	8.5	9.6
D-gluconate	$Ca(C_6H_{11}O_7)_2 + H_2O$	448.40	33	*

[a] at temperatures between 0 and 60°C
[b] at temperatures between 23 and 100°C
* data not available

Figure 16.4 The basic components of a table. Note that shading is included here to emphasise the heading and data sections and would not usually be present.

Definitions: data

Quantitative data: data that can be expressed in numbers, such as length, height or price (see **Ch 11**).

Qualitative data: data that are descriptive and non-numerical, such as colour, place of manufacture, or name (see **Ch 12**).

→ Important descriptive statistics

Descriptive statistics are used to simplify a complex data set, to summarise the distribution of data within the data set and to provide estimates of values of the population frequency distribution. Two aspects that are often quoted are:

- a measure of location – this is an estimate of the 'centre' of the frequency distribution;
- a measure of dispersion – this is an estimate of the spread of data within the frequency distribution.

Definition: frequency distribution

This is a description of the frequency of occurrence of values of a variable. You may be interested in the actual distribution in the sample you have taken, and you might use a frequency polygon (Figure 16.2(c)) to represent this. You might also be interested in the underlying population frequency distribution. This is often theoretical in nature and a smooth curve representing a model function might be used to represent it.

Different measures of location and dispersion are outlined in Table 16.1 and many of these values can be obtained simply, using a spreadsheet or statistical program. More complex descriptive statistics such as standard error (describing the precision of a mean), or quantifying the shape of frequency distributions, are outside the scope of this book and a specialist text should be consulted.

→ Concepts of hypothesis-testing statistics

Hypothesis testing in a statistical context is used to compare the properties of a data set with other samples or to compare the data set with some theory about it.

Error and variability exist in all data sets (see box below), which means that it is impossible to be 100 per cent certain about differences between sets. Are the differences 'genuine' and due to a true

Sources of random error and variability

The following are reasons why the values and hence the descriptive statistics of samples of data may vary.

- **Sampling error,** due to the selection of a small number of individuals from a larger, variable population.
- **Measurement error,** due to the method of measurement of the variable.
- **Rounding error,** due to an attempt to use an appropriate number of significant figures, but often compounded in calculations.
- **Human error,** due to inaccurate writing or copying of data, mixing up of samples, and so on.
- **Error from unknown sources,** or unappreciated effects of sampling.

Table 16.1 Descriptive statistics and their uses

Measure	Statistic	How to calculate*	Uses, advantages and disadvantages
Location	Mean	The sum of all the data values divided by the number of values, n	The most commonly used measure. It takes account of all the values in the data set, but can be influenced by the presence of outliers and is not representative of the whole body of data if this is asymmetric. Units are the same as the data
	Median	The mid-point of the data values when they are ranked in numerical order. For odd-sized data sets, it is the value of the middle datum, while for even-sized data sets, it is the mean of the two central values	May represent the location of the majority of the data better than the mean if the data set is asymmetric or there are outliers. Units are the same as the data
	Mode	The most common value in the data set	Easily found and unaffected by outliers; however, especially when the data set is small, it may be susceptible to 'random' variation in the distribution of values. Units are the same as the data
Dispersion	Range	The difference between the largest and the smallest values in the data set	Easy to determine, but its value is greatly affected by outliers and the size of the data set. Units are the the same as the data
	Semi-interquartile range	The difference between the first and third quartiles, which are the median values for the data ranked below and above the median value of the whole data set	Less easy to calculate than the range, but less affected by outliers and the size of the data set. Suitable to match with the median as a measure of location. Units are the same as the data.
	Variance	The sum of the squares of the difference between each data value and the mean, divided by $n - 1$	Measures the average difference from the mean for all the data values. Good for data sets that are symmetrical about the mean. Units are the square of those of the data.
	Standard deviation	The positive square root of the variance	A measure of the average difference from the mean for all the data values. Good for data sets symmetrical about the mean. Units are the same as the data, so preferable to the variance
	Coefficient of variation	The standard deviation multiplied by 100 and divided by the mean	A dimensionless (%) measure of variability relative to location. Allows the relative dispersion of data sets to be compared

dissimilarity between the samples, perhaps because of a treatment you have administered to one of them, or are the differences you observe just the result of random errors? Hypothesis testing works by trying to put a probability on these alternatives.

The norm is to set up a 'null hypothesis' (NH) that says that the samples are the same or that they conform to some theoretical description. By making certain assumptions about the data, calculating a hypothesis-testing statistic, and looking up tables of probability (or calculating), you can find the probability P of the NH being true. The lower P, the less likely you are to accept it in favour of the hypothesis that the differences were 'real' and due to your treatment or a genuine difference between the samples. Conventionally, if $P < 0.05$, then the NH is rejected.

Parametric and non-parametric statistical tests

The former make the assumption that the data are distributed according to a particular mathematical function, usually the so-called 'Normal' function; the latter make no assumptions of this kind, but are less powerful in distinguishing between samples that differ marginally.

Hypothesis-testing statistics differ in their assumptions about the data and what they set out to test. Some common ones and their uses are:

- ***t*-test:** for comparing two means;
- **χ^2 (Chi squared) test:** for comparing observed against expected values;
- **analysis of variance (ANOVA):** for comparing several means.

Precise details can be found in specialist texts.

Practical tips for producing graphs, tables and basic statistics

Learn how to manipulate spreadsheet chart output. If you are using a spreadsheet to compose your graph, it is important not to accept the default values without making a conscious decision to do so. Altering these attributes of charts is usually possible, although it may require some advanced knowledge of the program. Things you might wish to change include scale (often automatically selected), background, gridlines, symbols and lines.

Learn the table functions in your word processor. You should know how to create a table, add and delete columns and rows, manipulate the width of columns and rows, add and remove borders to the table 'cells', merge and split cells and sort data within tables. This will help you produce more presentable and user-friendly tables.

Research further on statistics. Statistics can be a little daunting, but like maths it is a subject in which you can greatly improve if you apply yourself. If you lack confidence in your statistical abilities, you may wish to enrol on a supplementary module or buy additional texts to help you improve. This is another aspect of maths where practice makes perfect.

GO And now . . .

16.1 **Examine critically the graphs produced by others.** You will see, for example, how graphs in newspapers are often presented in a way that supports the journalist's viewpoint, while presentations in academic articles tend to be less prone to bias because of the peer-review process. In all cases, you should think about why a particular graph format is shown, whether it is an aid to your understanding and how it might be improved, as this will help your own technique.

16.2 **Look at the chart options within Microsoft Excel.** Knowing your way round this program, or a similar spreadsheet available to you, and finding out what it offers will help you to choose the most appropriate chart and presentation for your purposes. It will also be useful to learn how to move charts from the spreadsheet to the word-processing software within your 'office' suite.

16.3 **Find out how tables are normally presented in your discipline.** This may vary, for example in the use of cell borders and lines, and you will probably be expected to adopt the style evident in text and journal articles in your area. If in doubt over a specific example, ask a colleague or your supervisor.

Addressing issues of plagiarism, referencing and ethics

17 Plagiarism and copyright infringement

How to avoid being accused of 'stealing' the ideas and work of others

Many students have only a vague understanding of plagiarism and copyright issues. However, failing to take account of them means you may risk loss of marks and serious disciplinary action. This chapter provides an insight into both types of potential infringement.

Key topics:

→ What is plagiarism?
→ What is copyright infringement?

Key terms
Copyright Paraphrase Plagiarism Synonym Verbatim

Plagiarism and copyright are topics that are extremely important academically and legally, but which are often misunderstood by students. Dissertations and project reports, by virtue of length, structure and depth, tend to require more citations than simpler types of academic writing. You therefore need to be fully aware of the issues involved so you can acknowledge intellectual property appropriately and avoid losing marks or being involved in further disciplinary action.

→ What is plagiarism?

Plagiarism can be defined as: 'the unacknowledged use of another's work as if it were one's own' (University of Dundee, 2005).

Alongside other forms of academic dishonesty, universities regard intentional plagiarism as a very serious offence. The regulations normally prescribe a range of penalties depending on the severity of the case, from a simple reduction in marks, to the ultimate sanctions of exclusion

Punishments for copying

Copying an essay or other piece of work by a fellow student (past or present) is cheating. The punishment is often an assessment mark of zero *for both parties*, and further disciplinary measures may be taken.

from the university or refusal to award a degree. You will find the exact penalties for your institution specified in institutional regulations.

Plagiarism is thus something to be avoided, and it is assumed that no one would deliberately set out to cheat in this way. The problem is that it is easy to plagiarise unwittingly. Regarding such 'unintentional plagiarism', you should note the following:

- The concept of 'work' in the definition of plagiarism given above includes ideas, writing or inventions, and not simply words.
- The notion of 'use' in the definition does not only mean 'word for word' (an exact copy) but also 'in substance' (a paraphrase of the notions involved).
- Use of another's work *is* acceptable, *if* you acknowledge the source.

The first two of these aspects give an indication of the potential dangers for students, but the third provides a remedy. To avoid the risk of unintentional plagiarism, adopt the following advice: if you think a particular author has said something particularly well, then quote them directly *and* provide a reference to the relevant article or book beside the quote. Note that the convention in academic writing is to use inverted commas (and sometimes italics) to signify clearly that a quotation is being made. The reference or citation is generally given in one of several standard forms that are discussed in Table 18.1.

Examples of plagiarism are given in Table 17.1. Each aspect of plagiarism is explained and a suggestion is made for an acceptable method of paraphrasing the material used.

What constitutes acceptable paraphrasing?

Good paraphrasing involves a significant rewrite of the original that retains the meaning and, possibly, adds extra points. Look particularly at the use of reporting verbs (**Ch 18**). Poor paraphrasing, which may be considered plagiarism (Table 17.1), involves merely changing the odd word or reconfiguring the order of the words (**Ch 18**).

included in the reference list at the end of the text. Explanations for several points made in the Comments column are given in **Ch 18**.

Category of plagiarism	Example	Revision or suggestion	Comment
Case study 1 Not giving credit to the source at all	*Danny has used material direct from the source without any acknowledgement. This is perceived as blatant **plagiarism**.*		
	Original: Most accidents are alcohol-related: 50% are fatalities but not necessarily of those under alcoholic influence (Annual Police Statistics, 2004; in Milne, 2006). Danny's text: The majority of road accidents are alcohol-related and 50% of these cases result in a death, but not always of the person who has consumed the alcohol.	Revision: A study of police statistics by Milne (2006) reported that approximately half of road accidents result in a death because one of the parties involved has been under the influence of alcohol.	Danny has rearranged the order slightly without noting the source of the data that he cites. Plagiarism aside, he's not explained how these figures were derived and hence they are represented as hearsay rather than hard fact.
Case study 2 Word substitution with some minor re-ordering of the original	*Xi thinks he can avoid plagiarism by changing odd words and word order of the original text. That is still considered to be **plagiarism**.*		
	Original: Post-operative physiotherapy is vital to the improvement in the quality of life of the elderly patient (Kay, 2003). Xi's version: Therapy after surgery is critical to the recovery of the older patient and their quality of life (Kay, 2003).	Revision: Kay (2003) attributes the improved quality of life levels of elderly patients who have undergone surgery to physiotherapy treatment.	Xi has used a thesaurus to find synonyms and has reversed two points. This does not show understanding of the issue. The revision uses the verb 'attributes' to indicate that this is a claim made by Kay, but is not necessarily a view shared by the author reporting it.
Case study 3 Using words from text and inserting citation, but omitting quotation marks	*Eileen's quoted the exact words from the original text. She has cited the source but has not inserted the quotation marks. However, this is still **plagiarism**.*		
	Original: It could be assumed that undergraduate students wrote what they could write and not what they actually know. Eileen's version: Sim (2006) asserted that students wrote what they could and not what they actually know.	Revision: Sim (2006) asserted that students 'wrote what they could and not what they actually know'.	Although Eileen has cited the source, by lifting the exact words taken from the text she is only doing half the job. She must place the exact words within inverted commas (quotation marks). See p. 198 for appropriate formats.

▼

Table 17.1 continued

Category of plagiarism	Example	Revision or suggestion	Comment
Case study 4 Using words from text and inserting quotation marks but omitting the citation	*Ed's copied the words from the original text and placed these within inverted commas but has not sourced the quotes. This, too, is a form of* ***plagiarism****.*		
	Original: It could be assumed that undergraduate students wrote what they could write and not what they actually know. Ed's version: Essentially, what was noted was that the students 'wrote what they could write and not what they actually know'.	Revision: Essentially, it was noted that students 'wrote what they could write and not what they actually know' (Sim, 2006). Or Sim (2006) noted that students 'wrote what they could write and not what they actually know'.	Although he has put in the inverted commas, by not including the source , Ed has failed to give recognition to the intellectual property of Sim. Furthermore, he has failed to understand that the citation brings credibility to his own work.
Case study 6 Stringing together a series of direct quotations with very little input from the student.	*Sally's struggling to understand her subject and lacks confidence in her own writing abilities. She tends to do more and more reading and picks out the bits she thinks are relevant. She puts those bits that seem to be related together in the same paragraph. She adds the sources and hopes that this evidences her understanding because she has clearly read widely. This does not reflect her understanding of the ideas that she is using to illustrate her argument. This is poor academically and could also be considered to be* ***plagiarism****.*		
	Sally's version: Brown (2000) noted 'insomnia is the ailment of the elderly'. Smith (2004) stated 'insomnia is a function of stressful living'. Jones (2001) said 'insomnia is a figment of those who sleep for an average of 5 hours a night'. This means that insomnia is a problem.	Revision: Perceptions about the incidence of insomnia are varied. Insomnia is problematic for the elderly (Brown, 2000) and for the stressed (Smith, 2004). However, Jones (2001) contends that people who claim to be insomniacs actually sleep for an average of 5 hours per night. This suggests that insomnia is often a perception rather than a reality.	Sally has created a kind of 'shopping list' of sources, but her list does not make the connection between the explicit point about types of people who suffer insomnia and the implicit point that those who claim insomnia do not actually suffer from it. Often students string together citations like this without making the underpinning connections or interpretations.

<table>
<tr><td rowspan="2">Case study 7
Downloading from the internet by cutting and pasting.</td><td colspan="3">Jeff has done the prescribed reading and has produced a piece of text that seems slightly too good when compared with the rest of what he has written. The hypertext links suggest that the words are not his own. There is no citation. This is an example of Internet plagiarism.</td></tr>
<tr><td><u>Jeff's version</u>: The incidence of drug misuse is something that invites action from international agencies including the <u>WHO</u>. There are also <u>European organisations</u> that have recognised the need to counter drug trafficking as well as establishing drug rehabilitation regimens throughout the European theatre.</td><td><u>Revision</u>: International and European organisations have engaged in tackling drug trafficking, misuse, and rehabilitation. (<u>www.drugfree.org</u> accessed 1.1.07)</td><td>Jeff's use of this text shows that he has not processed the material. Apart from his reliance on a source that may not be robust in that there is no certainty that his source is monitored or authenticated, he has shown that he has not engaged with the literature from more academic sources.</td></tr>
<tr><td rowspan="2">Case study 8
'Sharing' (copying?) work created with another student</td><td colspan="3">Marie has worked closely with her student buddy, Tim. They've shared material and both have included the same diagram which is a product of their collaboration. No explanation has been given. This is plagiarism.</td></tr>
<tr><td><u>Marie's version</u>:
Figure 3 shows that . . .
(diagram inserted)
<u>Tim's version</u>:
Figure 3 illustrates that . . .
(diagram inserted)</td><td colspan="2"><u>Suggested strategy</u>: It is good to work with a buddy to discuss and sketch the diagram. However, for the final version, both parties should work independently and should acknowledge the contribution of their partner, at an appropriate point, either in the text, the figure legend, the acknowledgements, or the reference list.</td></tr>
</table>

Three good reasons for paraphrasing

- It shows that you understand the concepts and ideas from the original text.
- It gives your reader a broad idea of the key ideas or argument without having to read all the source material.
- It demonstrates your capacity for critical thinking.

Cutting and pasting

The practice of cutting (copying) and pasting electronically (for example, taking material from websites) and using this in a project or dissertation without citing it, is regarded as plagiarism and will be punished if detected. Academics now have sophisticated electronic means of identifying where this has occurred.

→ What is copyright infringement?

Copyright law 'gives the creators of a wide range of material, such as literature, art, music and recording, film and broadcasts, economic rights' (Intellectual Property Office, 2007). Copyright infringement is regarded as equivalent to stealing, and legal rights are sometimes jealously guarded by companies with the resources to prosecute.

In the UK, authors have literary copyright over their material for their life, and their estate has copyright for a further 70 years. Publishers have typographical copyright for 25 years. This is why the copyright symbol © is usually accompanied by a date and the owner's name. You'll find this information on the publication details page at the start of a book.

Use of the copyright symbol

The © symbol indicates that someone is drawing your attention to the fact that something is copyright. However, even if © does not appear, the material may still be copyright.

You will be at risk of breaking the law if you copy (for example, photocopy, digitally scan or print out) material to which someone else owns the copyright, unless you have their express permission, or unless the amount you copy falls within the limits accepted for 'fair dealing'.

'Educational copying', *for non-commercial private study or research*, is sometimes allowed by publishers (they will state this on the material, and may allow multiple copies to be made). Otherwise, for single copies *for private study or research*, you should only copy what would fall under the 'fair dealing' provision, for which there is no precise definition in law.

Private study or research

This means what it says: the limits discussed here apply to that use and not to commercial or other uses, such as photocopying an amusing article for your friends. Copying of software and music CDs (including 'sharing' of MP3 files) is usually illegal, although you are usually permitted to make a *personal* back-up copy of a track or CD you already own.

Established practice suggests that you should photocopy no more than 5 per cent of the work involved, or:

- one chapter of a book;
- one article per volume of an academic journal;
- 20 per cent (to a maximum of 20 pages) of a short book;
- one poem or short story (maximum of 10 pages) from an anthology;
- one separate illustration or map up to A4 size (note: illustrations that are parts of articles and chapters may be included in the allowances noted above);
- short excerpts of musical works - not whole works or movements (note: copying of any kind of public performance is not allowed without permission).

Approved copyright exceptions

Some copying for academic purposes may be licensed by the Copyright Licensing Agency (CLA) on behalf of authors. Other electronically distributed material may be licensed through the HERON (Higher Education Resources On-Demand) scheme. In these cases you may be able to copy or print out more than the amounts listed opposite, including multiple copies. Your university may also 'buy in' to licensing schemes, such as those offered by the NLA (Newspaper Licensing Agency) and the Performing Rights Society. As these can refer to very specific sources, consult your library's staff if in doubt.

These limits apply to single copies - you can't take multiple copies of any of the above items, or pass on a single copy for multiple copying to someone else, who may be in ignorance of the source or of specific or general copyright issues.

In legal terms, it doesn't matter whether you paid for the source or not: copyright is infringed when the whole or a substantial part is copied without permission - and 'substantial' here can mean a qualitatively significant section even if this is a small part of the whole.

The same rules apply to printing or copying material on the Web unless the author gives explicit (i.e. written) clearance. This applies to copying images as well as text from the Internet, although a number of sites do offer copyright-free images. A statement on the author's position on copying may appear on the home page or a page linked directly from it.

Complexity of copyright law

Note that the material in this chapter is a summary, and much may depend on individual circumstances.

Practical tips for avoiding plagiarism

Avoid copying material by electronic means. You may only do this if you are prepared to quote the source. If you use the material in your work, and fail to add an appropriate citation, this would be regarded as cheating.

When making notes, always write down your sources. You may risk plagiarising if you cannot recall or find the source of a piece of text. Avoid this by getting into the habit of making a careful note of the source on the same piece of paper that you used to summarise or copy it out. Always use quote marks ('. . .') when taking such notes verbatim from texts and other materials, to indicate that what you have written down is a *direct copy* of the words used, as you may forget this at a later time. You do not need to quote directly in the final version of your work, but if you paraphrase you should still cite the source.

Try not to paraphrase another person's work too closely. Taking key phrases and rearranging them, or merely substituting some words with synonyms is still regarded as plagiarism.

Follow the academic custom of quoting sources. You should do this even if you prefer to use your own wording rather than a direct copy of the original. The reference to the source signifies that you are making that statement on the basis of the ideas reported there. If you are unclear about the different methods of mentioning sources and constructing a reference list, consult **Ch 18**.

Avoid overuse of quotations. Plagiarism still occurs if a considerable percentage of your report or dissertation is comprised of quotations. In general, quotations should be used sparingly.

Double-check on your 'original' ideas. If you have what you think is a novel idea, do not simply accept that your brainwave is unique. It's common for people to forget the original source of an idea, which may resurface in their mind after many years and perhaps in a different context - this may have happened to you. Think carefully about possible sources that you may have forgotten about; ask others (such as your tutor or supervisor) whether they have come across the idea before; and consult relevant texts, encyclopaedias or the Web.

And now . . .

17.1 Double-check your department's plagiarism policy. This should spell out the precise situations in which you might break rules. It may also give useful information on the department's preferred methods for citing sources.

17.2 Next time you are in the library, read the documentation about photocopying often displayed beside the photocopiers. This will provide detailed information about current legislation and any local exceptions.

17.3 Modify your note-taking technique. Put any direct transcriptions in quotes and add full details of the source whenever you take notes from a textbook or paper source.

18 Citing and listing references

How to refer appropriately to the work of others

The convention in academic writing is that you must support your discussion of a topic by referring to the relevant literature. There are several methods in use and which one you will be required to adopt will depend on the conventions within your discipline. This chapter outlines four of the more common styles showing you how to reference your source in text and how to list these in your reference list or bibliography.

Key topics:

→ Why you need to cite your sources
→ Using information within your text
→ How to cite the work in the text
→ Different reference methods

Key terms

Bibliography Citation Ellipsis Ibid. Indentation Op. cit. Reference list Superscript

When you write any kind of academic paper - such as a project report, dissertation or a thesis - you are expected to give the sources of information and ideas you have drawn from your in-depth reading on the subject. This means that you have to give your reader sufficient information to be able to locate your source. This is done in the body of the text at the point where you refer to (cite) the source. You then give full details of it either in a footnote, endnote or separate reference list at the end of the paper. Methods vary (see Table 18.1).

The preferred referencing method for your dissertation or project report will be stipulated in your course regulations, or may be recommended by your supervisor. However, you must be able to recognise the alternative styles used in other sources (Table 18.1) in order to interpret the information given. If you are unable to obtain style guide information, then seek the help of a librarian. Your library website may also provide useful links.

Table 18.1 Choosing a referencing style. Departments normally specify the referencing style. Where no guidance is given, then the choice is up to you. This table shows the most significant features, advantages and disadvantages of four common styles used in all forms of academic writing.

Harvard	
Features	• **Name/date** system used in the text (page number included only if making a reference to a specific quote or data) • Name of author can be included as part of the sentence (date in round brackets immediately after the name) *or* • Name and date both in round brackets at end of sentence
Advantages	• Minimal typing: once-only entry in alphabetical order by author name in the reference list • Easy to identify sources from the citations shown in the text • Easy to make adjustments in the text and the reference list
Disadvantages	• Name/date references can be intrusive in text • Not well suited to citing archive material, e.g. historical documents (insufficient detail to comply with the system)
Modern Languages Association (MLA)	
Features	• **Name/page** system in text; date at end of reference • Name of author can be included as part of the sentence (page number comes in brackets at the end of the sentence or clause) *or* • Name and page number(s) (no punctuation) both placed in brackets at the end of the sentence
Advantages	• Minimal typing as details are printed only once in alphabetical order by author name in the reference list, which makes it easy to locate the source information • Easy to identify contributors in a field from the citations shown in the text
Disadvantages	• Date of publication of source not in the text and not immediately evident in the reference list because of the position at the end of the reference • Indentation in 'follow-on' lines in the reference list can give a 'ragged' appearance to the layout of the reference list

▶

Software referencing packages

These can fit your reference list to any of several conventions. However, it is worth reflecting on whether it is worth while learning how to use a relatively complex package and key in the data, when you could achieve a similar end result using a list typed straight into a word-processed table, which could be sorted alphabetically.

Table 18.1 continued

	Vancouver
Features	• **Numerical** system with full-size numerals in brackets after the reported point • If another reference is made to a source in the text, the second and subsequent references use the number given to the reference when it was used for the first time
Advantages	• Numbers are less intrusive in the text • Numbers are listed in numerical order at the end of the text, thus it is easy to locate the reference
Disadvantages	• No bibliographical information in the text, thus difficult to gauge significance of the sources • Use of one number each time the source is used involves a considerable amount of checking and slows down the writing process
	Chicago
Features	• **Superscript numbers** used in the text • Relates superscript numbers to footnotes on the same page • Provides reference information in footnotes and reference list (format differs between the two)
Advantages	• Numbering system is unobtrusive and does not interrupt the flow of the text • Use of *op. cit.* and *ibid.* in the referencing saves retyping of bibliographical information
Disadvantages	• First mention of a source gives full details, subsequent references give only name/page • More difficult to track the main contributors • Layout of footnote references differs from the bibliographical reference (if used) • Intensive checking to ensure that all superscript references are consistent after any changes

Definitions: listing terms

Bibliography: list at the end of your work of all books, journals, web and online materials that you have consulted as preparation for your paper (not necessarily referred to in the text).

Reference list: at the end of the work all the books, journals, web and online materials you have referred to in your paper.

Citations: details of authorship and publication included directly or indirectly in the text to show source of information (see p. 268).

→ Why you need to cite your sources

Academic convention requires you to give this information in order to:

- acknowledge the use of other people's work - you must demonstrate clearly where you have borrowed text or ideas from others; even if you cite an author's work in order to disagree with it, you have made use of their intellectual property and you must show that you recognise this (there is more discussion on intellectual property and plagiarism in **Ch 17**);
- help your readers understand how your argument/discussion was assembled and what influenced your thinking - this will help them form opinions about your work;
- help your reader/supervisor evaluate the extent of your reading. This may help them to assess your work and to advise you on further or more relevant reading; and
- provide your readers with sufficient information to enable them to consult the source materials for themselves, if they wish.

→ Using information within your text

Essentially there are three means by which you can introduce the work of others into your text - by giving information in footnotes and endnotes, by *quoting* exact words from a source, or by *citation*, which involves summarising the idea in your own words. In all instances you need to indicate the source material by means of the chosen style of citation (Table 18.1).

Footnotes and endnotes

In some disciplines, footnotes and endnotes, generally using superscript numbers, lead readers to the source information. However, in other disciplines, footnotes and endnotes are used simply to provide additional information, commentary or points of discussion about the content of the text. Footnotes generally appear at the bottom of the page where the link appears; endnotes are recorded in number order at the end of the body of the work.

Quotation in the text

There are two possibilities. If the quotation is short, then the exact words are placed within single inverted commas within the sentence (e.g. xxxx 'zzzz zz zzzz zz zzzz' xxx). If you are using a longer quotation, usually 30 words or more, then no inverted commas are used (see pp. 269-70). The status of the text as a quotation is indicated by the use of indentation where several lines quoted from another source are indented within your own text and in single-line spacing. If you deliberately miss out some words from the original, then the 'gap' is represented by three dots. This is called ellipsis. For example:

> xxxxxxxx xxxxx xxxxx xxxx xxx xx xxxxxxxxx xxxx xx xxxxxx xx xx xxxx xxxxxx:
>
> > . . . zzzz z zzzzzz zzzzzzz zzz zzzzzzz zzzz zz z zz zzzz z zzzz zz z zzzzzz zzzzzzzzz. Zz zzzzz zzz zzzz zzzzzzz zzzz zz zzz zzzzzz. Zzzzzzzz zz zzzzz zzzz zzzzz z zzzzzzzzz zzz zzz z zz zzzz.
> >
> > (source and date)
>
> xxxxxxx xxxx xxx xxxx xx xx xx xxxxxxxxxx xxxxx xxxxxxx xxxxx xxxxxxxxxxxxxxx.

See **Ch 25** for further examples of presenting quotes.

How do I punctuate a quote within a quote?

The convention of British English is to use single inverted commas to cover the whole quotation and double inverted commas (quotation marks) for the quotation within the quotation. For example, 'xxxxxx "zzzz" xxx'. The convention in American English is the opposite.

Definition: ellipsis

The three dots used to substitute for words that have been omitted from a quotation are often used at the beginning of a quote as in the example opposite, or where some information that is irrelevant to your point has been omitted for brevity. Obviously, you should not omit words that change the sense of the quotation. As an extreme example, omitting the word 'not' in the following quotation would entirely change its sense: 'The adoption of the Euro as the common currency of the EU is *not* universally acceptable'.

→ How to cite the work in the text

There are essentially two ways in which to cite sources: the information-prominent and author-prominent methods. These depend on the style of referencing you have elected to follow. The broad principles are outlined below.

- **Information-prominent method.** Here the statement is regarded as being generally accepted within the field of study. For example:

  Children express an interest in books and pictures from an early age (Murphy, 1995).

- **Author-prominent method.** Here the author and date of publication form part of the construction of the sentence. This formulation can be used with appropriate reporting words (see below) to reflect a viewpoint. For example:

  Murphy (1995) claimed that children as young as six months are able to follow a simple story sequence.

smart tip

Reporting words

There is a considerable range of verbs that can be used to report the views of others. Here are some examples:

allege assert claim consider contend declare demonstrate explain found judge report show state suggest warn

Note that some of these words are 'stronger' than others and you need to consider carefully which you use so that they reflect your view of the reported work.

→ Different reference methods

Reference methods evolve as technology and preferences alter. Publishers of journals have been particularly influential in dictating styles that should be adopted in their publications. This has had the result that, even in the most commonly used styles, there have been modifications to create variants of the original format. The tables on the following pages illustrate common methods: Harvard (Table 18.2); Modern Languages Association (Table 18.3); Vancouver (Table 18.4); and Chicago (Table 18.5).

Table 18.2(a) Outline of the Harvard method for citing references. This referencing system has the advantage of being simpler, quicker and possibly more readily adjustable than other systems. It is used internationally in a wide range of fields and provides author and date information in the text. Note that there are various interpretations of the method. This one generally follows BS5605:1990.

How to cite the reference in the text	How to lay out the reference list or bibliography
The cause of European integration has been further hampered by the conflict between competing interests in a range of economic activities (Roche, 1993). However, Hobart and Lyon (2002) have argued that this is a symptom of a wider disharmony which has its roots in socio-economic divisions arising from differing cultural attitudes towards the concept of the market economy. Morrison *et al.* (2001) have identified 'black market' economic activity in post-reunification Germany as one which exemplified this most markedly. Scott (2004) suggests that the black economy which existed prior to reunification operated on strong market economy principles. However, Main (2003 cited in Kay, 2004) has supported the view that black market economies are not culture dependent. Statistics presented by Johannes (2000) suggest that, in the UK, as many as 23 per cent of the population are engaged at any one time in the black economy. European-wide statistics indicate that figures for participation in the black economy may be as high as 30 per cent (Brandt, 2001).	Brandt, K-H., 2001. *Working the system* [online]. Available from: http://www.hvn.ac.uk/econ/trickco.htm [accessed 1.4.01]. *Ferry Times*, 1999. Where the money moves. *Ferry Times*, 12 April, p. 24. Hobart, K. and Lyon, A., 2002. *Socio-economic divisions: the cultural impact*. London: Thames Press. Johannes, B., 2000. Functional economics. In M. Edouard ed., *The naked economy*. Cologne: Rhein Verlag, 2000, pp. 120–30. Kay, W., 2004. *The power of Europe*. Dover: Kentish Press. Morrison, F., Drake, C., Brunswick, M. and Mackenzie, V., 2001. *Europe of the nations*. Edinburgh: Lothian Press. Roche, P., 1993. *European economic integration*. London: Amazon Press. Saunders, C., ed., 1996. *The economics of reality*. Dublin: Shamrock Press. Scott, R., 2004. Informal integration: the case of the non-monitored economy. *Journal of European Integration Studies*, 3 (2), pp. 81–9.
Quotations in the text	
The movement of money within the so-called black economy is regarded by Finance Ministers in Europe as 'a success story they could emulate' (*Ferry Times*, 12.4.99). According to Saunders (1996, p. 82) 'black economies build businesses'.	

Table 18.2(b) How to list different types of source following the Harvard method

Type of source material	Basic format: author surname | author initial | date | title | place of publication | publisher
Book by one author	Roche, P., 1993. *European economic integration*. London: Amazon Press.
Book by two authors	Hobart, K. and Lyon, A., 2002. *Socio-economic divisions: the cultural impact*. London: Thames Press.
Book with more than three authors	Morrison, F., Drake, C., Brunswick, M. and Mackenzie, V., 2001. *Europe of the nations*. Edinburgh: Lothian Press.
Book under editorship	Saunders, C., ed., 1996. *The economics of reality*. Dublin: Shamrock Press.
Chapter in a book	Johannes, B., 2000. Functional economics. In M. Edouard ed., *The naked economy*. Cologne: Rhein Verlag, 2000, 120–30.
Secondary referencing - where the original text is not available and the reference relates to a citation in a text that you have read, refer to the latter	Kay, W., 2004. *The power of Europe*. Dover: Kentish Press.
Journal article	Scott, R., 2004. Informal integration: the case of the non-monitored economy. *Journal of European Integration Studies*, 3 (2), 81–9.
Newspaper article	*Ferry Times*, 1999. Where the money moves. *Ferry Times*, 12 April, p. 24.
Internet references including e-books	Brandt, K-H. 2001. *Working the system* [online]. Available from: http://www.hvn.ac.uk/econ/trickco.htm [accessed 1.4.01].
Internet references: e-journals	Ross, F., 2000. Coping with dementia. *Geriatric Medicine* [online], 5 (14). Available from: http://germed.ac.ic/archive00000555/[accessed 11.01.04].

Notes:

- In this version of the Harvard method only the first word of a title is capitalised. With the exception of proper nouns, other words are in lower case. Each entry is separated by a double line space.
- If you need to cite two (or more) pieces of work published within the same year by the same author, then the convention is to refer to these texts as 2005a, 2005b and so on.
- In some interpretations of this method the first line of every entry is indented five character spaces from the left margin. However, this can create an untidy page where it is difficult to identify the author quickly.

Table 18.3(a) Outline of the Modern Languages Association (MLA) method for citing references. This is claimed to be one of the 'big three' referencing systems used in the USA. It provides author and page information in the text, but no date is included within the text, only the page number(s).

How to cite the reference in the text	How to lay out the reference list or bibliography
The cause of European integration has been further hampered by the conflict between competing interests in a range of economic activities (Roche 180). However, Hobart and Lyon have argued that this is a symptom of a wider disharmony which has its roots in socio-economic divisions arising from differing cultural attitudes towards the concept of the market economy (101). Morrison *et al*. have identified 'black market' economic activity in post-reunification Germany as one which exemplified this most markedly (99–101). Scott suggests that the black economy which existed prior to reunification operated on strong market economy principles (83). However, Main has supported the view that black market economies are not culture dependent (cited in Kay 74). Statistics presented by Johannes suggest that, in the UK, as many as 23 per cent of the population are engaged at any one time as part of the black economy (121). European-wide statistics indicate that figures for participation in the black economy may be as high as 30 per cent (Brandt 12).	Brandt, K-H. 'Working the System.' 31 December 2000. 1 April 2001. <http://www.hvn.ac.uk/econ/trickco.htm> Hobart, K. and A. Lyon, *Socio-economic Divisions: the cultural impact*. London: Thames Press, 2002. Johannes, B. 'Functional Economics.' *The Naked Economy*. M. Edouard. Cologne: Rhein Verlag, 2000: 120–30. Kay, W. *The Power of Europe*. Dover: Kentish Press, 2004. Morrison, F., *et al. Europe of the Nations*. Edinburgh: Lothian Press, 2001. Roche, P. *European Economic Integration*. London: Amazon Press, 1993. Saunders, C. ed. *The Economics of Reality*. Dublin: Shamrock Press, 1996. Scott, R. 'Informal Integration: the case of the non-monitored economy.' *Journal of European Integration Studies* 2 (2004): 81–9. 'Where the money moves.' *Ferry Times* 12 April 1999: 24.
Quotations in the text	
The movement of money within the so-called black economy is regarded by Finance Ministers in Europe as 'a success story they could emulate' (*Ferry Times* 24). Some commentators appear to give approval to non-conventional economic activity: 'black economies build businesses' (Saunders 82).	

Table 18.3(b) How to list different types of source following the Modern Languages Association (MLA) method

Type of source material	Basic format: author surname | author initial | title | place of publication | publisher | date |
Book by one author	Roche, P. *European Economic Integration*. London: Amazon Press, 1993.
Book by two authors	Hobart, K. and Lyon, A. *Socio-economic Divisions: the cultural impact*. London: Thames Press, 2002.
Book with more than three authors	Morrison, F. *et al. Europe of the Nations*. Edinburgh: Lothian Press, 2001.
Book under editorship	Saunders, C. (ed.) *The Economics of Reality*. Dublin: Shamrock Press, 1996.
Chapter in a book	Johannes, B. 'Functional Economics.' *The Naked Economy*. M. Edouard. Cologne: Rhein Press, 2000: 120-30.
Secondary referencing - where the original text is not available and the reference relates to a citation in a text that you have read. This is the secondary source and is the one that you should cite in your reference list	Kay, W. *The Power of Europe*. Dover: Kentish Press, 2004.
Journal article	Scott, R. 'Informal Integration: the case of the non-monitored economy.' *Journal of European Integration Studies* 2 (2004): 81-9.
Newspaper article	'Where the money moves.' *Ferry Times* 12 April 1999: 24.
Internet reference	Brandt, K-H. 'Working the System.' 31 December 2000. 1 April 2001. <http://www.hvn.ac.uk/econ/trickco.htm>

Notes:

- Successive lines for the same entry are indented by five character spaces.
- If two (or more) pieces of work published within the same year by the same author are cited, then refer to these texts as 1999a, 1999b and so on.

Table 18.4(a) Outline of the Vancouver method (numeric style) for citing references. This system is widely used in Medicine and the Life Sciences, for example. In the text, numbers are positioned in brackets, that is, like this (1). These numbers relate to corresponding numbered references in the reference list. This style has the advantage of not interrupting the text with citation information. However, this means that the reader cannot readily identify the source without referring to the reference list. The Vancouver style resembles in some ways the style adopted by the Institute of Electrical and Electronic Engineers (IEEE).

How to cite the reference in the text	How to lay out the reference list or bibliography
The cause of European integration has been further hampered by the conflict between competing interests in a range of economic activities (1). However, Hobart and Lyon (2) have argued that this is a symptom of a wider disharmony which has its roots in socio-economic divisions arising from differing cultural attitudes towards the concept of the market economy. Morrison *et al*. (3) have identified 'black market' economic activity in post-reunification Germany as one which exemplified this most markedly. Scott (4) suggests that the black economy which existed prior to reunification operated on strong market economy principles. However, Kay (5) has supported the view of Main that black market economies are not culture dependent. Statistics presented by Johannes (6) suggest that, in the UK, as many as 23 per cent of the population are engaged at any one time as part of the black economy. European-wide statistics indicate that figures for participation in the black economy may be as high as 30 per cent (7).	1 Roche P. European Economic Integration. London: Amazon Press; 1993. 2 Hobart K. and Lyon A. Socio-economic Divisions: the cultural impact. London: Thames Press; 2002. 3 Morrison F., Drake C., Brunswick M. and Mackenzie V. Europe of the Nations. Edinburgh: Lothian Press; 2001. 4 Scott R. Informal Integration: the case of the non-monitored economy. Journal of European Integration Studies. 2004; 2, 81–9. 5 Kay W. The Power of Europe. Dover: Kentish Press; 2004. 6 Johannes B. Functional Economics. In Edouard M. The Naked Economy. Cologne: Rhein Verlag; 2000; pp. 120–30. 7 Brandt K-H. Working the System. 2000 [cited 1 April 2001]. Available from: http://www.hvn.ac.uk/econ/trickco.htm. 8 Where the money moves. Ferry Times. 12 April 1999; 24. 9 Saunders C. editor. The Economics of Reality. Dublin, Shamrock Press; 1996.
Quotations in the text	
The movement of money within the so-called black economy is regarded by Finance Ministers in Europe as 'a success story they could emulate' (8). According to Saunders, 'black economies build businesses' (9).	

Table 18.4(b) How to list different types of source following the Vancouver method

Type of source material	Basic format: author surname | author initial | title | place of publication | publisher | date
Book by one author	Roche P. European Economic Integration. London: Amazon Press; 1993.
Book by two authors	Hobart K. and Lyon A. Socio-economic Divisions: the cultural impact. London: Thames Press; 2002.
Book with more than three authors	Morrison F., Drake C., Brunswick M. and Mackenzie V. Europe of the Nations. Edinburgh: Lothian Press; 2001.
Book under editorship	Saunders C. editor. The Economics of Reality. Dublin: Shamrock Press; 1996.
Chapter in a book	Johannes B. Functional Economics. In Edouard, M. The Naked Economy. Cologne: Rhein Verlag; 2000; pp. 120–30.
Secondary referencing – where the original text is not available and the reference relates to a citation in a text that you have read. This is the secondary source, which is the one you cite	Kay W. The Power of Europe. Dover: Kentish Press; 2004.
Journal article	Scott R. Informal integration: the case of the non-monitored economy. Journal of European Integration Studies. 2004; 2, 81–9.
Newspaper article	Where the money moves. Ferry Times. 12 April 1999; 24.
Internet reference	Brandt K-H. Working the System. 2000 [cited 1 April 2001]. Available from: http://www.hvn.ac.uk/econ/trickco.htm.

Notes:

- In some interpretations of this style, superscript numbers[8] are used instead of the full-size number in brackets (8) shown in the example in Table 35.4(a).
- In this system, titles are not italicised.

Table 18.5(a) Outline of the Chicago method (scientific style) for citing references. This is a footnote style of referencing that enables the reader to see the full bibliographical information on the first page the reference is made. However, subsequent references of the same source do not give the same detail. If the full bibliographical information is not given in the footnote for some reason, then a full bibliography is given at the end of the work. To save space here, this method has been laid out in single-line spacing. The *Chicago Manual of Style* (2003) stipulates double-space throughout - texts, notes and bibliography.

How to cite the reference in the text
The cause of European integration has been further hampered by the conflict between competing interests in a range of economic activities.[1] However, Hobart and Lyon[2] have argued that this is a symptom of a wider disharmony which has its roots in socio-economic divisions arising from differing cultural attitudes towards the concept of the market economy. Morrison *et al.*[3] have identified 'black market' economic activity in post-reunification Germany as one which exemplified this most markedly. Scott[4] suggests, however, that the black economy which existed prior to reunification operated on strong market economy principles, while Main[5] has supported the view that black market economies are not culture dependent. Statistics presented by Johannes[6] suggest that as many as 23 per cent of the population are engaged at any one time as part of the black economy. This does not support the findings of Hobart and Lyon,[7] but it has been suggested by Scott[8] that this is probably an exaggerated statistic which it is impossible to verify. Scott[9] estimates a more modest 10 per cent of people of working age are actively involved in the black economy. Brandt[10] has conducted research into the phenomenon of the black economies of Europe but has been unable to confirm such estimates.
[1] P. Roche, *European Economic Integration* (London: Amazon Press, 1993), 180. [2] K. Hobart, and A. Lyon, *Socio-economic Divisions: The Cultural Impact* (London: Thames Press, 2002), 101. [3] F. Morrison, C. Drake, M. Brunswick, and V. Mackenzie, *Europe of the Nations* (Edinburgh: Lothian Press, 2001), 99. [4] R. Scott, 'Informal Integration: the case of the non-monitored economy,' Journal of European Integration Studies, 2 (2004): 81. [5] K. Main, *Power, Politics and People* (Plymouth: Maritime Press Co., 2003), 74, quoted in W. Kay, *The Power of Europe* (Dover: Kentish Press, 2004) 89. [6] B. Johannes, 'Functional Economics' in *The Naked Economy*, M. Edouard, 121 (Cologne: Rhein Verlag, 2000). [7] Hobart and Lyon *op. cit.*, 102. [8] Scott, *op. cit.*, 83 [9] *Ibid.* [10] K-H. Brandt, 'Working the System.' http://www.hvn.ac.uk/econ/trickco.htm (1.4.01).

Table 18.5(a) continued

Quotations in the text
The movement of money within the so-called black economy is regarded by Finance Ministers in Europe as 'a success story they could emulate'.[11] According to Saunders, 'black economies build businesses'.[12] [11] 'Where the money moves.' *Ferry Times*, 12 April 1999, 24. [12] C. Saunders, (ed.) *The Economics of Reality* (Dublin: Shamrock Press, 1996), 82.
How to lay out the reference list or bibliography (layout differs for the footnotes)
Brandt, K-H. 'Working the System.' Available from http://www.hvn.ac.uk/econ/trickco.htm (1.4.01). Hobart, K. and Lyon, A., *Socio-economic Divisions: The Cultural Impact*. London: Thames Press, 2002. Johannes, B. 'Functional Economics' in *The Naked Economy*, by M. Edouard, 120–30. Cologne: Rhein Verlag, 2000. Main, K. *Power, Politics and People*. Plymouth: Maritime Press Co., 2003, quoted in W. Kay, *The Power of Europe*. Dover: Kentish Press, 2004. Morrison, F., *et al. Europe of the Nations*. Edinburgh: Lothian Press, 2001. Roche, P. *European Economic Integration*. London: Amazon Press, 1993. Saunders, C., ed. *The Economics of Reality*. Dublin: Shamrock Press, 1996. Scott, R. 'Informal Integration: the case of the non-monitored economy.' *Journal of European Integration Studies* 2, (2004), 81–9. 'Where the money moves,' *Ferry Times*, 12 April 1999, 24.

Table 18.5(b) How to list different types of source following the Chicago method. The Chicago method uses footnote-style referencing. This table gives references as these would appear in the bibliography/reference list. Note that the layout differs for the presentation of the information in the footnotes.

Type of source material	Basic format: author initial | author surname | title | (place of publication | publisher | date) | page number
Book by one author	Roche, P. *European Economic Integration*. London: Amazon Press, 1993.
Book by two authors	Hobart, K. and Lyon, A. *Socio-economic Divisions: The Cultural Impact*. London: Thames Press, 2002.
Book with more than three authors	Morrison, F. *et al. Europe of the Nations*. Edinburgh: Lothian Press, 2001.
Book under editorship	Saunders, C., ed. *The Economics of Reality*. Dublin: Shamrock Press, 1996.
Chapter in a book	Johannes, B. 'Functional Economics' in *The Naked Economy*, by M. Edouard, 120-30. Cologne: Rhein Verlag, 2000.
Secondary referencing - where the original text is not available and the reference relates to a citation in a text that you have read	Main, K. *Power, Politics and People*. Plymouth: Maritime Press Co., 2003, quoted in W. Kay, *The Power of Europe*. Dover: Kentish Press, 2004.
Journal article	Scott, R. 'Informal Integration: the case of the non-monitored economy,' *Journal of European Integration Studies*, 2 (2004), 81-9.
Newspaper article	'Where the money moves.' *Ferry Times*, 12 April 1999, 24.
Internet reference	Brandt, K-H. 'Working the System.' Available from http://www.hvn.ac.uk/econ/trickco.htm (1.4.01).

Notes:

- Uses superscript numbers in the text ordered consecutively. These relate to a footnote on the same page as the reference. Where references are repeated, then a new number is assigned each time it occurs in the text.
- Some abbreviations are used in this style. The most commonly used are *op. cit.* (in the work already cited) and *ibid.* (in the same place - usually in the same place as the last fully cited reference.) Thus, in the example in Table 18.5(a) [9] relates to [8] which, in turn, relates to [4].
- In the footnotes the author's first name or initial precedes the surname.
- Second or further lines in the reference or bibliography list should be indented five character spaces.

Practical tips for citing and listing references

Record the bibliographical detail routinely. However you copy your notes - electronically, by photocopy or by writing - ensure that you record all the necessary bibliographical information, or you will waste time later on backtracking to find it.

Compile your reference list as you go along. Keep a list of the works you have read. Simply create a table within your software package and type in the details immediately you cite the source in the text. Doing this from time to time as you write saves you having to embark on a marathon of typing at the completion of the task. You will need to make a decision about the reference style at an early stage. You can do this routinely if you are using a software referencing program.

Don't mix referencing systems. Whichever method you use, make sure you follow its conventions to the letter, including all punctuation details. When no guidance is given, consult Table 18.1 to evaluate the possibilities.

Source quotations. If you note down a quotation speculatively for later use, then make sure that you write down full reference details alongside it. Never rely on your memory for referencing. Check everything and write it all down.

Check the detail. Allow plenty of time for final checking.

And now . . .

18.1 Identify the recommended referencing style in your regulations or library's style guide. These may differ from one subject to another. If no explicit information is given, then ask your supervisor or analyse the way that the list of books on your reading lists have been printed. Alternatively, look at a well-known journal in your field and identify the style used there. Often, very clear guidelines are given in a section in journals entitled 'Guidelines for contributors', or similar. If you compare this with the examples in Tables 18.2–18.5, then you may be able to identify the method by name.

18.2 Look at textbooks or journal articles in your subject area to identify what method is appropriate for quotations. Identify whether making direct quotations is common. In many academic areas, quotation from sources would be rare, and you need to be aware of this.

18.3 Check out availability of software referencing packages in your university's electronic systems. Your library advisor, or some one from your computing support service, will probably be able to give you guidance on how to use these packages. Learning the details of their use may be worthwhile if you know that your work may be needed to be presented in one format for your dissertation or project report but may need to change to a different citation and referencing method if the material is to be submitted for publication to a learned journal. Most software referencing packages can translate from one style to another.

19 Ethics in researching and reporting

How to follow good research practice

For many research topics and methodologies, it is important to review the ethical position regarding your study. The precise details differ according to discipline and the nature of the investigation. This chapter outlines the principles and procedures that may apply.

Key topics:

→ Ethical principles
→ Safe research
→ Consent and confidentiality
→ Obtaining ethical approval
→ Practical tips for ensuring your research is ethical

Key terms

Dissertation   Ethics   Ethics committee   Informed consent   Supervisor

The term 'ethics' in the research context refers to the principles, rules and standards of conduct that apply to investigations. Most disciplines have self-monitoring codes of ethical practice and your institution will operate its own internal research governance policy. The types of ethical requirements vary among disciplines and your study must comply with recognised practice in your field and your institution. It is imperative that you familiarise yourself with these codes and are able to bring that understanding to the initial discussion of the research project with your supervisor. He or she will be responsible for ensuring that your research proposal complies with ethical practice in your institution. Where necessary your supervisor will help you prepare an application to conduct the research for submission to your institution's Ethics Committee. Note that there may be different committees and rules for clinical and non-clinical research.

i

Ethics committees

These bodies are comprised of academics from within your institution and they monitor research activity at undergraduate and postgraduate levels. In addition to approving applications to conduct research, they also hear appeals where approval has not been granted, provide guidance on cases that are unclear, and refer cases of research misconduct to higher institutional authority. Their procedures are recorded in writing and are available for public scrutiny.

→ Ethical principles

Any research project involving human beings should be characterised by protection of the human rights, dignity, health and safety of participants and researchers. This is achieved by observing three fundamental tenets:

- the research should **do no harm**;
- consent should be **voluntary**; and
- **confidentiality** should be respected throughout.

smart tip

Codes of research practice

These are enshrined in the Universal Declaration of Human Rights (1948) and in the Nuremberg Code (1949). These codes have provided the basis for ethical research practices in academic research involving humans.

Ethical considerations may relate to non-human as well as human research activity. Controversial areas have included the use of animals in research, cloning, human embryo research, stem cell research, *in vitro* fertilisation, and nuclear research. In the UK, experiments involving animals are subject to Home Office approval. If this is required for your work, your supervisor will guide you through the procedures. Similarly, experiments involving genetic manipulation must comply with relevant legislation and you will be guided through relevant procedures if necessary.

→ Safe research

It is a fundamental of research activity in the spirit of international codes of practice that the health and safety of all those involved in research activity as participants or researchers should be a priority at all times. Thus, all research approved by the appropriate Ethics Committee must follow passed protocols exactly. Any modification to the original proposal has to be referred back to the Ethics Committee. For the purposes of undergraduate research proposals, although the student is acting as the 'Principal Investigator', the actual Principal Investigator responsibility remains with the Supervisor.

smart tip

Following safety procedures

Your university will have a safety office and policies in place for potentially dangerous procedures or to cover risks like exposure to hazardous chemicals. Completing paper work, such as Control of Chemicals Hazardous to Health (COSHH) forms, should be regarded as an opportunity to learn about the risks associated with your work, rather than a chore.

→ Consent and confidentiality

Participants may need to be informed in writing about certain aspects of your research. This is usually provided as a 'Participant Information Sheet', which usually includes the following information:

- ❑ Outline of the purpose of the study
- ❑ Invitation and reason for being selected
- ❑ Explanation of the voluntary nature of participation and of the freedom of the subject to terminate participation at any time
- ❑ Explanation of the procedure to be followed in the research and the time commitment involved
- ❑ Advantages and disadvantages of participation
- ❑ Assurance of confidentiality and anonymity
- ❑ Information about outcomes
- ❑ Information about the funding source

- Names of lead researcher and assistants
- Information about any sponsorship or affiliation connected to the project
- Information about refunding of expenses, if applicable

Particularly in the clinical area, a 'template' is often adopted to frame the explanation for participants. However, in many instances, this is often unsatisfactory because the language used, and the format and layout are often unclear to the non-specialist. Every effort should be made to inform participants about the project as concisely as possible in 'plain' English, that is, in language that can be easily assimilated and understood by people in all walks of life.

In response to this information, participants are then requested to complete an 'Informed Consent Form' that requires their signature. In some instances, a debriefing form will also need to be completed once the data-gathering phase is concluded.

How ethical is your research?

Unethical approaches to research can be inadvertent and unintended. For example, vulnerable groups may feel pressured into participating although members of such groups may not express this to the researcher. Patients may feel that they will receive better treatment if they participate in a study and risk a poorer level of treatment if they don't. Consequently, your research design and consent forms must reflect your awareness of such potential perceptions. Cases of unethical research procedures are legion and, thus, the field of ethics is a complex one. If you have any doubts at all about the ethical dimension of your study, then you should discuss these with your supervisor to ensure that neither you nor your subjects are compromised by the research activity.

Human participants must be assured that their identities will be protected by the promise of anonymity. This means that the confidentiality of any representation of data whether in aggregated forms (for example, mean value) or as qualitative material that might be obtained from individuals (for example, through questionnaires, interviews or focus groups) is protected in any printed format. It is essential that written permission to quote informants be sought from them at the time of participation in the enquiry, with the proviso that identities will be protected when findings are reported.

Data protection

The storage and use of personal information is an ethical issue. In the UK, the Data Protection Act covers procedures that must be adopted. Consult your university's web pages for information and guidance on local procedures if you plan to store information either in paper files or electronically. Legislation apart, it is simply good practice to time-limit the period in which data will remain on your records - and to inform participants how their data will be stored, and when it will be deleted or destroyed.

→ Obtaining ethical approval

You should first read the guidance notes provided by your university's ethics committee or department. Once you have satisfied yourself that you have made arrangements to cover the ethical dimensions of your research project, you will be in a position to frame your proposal for ethical approval. Institutions will vary in the formats required. In general, you will need to provide information on:

- the title, purpose and duration of the project, and the location of the study;
- the methodological approach to be adopted, and information on how data will be stored securely;
- if appropriate, the way in which participants will be recruited, plus information as to age, gender and any inclusion/exclusion criteria;
- measures taken to ensure that all ethical dimensions are covered in compliance with the appropriate research code of practice in your institution, including confidentiality in reporting results; and
- if appropriate, identification of the involvement of any funding body.

In your research plan (**Ch 5** and **Ch 6**), you should make due allowance for the time taken to obtain ethical approval (your supervisor can advise on normal delays). Make sure that you carry out some relevant work, such as a literature review, while you are waiting.

Practical tips for ensuring your research meets ethical requirements

Consult your university's website for up-to-date and detailed information on approaches to research ethics. In addition to the ethical policy, there may be general guidance information, discipline-specific advice, and links to useful websites.

Consult appropriate texts related to ethics. Potential starting points are Sana (2002) and Shamoo and Resnick (2003), but either consult the library catalogue or ask at your library for holdings specific to your discipline.

Visit websites for learned societies in your discipline to obtain up-to-date information about ethical aspects that may impact on your research study. This may be important if you are required to take an oral exam on your research project and your external examiner may wish to explore the ethics of your study in the wider discipline with you.

Be alert to publicity that covers instances of unethical behaviour in any field of research. This may raise issues that subsequently you could have to address in other projects in the course of your studies.

Where possible, discuss ethical dimensions of research with peers and academic staff. This debate will raise your awareness of issues that can arise and may also provide you with some benchmarks against which to judge your own study.

And now . . .

19.1 Brainstorm the ethical dimensions of your research. Write out the tentative title of your dissertation or project, add major branches for harm, consent and confidentiality (p. 212). Using this chapter as a guide, elaborate on these aspects and any others you should be taking into account.

19.2 Address ethical issues as soon as you can. If there are likely to be significant ethical dimensions to your project, ask to meet up with your supervisor at an early stage to discuss these issues and how they should be handled. Rehearse your points by writing them down beforehand and take this note with you to inform the discussion.

19.3 Familiarise yourself with the ethics guidelines that govern research activity in your specialist field. This is important to your personal development and is an aspect of your professional practice that will apply when you graduate. Often the guidelines are provided in the literature of your professional association. Look also at 'Materials and Methods' sections in relevant research papers to establish the norms for ethical behaviour your field of work. Use a search engine to identify any major cases that have raised ethical issues in the research context.

Writing a first draft

20 Structuring a dissertation

How to organise your writing within a standard framework

Regardless of the type of writing assignment you have to complete, the structure will follow a basic format. This chapter describes this design and explores some of the features that need to be included as you map your outline plan on to this structure.

Key topics:

→ Standard format
→ Taking word limits into account

Key terms
Citation Exemplify

The word 'dissertation' can have different meanings according to context. In this book it is used to refer to a formal written study of a specialist subject, submitted as part of the assessment for a university degree. A literature survey is a similar exercise, often shorter, and perhaps with more emphasis on reviewing of published work, rather than giving the views of the writer. Regarding structure, however, similar principles apply.

All works of this type essentially follow what can be described as standard academic format, namely introduction - main body - conclusion. This framework is easily adapted to most scenarios and within the main body, you can incorporate the various intellectual approaches you have adopted to analyse the topic (**Ch 5**).

→ Standard format

The basic structure follows the convention of moving from the general (the introduction) through to the specific (the main body) and back to the general (the conclusion).

Introduction

Generally, this should consist of three components:

- a brief explanation of the context of the topic;
- an outline of the topic as you understand it;
- an explanation of how you plan to address the topic in this particular text - in effect, a statement of intent.

This introductory section indicates to your reader where you expect to take them in the main body of text. The introduction also lays down the parameters that you have set yourself for this piece of text. For example, your topic may be multifaceted and the word limit imposed on the dissertation may not allow you to give a comprehensive coverage of all aspects. It is better to acknowledge the extensive nature of the topic and note that you are going to limit your discussion to only some of these aspects - usually those you consider to be most important. You need to explain the reasons for this decision at this stage.

smart tip

The importance of the introduction

This is the first contact that your reader makes with you as the author of the text. This means that it has to be well organised and clear. However, to achieve this, it is important to see this introductory section as 'work in progress' because, until you complete the entire text, you cannot really introduce the whole work accurately. Therefore, you should be prepared to factor in time to revisit your draft introduction, reviewing it as a preamble to the main body. Indeed, some people prefer to start writing the main body, move on to the conclusion, and only then write the introduction.

Main body

This section lays out your analysis of the topic based on the approach you decide to adopt in organising the content (**Ch 5**). You will have explained the approach in the introduction and this will mean that you should have mapped out your route for explaining your points. In this section, you may need to generalise, describe, define or exemplify as part of your analysis. Here it's important to keep this part of the writing as brief, yet as clear, as possible. The construction of your paragraphs will be dictated by what you are trying to achieve at any particular point (see **Ch 8**).

smart tip

Sub-headings

In some disciplines, and especially in report writing, sub-headings are acceptable. In others they are not. However, it's helpful to maintain the focus of your writing by using sub-headings in your draft. This helps to prevent you digressing into unrelated areas or presenting an apparently rambling paper. If you then 'translate' your sub-heading into a topic sentence (p. 74), this will provide a link with the previous paragraph or an introduction to the next theme.

Conclusion

This summarises the whole piece of work. You should review the entire text in three elements:

- a restatement of the question and what you feel are the important features of the topic;
- a summary of the specific evidence that you have presented in support of your views;
- a statement of your overall viewpoint on the topic.

What mainly distinguishes the conclusion from the introduction is language. In the introduction, your explanation should be given clearly, avoiding jargon or technical words as far as possible. In the conclusion, you will be writing about the detail of the content and, therefore, the terminology you use is more likely to contain technical or more sophisticated language because you will have introduced this in the main body. You should avoid introducing new ideas in the conclusion that have not already been discussed in the earlier part of the writing.

Mini-conclusions

As you become immersed in the writing process you will become very familiar with the material and conclusions you have drawn along the way. By the time you come to write the conclusion to the whole work this in-depth awareness may become diluted. To avoid this, it is a good idea, at the end of each section you write, to note down what main ideas you had considered and what your view is about these. If you note these down in a separate file, then this will provide the substance for your final conclusion.

→ Taking word limits into account

Word limits are imposed, not to relieve tutors of marking, but to train you to be concise in your writing and to analyse the topic carefully to decide what to keep in and what to leave out.

It's important to note that falling short of the word limit is just as bad as overrunning the maximum. Some students keep a running total of words they have used and as soon as they reach the minimum word limit, they stop abruptly. This is not a good approach because it is more likely to leave an incomplete or unbalanced piece of text that comes to an unexpected halt rather than one that is well planned, relevant and concisely written.

It's usually better to plan and write your first draft keeping only a casual eye on word count at this stage. When you come to editing that draft you can prune and reshape your writing so that it becomes a tighter piece of prose that falls within the maximum-minimum word limits imposed by the regulations.

How can I keep track of my word count?

Most word processors include a word-count feature. Microsoft Word has, in addition, a useful 'floating' toolbar that allows you to check running totals as you write or edit. You can access both features in this program from 'Tools > Word Count (> Show Toolbar)'.

Practical tips for structuring a dissertation

Keep the right proportions. Make sure that the three elements within your writing framework are well balanced in extent. The main body should be the most substantial piece of the writing, whereas the introduction and conclusion should occupy much less space. A common problem for many students is that they devote too much time to outlining the context in the introduction and leave themselves with too little time and space to get to the core of the dissertation.

Start writing as soon as you can. Word processors allow text fragments to be moved around with ease. This means that you can write up some components (especially descriptive parts) as you go along, and reorganise these when you have a better picture of the whole subject.

Pay adequate attention to the conclusion. By the time that you come to write the conclusion, this is often done at some speed because there may be other demands on your time, or the initial interest in the subject has waned, or you may simply be tired. Thus, conclusions often don't get the attention they deserve. Do reserve some time to give your conclusion a critical appraisal, and even consider writing this section before finishing the perhaps more 'mechanical' earlier parts. Alternatively, as suggested above, you could 'write it as you go' by keeping detailed notes of key points separately, which you can use to frame your conclusion once you have written the main body.

Review the introduction. Once you have completed your draft, go back to the introduction and make sure that you have actually done what you set out to do when defining the parameters of your work and in your statement of intent. The act of writing your text may have stimulated new thoughts and your initial intentions may have altered in the process of writing.

Think about appendices. Sometimes the length of your text may be seriously beyond the word limit. This means that some drastic 'surgery' is required. One strategy might be to remove some parts of the text and, while remaining within the word limit, reduce the information contained to bullet-point lists. The detail can then be placed in an appendix or appendices (plural of appendix), making appropriate cross-references in the main text. Clearly, this is a strategy that has to be used sparingly, but it can be useful in some situations.

Think about citations. In most disciplines you will be expected to include reference to recognised authorities within the field you are studying. In law, this could be cases; in the arts and humanities, it could be work by a renowned academic. This does not mean that you need to quote substantial pieces of text; you can summarise the idea in your own words and then follow the rules about citation that are given in **Ch 18**. All this needs to be taken into consideration in planning and drafting your writing.

Discuss drafts with your supervisor or a friend. Your supervisor may not ask to see your drafts, but you will probably gain valuable advice if you can persuade them to comment. A friend, even one who doesn't know your subject, will also be able to point out where your explanations are obscure or your view seems biased.

Review and edit what you have written. If at all possible, aim to finish your writing a week or so ahead of the submission date. Then, leave your work for a day to two and return to it, reading it in one sweep. This will help you take a more critical look at what you have written.

GO And now . . .

20.1 Compare textual patterns. Go back to a basic textbook or other dissertations or reports and identify the proportion of space allocated to introducing the entire book or a specific chapter and how much is reserved for the conclusion. This should be instructive in framing your own writing.

20.2 Track the pattern of your writing. Go back to an existing piece of your own writing and try to identify whether you have the basic elements and sub-elements of the standard writing format in place. Are the introduction, main body and conclusion identifiable? Does the introduction contain the elements of context, specific focus and statement of intent? For the conclusion, is your position laid out clearly and with supporting rationale? If any of the answers are negative, try to work out how you could improve things.

20.3 Practise converting sub-headings into topic sentences. Take a piece of your own writing or a section from a textbook where sub-headings have been used. Try to create a topic sentence that could replace that sub-heading. Decide which is more effective - the topic sentence or the original sub-heading. Consider why this is the case. Again, this should be instructive in shaping the style you adopt in your own writing.

21 Structuring a project report

How to select and shape your content appropriately

Project reports often have to follow discipline-specific formats. It is important to adhere to the guidelines provided and select the correct information to put into the different sub-sections. This chapter considers common formats that may be suitable for scientific project reports, literature surveys and business-style reports.

Key topics:

→ Common features of report writing
→ Representative formats for reports

Key words
Business report   Literature survey   Scientific report

The purpose of any report is to convey information, usually on a well-defined topic. Conventions have evolved for the structure, style and content of reports in different subjects, and, while the scholarship underlying the report will always be foremost in their assessments, presentational aspects are also judged as important, so you should follow the appropriate format very carefully. You can find out about aspects of the research that precedes the writing of experimental and business reports in **Ch 3**, **Ch 6**, **Ch 11**, **Ch 13** and **Ch 14**. Presentation is covered in **Ch 25**.

→ Common features of report writing

Writing a report is often a drawn-out task and may follow a lengthy period of research in the library, on the Internet, in the laboratory, or in the field. However, you should not consider the research and writing phases as separate. Your research must take into account the style and format of the report, while elements of writing up can and should be carried out as you continue to explore your topic.

Aspects of report writing

Description: reporting your experiments or summarising facts you have gathered.

Visual summaries: making diagrams, flow charts, graphs or tables to illustrate points.

Analysis: looking at results or facts and possibly working out descriptive or hypothesis-testing statistics.

Discussion: weighing up the pros and cons of a position.

Solution(s): explaining different options to solve an issue or problem being addressed.

Evaluation: deciding what's important and why.

Recommendation: identifying the best solution and giving supporting evidence.

Arriving at a conclusion: stating a position on the basis of your research.

→ Representative formats for reports

Table 21.1 lists alphabetically the general components of reports and summarises what each component should contain. Reports for different purposes and in different subjects follow different designs and include various components, not always in the same order. Table 21.2 provides some examples, but you should follow closely the guidelines published by your department.

Literature surveys

These follow the relatively uncomplicated format shown in Table 21.2(a). Aspects of finding and analysing the literature are discussed in **Ch 7** and **Ch 9**. Two important formatting aspects to consider are citation of literature references and presenting quotes from your sources (**Ch 18**).

Table 21.1 Typical components of reports, and notes on the expected content of each part. For ease of reference, these are arranged alphabetically and would not appear in this order in any report. For representative examples of report formats, see Table 21.2. *Always adopt the precise format specified in your course handbook or institutional guidelines.*

Section or part	Expected content
Abbreviations	A list of any abbreviations for technical terms used within the text (for example, 'DNA: deoxyribonucleic acid'). These are also given within the text at the first point of use, for example 'deoxyribonucleic acid (DNA)'.
Abstract	A brief summary of the aims of the experiment(s) or series of observations, the main outcomes (in words) and conclusions. This should allow someone to understand your main findings and what you think they mean. This is normally written last, but is usually positioned at the beginning of the report.
Acknowledgements	A list of people who you wish to thank for their help.
Appendix (pl: appendices)	Includes tabular information, usually, that only an expert would want or need to consult; a section where you can put items such as a questionnaire template, and data or results that would otherwise disrupt the flow of the report or make the results section too lengthy.
Bibliography/ references/ literature cited	An alphabetical list of sources cited in the text, following one of the standard formats (**Ch 18**).
Discussion (or conclusions)	• **Scientific-style reports.** A commentary on the results and an outline of the main conclusions. This could include any or all of the following: - comments on the methods used; - mention of sources of errors; - conclusions from any statistical analysis; - comparison with other findings or the 'ideal' result; - what the result means; - how you might improve the experiment(s); - how you might implement the findings (in a business report); - where you would go from here, given more time and resources. Sometimes you might combine the results and discussions sections to allow a narrative to develop – to explain, for example, why one result led to the next experiment or approach. Bear in mind that a large proportion of marks may be given for your original thoughts in this section. • **Non-scientific-style reports.** In this section you might restate the problem or issue to be addressed, outline the key 'solutions' or responses to the problem, and explain the reason for favouring one over another by providing evidence to support that choice. In some, but not all, instances, a set of recommendations might be appropriate.

▶

Table 21.1 continued

Section or part	Expected content
Executive summary	Takes the place of an abstract in a business report. Gives the key points of the report, usually no more than one A4 page long. It should start with a brief statement of the aims of the report, a summary of the main findings and/or conclusions, perhaps given as bullet points, and a summary of the main conclusions and/or recommendations. You would normally write this part last.
Experimental	A description of apparatus and method, similar to materials and methods.
Glossary	A list of terms that might be unfamiliar to the reader, with definitions.
Introduction	• **Scientific-style reports.** An outline of the background to the project, the aims of the experiment(s) and brief discussion of the techniques to be used. Your goal is to orientate the reader and explain what you have done and why. • **Non-scientific-style reports.** The context of the study and an outline of the problem or issue to be addressed, in other words, the aim of the report. This may require reference to the literature or other resource material to be used.
Main body of text	Your appraisal of the topic. It should systematically address solutions or issues in response to the report's purpose and provide an analysis of all pertinent matters. It may be subdivided into sections reflecting different aspects (**Ch 5**). In a scientific literature survey, the approach is often to give a chronological account of developments in the field, quoting key authors, their ideas and findings. This section may include tables comparing different approaches or results in different studies. Figures tend to be rare, but may be used to summarise concepts or illustrate key findings.
Materials and methods	A description of what was done. You should provide sufficient detail to allow a competent person to repeat the work.
Results	A description of the experiments carried out and the results obtained, usually presented in either tabular or graphic form (never both for the same data). You should point out meaningful aspects of the data, which need not be presented in the same order in which the work was done.
Table of contents	Effectively an index to allow the reader to find parts in which they are interested. May also include a table of diagrams. More likely to be included in a lengthy report.
Title page	The full names of the author or authors, the module title, code or course of study and the date. In a business report this may also include the company logo, client details and classification (for example, 'confidential'). • **Scientific-style reports.** A descriptive title that indicates what was done, indicates any restrictions, and sometimes describes the 'headline' finding. • **Non-scientific-style reports.** A concise but comprehensive title that defines the topic.

Table 21.2 Designs of different sorts of report. The literature review (a) has a simple structure. The main body is the largest part, and may be subdivided into sections. The general scientific report (b) has a focus on materials and methods, but in some disciplines the components may be presented in a different order, as shown in the model for the report in chemistry (c). The undergraduate lab reports you may have submitted in earlier years (d) will probably be a stripped-down and shorter version of (b). A non-scientific style of report (e) would not focus on materials and methods, but might have a main body of text dealing with the topic being considered. A typical business-style report (f) includes the conclusions or recommendations as part of the main body and provides an executive summary for quick reading. It often has appendices and a glossary for the non-specialist. See Table 21.1 for details of content for each section.

(a) Literature survey/dissertation	(b) General scientific report	(c) Scientific report in chemistry	(d) Laboratory report in the sciences	(e) Non-scientific report	(f) Typical business-style report
Title page	Title page	Title page	Title page	Title page	Title page
Abstract	Abstract	Abstract	Introduction	Introduction	Executive summary
Introduction	Abbreviations	Abbreviations	Materials and methods	Main body of text	Acknowledgements
Main body of text	Introduction	Introduction	Discussion/conclusions	Conclusion	Table of contents
Conclusions	Materials and methods	Results			Main body of text
References or literature cited	Results	Discussion			Bibliography/references
	Discussion	Materials and methods			Appendices
	Acknowledgements	Acknowledgements			Glossary
	References	References			

Scientific reports

Representative formats are shown in Table 21.2(b), (c) and (d). These tend to mirror the format of journal articles in the primary literature for each subject area (**Ch 9**). Aspects you should bear in mind are:

- Anyone reading your report should be able to assimilate your findings quickly, and should be able to find relevant information in the expected place.
- You should provide enough information to allow another competent scientist to understand and repeat your work.
- Your text should be objective and balanced, considering all possible interpretations of your results.
- Appropriate statistical analysis should be included (**Ch 16**).

Reports for non-scientific subjects

Increasingly report writing is becoming a feature in non-scientific subjects. A report-style response could be required for a case study, project or group problem-solving exercise, for example. Table 21.2(e) shows a representative structure. A good approach for the main body of text in these report-style tasks is to follow the situation - problem - solution - evaluation + (optional) recommendation (SPSER) model (p. 48). This provides a basic skeleton. You may wish to tailor the headings and sub-headings to fit the context of the topic or problem that you are addressing, but the essence of the SPSER model remains intact 'below the surface' of these headings.

Business-style reports

The main aim of a business report is to provide information that helps decision-making. These reports differ greatly in their style and formality and the chief factor to consider is your audience. Table 21.2(f) illustrates one possible format. Possible variations might include:

- A report aimed solely at a shop-floor manager: relatively short and informal, focussing on production statistics and limitations.
- A business plan aimed at an investor or bank manager: fairly brief, focussing on financial projections given in charts and tables.
- An academic analysis of a business sector: relatively lengthy and formal, quoting many sources and views.

Structurally, a business report is unlike an essay in that you should use headings and sub-headings so that your reader can find relevant information quickly.

Why are you required to write reports at university?

Report writing is regarded as important because it:

- compels you to complete your work and present it in a neatly organised form for assessment;
- helps you to develop important professional skills to enhance your employability;
- provides a record for replication or development of results for future research.

Practical tips for selecting and shaping report content

Find a model for the layout you need to adopt. This might be given in your course handbook or could be adopted from an example that you feel is well organised. Otherwise, the models shown in Table 21.2 may provide a template.

Be ruthless in rejecting irrelevant information. You must keep your report as short and to the point as you can. Especially if you have spent a long time obtaining information or conducting an analysis, you may be tempted to include it for this reason alone. Don't. Relevance must be your sole criterion.

Consider your writing style. Reports can be dense and difficult to read. Try to keep your sentences relatively simple and your paragraphs short. In reports you can use sub-headings and bullet points to break up the text (**Ch 22**). All these devices can make the content easier for your reader to assimilate.

Choose appropriate chart types. If you wish to present diagrams and graphs, keep these simple and use the title and legend to explain what you want to show in each case (**Ch 16**). Use a variety of types of chart if you can.

Think about your likely conclusions from an early stage. This may shape both the research you do and the content. However, make sure you keep an open mind if the evidence points you in another direction.

GO And now . . .

21.1 Compare Tables 21.2(a–f). You will see similarities and differences that reflect the purpose of each type of report. How does this relate to the specific format you have been asked to adopt?

21.2 Research types of graph. Add variety and impact to scientific and business reports, you should select the right type of chart – and you can only do this if you know about the different formats available. This is covered in **Ch 16**, but the 'Chart Wizard' in Microsoft Excel is another source of options. If you enter your data into the spreadsheet, use this feature to obtain a quick and easy indication of what each potential type would look like.

21.3 Focus on higher-level academic thinking skills. In most forms of report, you will be assessed on the analysis and evaluation you make, based on a thorough summary of the topic. If you aren't 100 per cent certain of what is involved in these skills, consult **Ch 14** and read examples from your subject area with this in mind.

22 Academic writing style

How to adopt the appropriate language conventions

Writing for academic purposes is a vital skill, yet the stylistic codes you need to follow are rarely comprehensively defined. This chapter will help you understand what it means to write in an academic style and outlines some forms of language to avoid.

Key topics:

→ What is academic style?
→ Being objective
→ Appropriate use of tense
→ Appropriate use of vocabulary
→ Appropriate use of punctuation
→ Transforming non-academic to academic language

Key words

Acronym Colloquial Idiom Noun Phrasal verb Pronoun Register Rhetorical question Verb

The format, the content and the presentation of projects and dissertations differ according to discipline. One thing that is common to all these types of writing is that they need to follow academic style. While it is possible to identify differences between 'scientific' and 'humanities' styles in the finer detail, this chapter covers the common features of all types of academic writing.

→ What is academic style?

Academic style involves the use of precise and objective language to express ideas. It must be grammatically correct, and is more formal than the style used in novels, newspapers, informal correspondence and everyday conversation. This should mean that the language is clear and simple. It does not imply that it is complex, pompous and dry. Above all, academic style is *objective*, using language techniques that generally maintain an impersonal tone and a vocabulary that is more succinct, rather than involving personal, colloquial, or idiomatic expressions.

British English (BE) versus American English (AE)

Academic writing in the UK nearly always adopts BE. The differences are most evident in spelling; for example, 'colour' (BE) and 'color' (AE). However, there are also differences in vocabulary, so that in AE people talk of 'professor' for 'lecturer'; and in language use, so that in AE someone might write 'we have gotten results', rather than 'we have obtained results'. In some disciplines, there is an attempt at standardisation, for example, in chemistry the spelling of 'sulphur' (BE) has become 'sulfur' (AE) as the international standard.

→ Being objective

In academic writing, it is important that your personal involvement with your topic does not overshadow the importance of what you are commenting on or reporting. Generally, the main way of demonstrating this objectivity and lack of bias is by using impersonal language. This means:

- Avoiding personal pronouns - try not to use the following words:

  I/me/one

  you (singular and plural)

  we/us.

- Using the passive rather than active voice - try to write about the action and not about the actor (the person who performed the action).

You can use other strategies to maintain an impersonal style in your writing. For general statements, you could use a structure such as 'it is . . .', 'there is . . .' or 'there are . . .' to introduce sentences. For more specific points relating to statements you have already made, you could use the structures 'this is . . .' or 'these are . . .'; 'that is . . .' or 'those are . . .' with appropriate tense changes according to the context. Don't forget that when you use words like 'it', 'this', 'these', 'that' or 'those', there should be no ambiguity over the word or phrase to which they refer.

Another way in which you can maintain objectivity by writing impersonally is to change the verb in the sentence to a noun and then reframe the sentence in a less personal way, for example:

> We **applied** pressure to the wound to stem bleeding (*verb in bold*).
> The **application** of pressure stemmed bleeding (*noun in bold*).

This kind of text-juggling will become second nature as you tackle more and more assignments.

Passive and active voice

This is best explained from examples:

- Pressure was applied to the wound to stem bleeding (passive).
- We applied pressure to the wound to stem bleeding (active).

Some would argue that the second example is clearer, but their opponents would counter-argue that the use of 'we' takes attention away from the action.

You may find that the grammar checkers in some word-processing packages suggest that passive expressions should be changed to active. However, if you follow this guidance, you will find yourself having to use a personal pronoun, which is inconsistent with impersonal academic style. If in doubt, ask your tutors for their preference.

→ Appropriate use of tense

The past tense is used in academic writing to describe or comment on things that have already happened. However, there are times when the present tense is appropriate. For example, in a report you might write 'Figure 5 shows . . .', rather than 'Figure 5 showed . . .', when describing your results. A material and methods section, on the other hand, will always be in the past tense, because it describes what you *did*.

In colloquial English, there is often a tendency to misuse tenses. This can creep into academic writing, especially where the author is narrating a sequence of events. This can be seen by contrasting:

Napoleon ***orders*** his troops to advance on Moscow. The severe winter ***closes*** in on them and they ***come back*** a ragbag of an army. (Present tense in bold.)

and:

Napoleon ***ordered*** his troops to advance on Moscow. The severe winter ***closed*** in on them and they ***came back*** a ragbag of an army. (Simple past tense in bold.)

While the first of these examples might work with the soundtrack of a documentary on Napoleon's Russian campaign, it is too colloquial for academic written formats.

Plain English

There has been a growing movement in recent times that advocates the use of 'Plain English', and it has been very successful in persuading government departments and large commercial organisations to simplify written material for public reference. This has been achieved by introducing a less formal style of language that uses simpler, more active sentence structures, and a simpler range of vocabulary avoiding jargon. This is an admirable development. However, academic writing style needs to be precise, professional and unambiguous, and the strategies of 'Plain English' campaigners may not be entirely appropriate to the style expected of you as an academic author. For the same reasons, some of the suggestions offered by software packages may be inappropriate to your subject and academic conventions.

→ Appropriate use of vocabulary

Good academic writers think carefully about their choice of words. The 'Plain English' movement (see above) recommends that words of Latin origin should be replaced by their Anglo-Saxon, or spoken, alternatives. However, this does not always contribute to the style and precision appropriate to academic authorship. For example, compare:

If we ***turn down*** the volume, then there will be no feedback.

and

If we ***turn down*** the offer from the World Bank, then interest rates will rise.

Both sentences make sense, but they use the two-word verb 'turn down' in different senses. These verbs are properly called phrasal verbs and they often have more than a single meaning. Furthermore, they are also used more in speech than in formal writing. Therefore, it would be better to write:

If we ***reduce*** the volume, then there will be no feedback.

and

If we ***reject*** the offer from the World Bank, then interest rates will rise.

By using 'reduce' and 'reject' the respective meanings are clear, concise and unambiguous. If you are restricted to a word limit on your work, using the one-word verb has additional obvious advantages.

→ Appropriate use of punctuation

In formal academic writing good punctuation is vital to convey meaning. However, punctuation standards are being eroded as corporate logos and design practice seek to attract the eye with unconventional print forms that ignore the correct use of capitals, apostrophes, commas and other punctuation marks. Consider the following:

1. visitors car park	(meaningless - simply a list of words)
2. Visitor's car park	(car park for a single visitor)
3. Visitors' car park	(car park for more than one visitor)
4. Visitor's car, park!	(instructing a single visitor to park)
5. Visitors, Car Park	(greeting many visitors and, rather oddly, inviting them to park or it could be a sign (a) giving directions for visitors to follow and (b) directions to a car park)

Either versions 2 or 3 could be valid and the remainder are likely to be nonsensical. This example serves to demonstrates how clear punctuation avoids ambiguity. Without punctuation or with inappropriate punctuation, sentences become meaningless or, worse still, confusing and/or impenetrable. Table 22.1 illustrates some of the more common errors that appear regularly in student writing, models the correction and explains the error.

Table 22.1 Common punctuation errors and their corrections. The following common errors with their corrections should help you to find an answer to most punctuation dilemmas.

Punctuation mark	Error	Correction	Explanation
1.1 Apostrophes: singular	The **Principals'** Committee will meet at noon today.	Principal's	There is only one Principal, therefore the apostrophe goes immediately after the word 'Principal'. Then add the s to make it correctly possessive.
1.2 Apostrophes: plural	The **womens'** team beat the mens' team by 15 points and the **childrens'** team beat them both. The **boy's** team won the prize.	women's men's children's boys'	The words 'women', 'men' and 'children' are plural words. To make them possessive, just add an apostrophe after the plural word and add 's'. The word 'boys' is a plural and is a regularly formed plural, thus, the apostrophe comes after the 's'.
1.3 Apostrophes: contractions	**Its** not a good time to sell a property. **Its** been up for sale for ages. **Well** need to lower the price.	It's = it is It's = it has We'll = we shall	'It's' is a contracted form of the words 'it is' or 'it has'. In this case, the sentence means: 'It is not a good time to sell a property'.
1.4 Apostrophes: not needed	The **tomatoes'** cost 60 pence a kilo.	tomatoes	The word 'tomatoes' is a plural. No apostrophe is needed to make words plural.
1.5 Apostrophes: not needed	The Charter includes human rights in **it's** terms.	its	No apostrophe needed to show possession.
2.1 Capital letters: sentences	**the** first day of the term is tomorrow.	The	The first letter of the first word of a sentence in English always needs a capital letter.
2.2 Capital letters: proper names	The **prime minister** is the first **lord** of the **treasury**. The **north atlantic treaty organisation** is a regional organisation. Pearls found in the **river tay** are of considerable value.	Prime Minister; First Lord of the Treasury North Atlantic Treaty Organisation River Tay	Proper nouns for roles, names of organisations, rivers, mountains, lochs, lakes and place names. These all require a capital for all parts of the name.

3 Colon	A number of aspects will be covered, **including** • Energy conservation • Pollution limitation • Cost control	. . . including: • energy conservation; • pollution limitation; • cost control.	A colon to introduce the list. Each item, except the last one, should be finished with a semicolon. No capital is necessary at each bullet if the list follows from an incomplete sentence introducing the list.
4.1 Commas	**The leader of the group Dr Joan Jones** was not available for comment.	The leader of the group, Dr Joan Jones, was not available for comment.	This is a common error. The name of the person gives more information about the leader; thus, the person's name needs to be inserted with commas before and after.
4.2 Commas	There are several member-states that do not support this view. They are **Britain France Germany Portugal and Greece.**	There are several member-states that do not support this view. They are Britain, France, Germany, Portugal, and Greece.	Strictly speaking, when making a list such as in the example, a comma should come before 'and'. This is called the 'Oxford comma' and its use has caused much debate. However, increasingly, the comma is being omitted before the word 'and' in lists such as this one.
4.3 Commas	**However** we have no evidence to support this statement.	However, we have no evidence to support this statement.	The 'signposting' words often used at the beginning of sentences are followed by a comma. Some of the more common of these words are: however, therefore, thus, hence, nevertheless, moreover, in addition.
4.4 Commas	**Although we have had significant** rainfall the reservoirs are low.	Although we have had significant rainfall, the reservoirs are low.	When a sentence begins with 'although', then the sentence has two parts. The part that gives the idea of concession in this sentence is 'Although we have had significant rainfall'. The second part gives us the impact of that concession, in this case, that 'the reservoirs are low'. A comma is used to divide these parts.
4.5 Commas	**To demonstrate competence** it is important to be able to face challenges.	To demonstrate competence, it is important to be able to face challenges.	Another way to write this sentence would be: 'It is important to be able to face challenges to demonstrate competence'. By putting the phrase 'to demonstrate competence' at the beginning of the sentence, it places emphasis on the idea of competence and, in order to make that word-order distinction, a comma is needed.
5 Ellipsis	There is a deficit in the budget . . . . . . brought on by mismanagement at the highest level.	There is a deficit in the budget . . . brought on by mismanagement at the highest level.	Ellipsis marks always consist of three dots, no more.

→ Transforming non-academic to academic language

Thinking about the style of your writing should be a feature of any review you make of drafts of your written work Table 22.2 gives a specific example of text conversion from informal to formal style. Table 22.3 provides several pointers to help you achieve a more academic style.

Table 22.2 Example of converting a piece of 'non-academic' writing into academic style. Note that the conversion results in a slightly longer piece of text (47 versus 37 words): this emphasises the point that while you should aim for concise writing, precise wording may be more important.

Original text (non-academic style)	'Corrected' text (academic style)
In this country, we have changed the law so that the King or Queen is less powerful since the Great War. But he or she can still advise, encourage or warn the Prime Minister if they want.	In the United Kingdom, legislation has been a factor in the decline of the role of the monarchy in the period since the Great War. Nevertheless, the monarchy has survived and, thus, the monarch continues to exercise the right to advise, encourage and warn the Prime Minister.
Points needing correction	**Corrected points**
• Non-specific wording (*this country*)	• Specific wording (country specified: *in the United Kingdom*)
• Personal pronoun (*we*)	• Impersonal language (*legislation has*)
• Weak grammar (*but* is a connecting word and should not be used to start a sentence).	• Appropriate signpost word (*nevertheless*)
• Word with several meanings (*law*)	• Generic, yet well-defined term (*legislation*)
• Duplication of nouns (*king or queen*)	• Singular abstract term (*monarch*)
• Inconsistent and potentially misleading pronoun use (*he or she, they*)	• Repeated subject (*monarch*) and reconstructed sentence
• Informal style (*can still*)	• More formal style (*continues to exercise*)

Table 22.3 Fundamentals of academic writing. These elements of academic writing are laid out in alphabetical order. Being aware of these elements and training yourself to follow them will help you to develop as an academic author and will ensure that you don't lose marks by making some basic errors of usage or expression.

Abbreviations and acronyms

It is acceptable to use abbreviations in academic writing to express units, for example, SI units. Otherwise, abbreviations are generally reserved for note-taking. Thus, avoid: e.g. (for example), i.e. (that is), viz. (namely) in formal work.

Acronyms are a kind of abbreviation formed by taking the initial letters of a name of an organisation, a procedure or an apparatus, and then using these letters instead of writing out the title in full. Thus, World Health Organisation becomes WHO. The academic convention is that the first time that you use a title with an acronym alternative, then you should write it in full with the acronym in brackets immediately after the full title. Thereafter, within that document you can use the acronym. For example:

The European Free Trade Association (EFTA) has close links with the European Community (EC). Both EFTA and the EC require new members to have membership of the Council of Europe as a prerequisite for admission to their organisations.

In some forms of academic writing, for example, formal reports, you may be expected to include a list of abbreviations in addition to these first-time-of-use explanations.

'Absolute' terms

In academic writing, it is important to be cautious about using absolute terms such as:

always and **never; most** and **all; least** and **none.**

This does not prevent you from using these words; it simply means that they should be used with caution, that is, when you are absolutely certain of your ground (see p. 149).

Clichés

Living languages change and develop over time. This means that some expressions come into such frequent usage that they lose their meaning; indeed, they can often be replaced with a much less long-winded expression. For example:

First and foremost (first); **last but not least** (finally); **at this point in time** (now).

This procedure is the **gold standard** of hip replacement methods.
(This procedure is the best hip replacement method.)

In the second example, 'gold standard' is completely inappropriate; correctly used, it should refer to monetary units, but it has been misused by being introduced into other contexts.

Table 22.3 continued

Colloquial language
This term encompasses informal language that is common in speech. Colloquialisms and idiomatic language should not be used in academic writing. This example shows how colloquial language involving cliché and idiom has been misused: **Not to beat about the bush**, increasing income tax did the Chancellor **no good at the end of the day** and he **was ditched** at the next Cabinet reshuffle. (Increasing income tax did not help the Chancellor and he was replaced at the next Cabinet reshuffle.)
'Hedging' language
For academic purposes, it is often impossible to state categorically that something is or is not the case. There are verbs that allow you to 'hedge your bets' by not coming down on one side or another of an argument, or which allow you to present a variety of different scenarios without committing yourself to any single position, for example: **seems that looks as if suggests that appears that.** This involves using a language construction that leaves the reader with the sense that the evidence presented is simply supporting a hypothetical, or imaginary, case. To emphasise this sense of 'hedging', the use of a special kind of verb is introduced. These are: **can/cannot could/could not may/may not might/might not.** These can be used with a variety of other verbs to increase the sense of tentativeness. For example: These results **suggest** that there has been a decline in herring stocks in the North Sea. Even more tentatively, this could be: These results **could suggest** that there has been a decline in herring stocks in the North Sea.
Jargon and specialist terms
Most subjects make use of language in a way that is exclusive to that discipline. It is important, therefore, to explain terms that a general reader might not understand. It is always good practice to define specialist terms or 'regular' words that are being used in a very specific way.
Rhetorical questions
Some writers use direct rhetorical questions as a stylistic vehicle to introduce the topic addressed by the question. This is a good strategy if you are making a speech and it can have some power in academic writing, although it should be used sparingly. Example: **How do plants survive in dry weather?** This might be a question starting a chapter. It could be rephrased as: **It is important to understand how plants survive in dry weather.** (Note: no question mark needed.)

Table 22.3 continued

Split infinitives
The most commonly quoted split infinitive comes from the TV series *Star Trek* where Captain James T. Kirk states that the aim of the Star Ship Enterprise is 'to boldly go where no man has gone before'. This means that an adverb (boldly) has split the infinitive (to go). It should read as 'to go boldly'. Many traditionalists consider that the split infinitive is poor English, although modern usage increasingly ignores the rule. Nevertheless, it is probably better to avoid the split infinitive in academic writing, which tends to be particularly traditional.
Value judgements
These are defined as statements in which the author or speaker is imposing their views or values on to the reader. For example, a writer who states that 'Louis XIV was a rabid nationalist' without giving supporting evidence for this statement is not making an objective comment in a professional manner. Rewording this statement to: 'Louis XIV was regarded as a rabid nationalist. This is evident in the nature of his foreign policy where he . . .' offers the reader some evidence that explains the claim (see p. 148).

Practical tips for ensuring that you write in an academic style

Think about your audience. Your readers should direct the style you adopt for any writing you do. For example, if you were writing to your bank manager asking for a loan, you would not use text-messaging or informal language. For academic writing, you should take into account that your reader(s) will probably be assessing your work and, in addition to knowledge and content, they will be looking for evidence of awareness and correct use of specialist terms and structures.

Avoid contractions. In spoken English, shortened forms such as, don't, can't, isn't, it's, I'd and we'll are used all the time. However, in academic written English, they should not be used. Texting contractions are also inappropriate.

Avoid personal pronouns. Experiment with other language structures so that you avoid the personal pronouns, I/me/one, you and we/us, and their possessive forms, my, your and our.

Take care with style in reflective writing. Some subjects, such as Nursing, Education and Social Work, involve student practitioners in a process of reflection on professional contexts and their roles within them. When this type of requirement is part of a written assessment, then moderate use of the first person (I or we) is expected. If your subject requires this approach, then balance your use of personal identification with the more neutral style expected more generally in academic circles. In other words, don't overuse the words 'I' or 'we'.

Avoid sexist language. The Council of Europe recommends that, where possible, gender-specific language be avoided. Thus: 'S/he will provide specimens for her/his exam'. This is rather clumsy, but, by transforming the sentence into the plural, this is avoided: 'They will provide specimens for their exams'. Alternatively, 'you' and 'your' could be used.

GO And now . . .

22.1 **Take steps to improve your grammar.** You may be able to find repeated errors that your supervisor or other lecturers may have identified in your work. Highlight points that you do not know how to rectify at present and resolve to find further information. You can do this by consulting a grammar book - for example, Foley and Hall (2003) - to find out more about the relevant grammar point. You can consolidate your understanding by doing the exercises provided in such books.

22.2 **Ask a friend to work with you on your writing style.** Swap a piece of writing and check over your friend's writing and ask them to do the same for yours. When you have done this, compare the points you have found. Try to explain what you think could be improved. Together, you may be able to clarify some aspects that you were unaware were problematic. Afterwards, follow the suggestion in point 22.1 above.

22.3 **Learn from published academic writing in your discipline.** Look at a textbook or journal article - especially in the area that discusses results or evidence or recommendations. Try to find examples of the use of 'hedging' language (Table 22.3) and note what else authors do with language in order to ensure that they avoid implying absolute judgements.

Editing, revising and presenting

23 Reviewing, editing and proof-reading

How to make sure your writing is concise and correct

Looking critically at your own writing is essential if you want to produce work of the highest quality. These editing skills will allow you to improve the sense, grammar and syntax of your written assignments.

Key topics:

→ The reviewing, editing and proof-reading process
→ The value of reviewing, editing and proof-reading

Key terms
Annotate Syntax Typo

Writing is a process. It begins with a plan and it finishes with reviewing, editing and proof-reading. This means that you should read your text critically before submitting it for assessment. The effort you invest in this final stage will contribute to the quality of your work and to your final grade. Ideally, you should leave a gap of time between completing the writing and beginning the reviewing process, as this allows you to 'distance' yourself from the work and helps you look at it as a new reader would.

→ The reviewing, editing and proof-reading process

At this stage you are performing the role of editor. This means that you are looking critically at your text for content, relevance and sense, as well as for flaws in layout, grammar, punctuation and spelling. You should also check for consistency in all aspects, for example, in the use of terminology, in spelling, and in presentational features such as font and point size, layout of paragraphs, and labelling of tables and diagrams.

Clearly, there are a lot of aspects to cover, and some degree of overlap in different parts of the process. Some people prefer to go through their text in one sweep, amending any flaws as they go; others, in particular professional writers, take a staged approach, reading through their text several times looking at a different facet each time.

Definitions

Reviewing: appraising critically; that is, examining a task or project to ensure that it meets the requirements and objectives of the task and that the overall sense is conveyed well.

Editing: revising and correcting later drafts of an essay, to arrive at a final version. Usually, this involves the smaller rather than the larger details, such as details of punctuation, spelling, grammar and layout.

Proof-reading: checking a printed copy for errors of any sort.

Table 23.1 gives some strategies you can adopt when going through the editing process. Table 23.2 illustrates some of the more commonly used symbols that professional proof-readers have developed to speed up the editing and proof-reading process. You may wish to adopt some of these yourself, and you are certainly likely to see them, as well as other 'informal' marks, on drafts returned by your supervisor.

There are five aspects to consider in the reviewing process:

- content and relevance
- clarity, style and coherence
- grammatical correctness
- spelling and punctuation
- presentation.

Table 23.3 provides a quick checklist of key aspects to consider under each of these themes. This has been designed for photocopying so that you can, if you wish, use it as a checklist each time you complete a piece of work.

smart tip

Technical aids for reviewing

The word processor has made the reviewing and editing task much easier. Here are some tips for using this software effectively:

- Use the word-count facility to check on length.
- Use the 'View' facility to check page breaks and general layout before you print out.
- Don't rely 100 per cent on the spell- and grammar checker.
- Sometimes the grammar checker will announce that you have used the passive voice. This is often a standard academic usage and, therefore, is not an error (see p. 237).
- Sometimes staff add comments to students' work using 'Tools/Track Changes' or Insert/Comments in Microsoft Word software. Depending on the version you are using, feedback information can usually be accepted or rejected by right-clicking on the word or punctuation point that has been marked for alteration.

Table 23.1 Editing strategies. The reviewing/editing/proof-reading process can be done in a single 'sweep'. As you become more experienced, you will become adept at doing this. However, initially, it might help you to focus on each of these three broad aspects in a separate 'sweep' of the text.

Content and relevance; clarity, style and coherence
• Read text aloud - your ears will help you to identify errors that your eyes miss. • Revisit the task or question. Check your interpretation against the task as set. • Work on a hard copy using editing symbols to correct errors. • Identify that the aims you set out in your introduction have been met. • Read objectively and assess whether the text makes sense. Look for inconsistencies in argument. • Check that all your facts are correct. • Insert additional or overlooked evidence that strengthens the whole. • Remove anything that is not relevant or alter the text so that it is clear and unambiguous. Reducing text by 10-25 per cent can improve quality considerably. • Honestly and critically assess your material to ensure that you have attributed ideas to the sources, that is, check that you have not committed plagiarism. • Remodel any expressions that are too informal for academic contexts. • Eliminate gendered or discriminatory language. • Consider whether the different parts link together well - if not, introduce signpost words to guide the reader through the text.

▶

Table 23.1 continued

Grammatical correctness, spelling and punctuation
• Check for fluency in sentence and paragraph structure - remodel as required. • Check sentence length - remodel to shorter or longer sentences. Sometimes shorter sentences are more effective than longer ones. • Ensure that you have been consistent in spelling conventions, for example, either following British English or American English spelling. • Spelling errors - use the spellchecker but be prepared to double-check in a standard dictionary if you are in doubt. • Check for cumbersome constructions - divide or restructure sentence(s); consider whether active or passive is more suitable. Consider using vocabulary that might convey your point more eloquently. • Check use of 'absolute' terms to maintain objectivity.
Presentation
• Check titles and subtitles are appropriate to the style of the work and stand out by using bold or underlining (not both). • Check that you have made good use of white space, that is, not crammed the text into too tight a space, and that your text is neat and legible. • If word-processed, check that you have followed standard typing conventions. Follow any 'house style' rules stipulated by your department. • Check that your reference list consistently follows a recognised method. • Check that all citations in the text are matched by an entry in the reference list and *vice versa*. • Ensure all pages are numbered and are stapled or clipped, and, if appropriate, ensure that the cover page is included. • Check that your name, matriculation number and course number are included. You may wish to add this information as a footnote that appears on each page. • Check that numbering of diagrams, charts and other visual material is in sequence and consistently presented. • Ensure that supporting material is added in sequence as appendices, footnotes, endnotes or as a glossary as applicable.

Table 23.2 Common proof-reading symbols. University lecturers and tutors use a variety of symbols on students' work to indicate errors, corrections or suggestions. These can apply to punctuation, spelling, presentation or grammar. The symbols provide a kind of 'shorthand' that acts as a code to help you see how you might be able to amend your text so that it reads correctly and fluently. In this table some of the more commonly used correction marks are shown alongside their meanings. The sample text shows how these symbols may be used either in the text or the margin to indicate where a change is recommended.

Correction mark	Meaning
⅃ (np)	(new) paragraph
≢	change CAPITALS to small letters (lower case)
~~	change into **bold** type
≡	change into CAPITALS
⊂⊃	close up (delete space)
/ or ꝺ or ⊢⊣	delete
⅄	insert a word or letter
Y	insert space
.... or (STET)	leave unchanged
Insert punctuation symbol in a circle (,)	punctuation
plag.	plagiarism
⟵⟶	run on (no new paragraph)
Sp.	spelling
⊔⊓	transpose text
?	what do you mean?
??	text does not seem to make sense
✓	good point/correct
×	error

Example

Text	*margin*
The correction marks that tutors	⊂⊃
use in students' texts aregenerally	Y
made to help identify where there	
have been errors of spllinor	⅄e ⅄g
punctuation. They can ~~often~~	(STET)
indicate where there is lack of	
paragraphing or grammatical	
accuracy. If you find that work is	(np)
returned to you with such	
marks correction, then it is	⊔⊓
worthwhile spending some time	
analysing the common errorrs as	ꝺ
well as the comments, because this	
will help you to improve the	
quality of presentation and content	
of your work this reviewing can	⊙/≡
have a positive effect on your	
assessed mark.	

In the margin, the error symbols are separated by a slash (/).

Table 23.3 Proof-reading and editing checklists. Each heading represents a 'sweep' of your text, checking for the aspects shown. The text is assumed to be a piece of writing produced for assessment. This table is copyright-free for use when reviewing your work.

Content and relevance
❑ The intent of the title has been observed ❑ The structure is appropriate ❑ The text shows objectivity ❑ The examples are relevant ❑ All sources are correctly cited ❑ The facts presented are accurate
Clarity, style and coherence
❑ The aims and objectives are clear ❑ What you wrote is what you meant to write ❑ The text is fluent, with appropriate use of signpost words ❑ Any informal language has been removed ❑ The style is academic and appropriate for the task ❑ The content and style of each section is consistent ❑ The tense used in each section is suited to the time frame of your text and is consistent ❑ The length of the text sections are balanced appropriately
Grammatical correctness
❑ All sentences are complete ❑ All sentences make sense ❑ Paragraphs have been correctly used ❑ Suggestions made by grammar checker have been accepted/rejected ❑ The text has been checked against your own checklist of recurrent grammatical errors ❑ The text is consistent in adopting British or American English
Spelling and punctuation
❑ Any blatant 'typos' have been corrected by reading for meaning ❑ The text has been spellchecked and looked at for your 'own' most often misspelled words ❑ A check has been made for spelling of subject-specific words and words from other languages ❑ Punctuation has been checked, if possible, by the 'reading aloud' method (p. 252) ❑ Proper names are correctly capitalised ❑ Overlong sentences have been divided
Presentation
❑ The text length meets the word-count target – neither too short nor too long ❑ If no word-count target is given, the overall length is as might be expected for the standard of this level of work ❑ Overall neatness checked ❑ The cover-sheet details and presentation aspects are as required by your department ❑ The bibliography/reference list is correctly formatted ❑ Page numbers have been included (in position stipulated, if given) ❑ The figures and tables are in appropriate format and are appropriately titled

→ The value of reviewing, editing and proof-reading

Although the editing process may seem tedious and more complex than it might have appeared at first, a text that is not revised in this way will be unlikely to receive as favourable a reading - and possibly as high a mark - as one that has been fully reviewed, edited and proofed. It is the mix of style, content, structure and presentation that will gain you marks, and anything you can do to increase your 'mark-earning' power will be to your advantage. In the longer term, learning how to edit your work properly will help you to develop a skill of critical analysis that will stand you in good stead throughout your career.

Practical tips for reviewing, editing and proof-reading your work

Make time for checking. When planning the writing, ensure that you have allowed adequate time for reviewing and proof-reading. You don't want to spoil all your hard work by skimping on the final stage. Leave some time between finishing the final draft and returning to check the whole text, because you will return to your work with a fresh and possibly more critical eye

Work from a hard copy. Reading through your work laid out on paper, which is the format in which your marker will probably see it, will help you identify errors and inconsistencies more readily than might be possible on the screen. A paper version is also easier to annotate (although this can also be done using the 'Track Changes' facility on your word processor). A printout also allows you to see the whole work in overview, and focus on the way the text 'flows'. If necessary, spread it out on the desk in front of you.

Follow the 'reading aloud' check. This is a tried and tested technique to ensure that what you have written actually makes sense. Simply read your text aloud to yourself. Your ears will hear the errors that your eyes might miss on a silent reading of the text. This will help you correct grammatical and spelling inconsistencies, as well as punctuation omissions.

Map your work to obtain an overview. 'Label' each paragraph with a topic heading and list these in a linear way on a separate paper.

This will provide you with a 'snapshot' of your text and will allow you to appraise the order, check against the original plan, and adjust the position of parts as you feel necessary.

Check for relevance. Ensure that section headings relate to content.

Check for consistency in the elements of your text. For example, ensure that your introduction and conclusion complement and do not contradict each other.

Check for factual accuracy. Ensure that all the facts are correct, for example, in a history dissertation that the date sequences are consistent, or in a scientific report that a numerical result you have included is realistic.

Stick to your word limits/targets. Remember that too few words can be just as bad as too many. The key point is that your writing must be clear to your reader. Sometimes this means giving a longer explanation; sometimes it means simplifying what you have written. However, at this stage, if you are over the word-count limit, then check for ways in which you can reword the text to eliminate redundant words while maintaining the sense you intended to convey.

Create 'white space'. To help produce a more 'reader-friendly' document that will not deter the markers, try to create 'white space' by:

- leaving space (one 'return' space) between paragraphs;
- justifying only on the left side of the page;
- leaving space around diagrams, tables and other visual material;
- leaving spaces between headings, sub-headings and text.

Check that all the 'secretarial' aspects are in place. Neat presentation, punctuation and spelling all help your reader to access the information, ideas and argument of your writing. While this may not gain you marks, it will certainly ensure that you do not lose marks even indirectly by making the marker struggle to 'decode' your work.

Check other visual aspects. Diagrams, tables and figures should be drawn using a ruler, if you cannot create these electronically. Only in some subjects would freehand drawing be acceptable, for example, in the study of Architecture.

GO And now . . .

23.1 Reflect on past writing. Look at an assignment that you have produced and go through it using the checklist in Table 23.3. Concentrate on two pages and, using a highlighter, mark all flaws, inconsistencies or errors. Look at the overall effect of these errors and reflect on the extent to which this may have lost you marks; then consider how you might allow for more time for the editing/proof-reading phase for your dissertation.

23.2 Practise using the standard proof-reading marks. When editing your own work, learn how to use some of these symbols as this will help you speed up the proof-reading process.

23.3 Try condensing a piece of your text. This is an acknowledged way of improving your work, though you have to bear in mind any word targets that have been set. Look at your text for irrelevant points, wordy phrases, repetitions and excessive examples; if you can reduce its original length by 10–25 per cent, you will probably find that you have created a much tighter, easier-to-read piece of writing.

24 Exploiting feedback

How to understand and learn from what your supervisor writes on your work

Your supervisor may provide some written feedback on drafts of your work. It is essential that you consider these comments if you want to improve your text. This chapter outlines some common annotations and describes how you should react to them.

Key topics:

→ Types of feedback
→ Examples of feedback comments and what they mean

Key terms
Feedback

Feedback from your supervisor or lecturer may be oral or written. Much will depend on your experience in your subject area and also on the topic you've chosen. However, a dissertation or report represents an extensive writing process and your supervisor may wish to monitor progress by reading through at least one draft version. This chapter looks at differet forms of feedback and provides some interpretation of what comments might mean.

→ Types of feedback

Written feedback may be provided on your scripts and other work. This may take the form of handwritten comments over your text, and a summary commenting on your work or explaining what changes are needed. Alternatively, your supervisor may use a facility in Microsoft Word that is found under Tools/Track changes. This allows amendments to your work. In addition, your supervisor may use the

How well are you performing?

When you are writing a dissertation or project report, you will not receive feedback in the form of marks or grades. Instead, you must be sensitive to the comments provided by your supervisor on drafts that you have provided, and try to match the standard requested. In some cases opportunities for this feedback may not exist, and you will need to resort to other routes to ensure that your work is of the required standard. For instance, you could swap drafts with a fellow student, or ask a family member to comment on your drafts.

Comments facility in Word, to add explanations or ideas. The Help menu explains how to accept or delete amendments and comments.

Some feedback may be verbal and informal, for example, a comment given as you work in the lab, or an observation on your contribution in a seminar. If you feel uncertain about why a particular comment was provided, you may be able to arrange a meeting with your supervisor to obtain further verbal explanations.

smart tip

Always read your feedback

The comments in your feedback should give you constructive direction for developing the structure and style of your work, as well as encourage you to develop a deeper understanding of the topic. It is wise to spend some time reviewing comments and considering how you intend to act on them. A student who ignores advice from a supervisor would be unwise.

→ Examples of feedback comments and what they mean

Different lecturers use different terms to express similar meanings, and because they work quickly, their handwritten comments are sometimes untidy and may be difficult to interpret. This means that you may need help in deciphering their meaning. Table 24.1 illustrates feedback comments that are frequently made and explains how you should react to obtain better grades in future. This should be viewed with Table 23.3 which explains some proof-reading symbols that lecturers may use. If a particular comment or mark does not make sense to you after reading these tables, then you may wish to approach the marker for an explanation.

Table 24.1 Common types of feedback annotation and how to act in response. Comments in the margin may be accompanied by underlining of word(s), circling of phrases, sentences or paragraphs.

Types of comment and typical examples	Meaning and potential remedial action
REGARDING CONTENT	
Relevance *Relevance?* *Importance?* *Value of example?* *So?*	An example or quotation may not be apt, or you may not have explained its relevance. Think about the logic of your narrative or argument and whether there is a mismatch as implied, or whether you could add further explanation; choose a more appropriate example or quote.
Detail *Give more information* *Example?* *Too much detail/ waffle/padding*	You are expected to flesh out your text with more detail or an example to illustrate your point; or, conversely, you may have provided too much information. It may be that your work lacks substance and you appear to have compensated by putting in too much description rather than analysis, for example.
Specific factual comment or comment on your approach *You could have included . . .* *What about . . . ?* *Why didn't you . . . ?*	Depends on context, but it should be obvious what is required to accommodate the comment.
Expressions of approval *Good!* *Excellent!* ✓ (may be repeated)	You got this right or chose a good example. Keep up the good work!
Expressions of disapproval *Poor* *Weak* *No!* ✗ (may be repeated)	Sometimes obvious, but may not be clear. The implication is that your examples, logic etc. could be improved.

Table 24.1 continued

Types of comment and typical examples	Meaning and potential remedial action
REGARDING STRUCTURE	
Fault in logic or argument *Logic!* *Non sequitur* (does not follow)	Your argument or line of logic is faulty. This may require quite radical changes to your approach to the topic.
Failure to introduce topic clearly *Where are you going with this?*	What is your understanding of the topic? What parameters will confine your discussion? How do you intend to develop this aspect?
Failure to construct a logical discussion *Imbalanced discussion* *Weak on pros and cons*	When you have to compare and contrast in any way, then it is important that you give each element in your discussion equal coverage.
Failure to conclude dissertation or report clearly *So what?*	You have to leave a 'take-home message' that sums up the most salient features of your writing and you should not include new material in this section. This is to demonstrate your ability to think critically and define the key aspects.
Heavy dependency on quotations *Watch out for over-quotation* *Too many quotations*	There is a real danger of plagiarism if you include too many direct quotations from text (**Ch 18**). You have to demonstrate that you can synthesise the information from sources as evidence of your understanding. However, in a subject like English literature or law, quotation may be a key characteristic of writing. In this case, quotation is permitted, provided that it is supported by critical comment.
Move text *Loops and arrows*	Suggestion for changing order of text, usually to enhance the flow or logic.

Table 24.1 continued

Types of comment and typical examples	Meaning and potential remedial action
	REGARDING PRESENTATION
Minor proofing errors *sp.* (usually in margin - spelling) ⋏ (insert material here) _⌐ (break paragraph here) ე (delete this material) *P* (punctuation error)	A (minor) correction is required. Table 23.2 provides more detail of likely proof-reading symbols.
Citations *Reference (required)* *Reference list omitted* *Ref!*	You have not supported evidence, argument or quotation with a reference to the original source. This is important in academic work and if you fail to do it, you may be considered guilty of plagiarism. If you omit a reference list, this will invalidate your work and imply that you have done no specialist reading.
Tidiness *Untidy* *Can't read*	Your document may be difficult to follow because of poor layout, inconsistent numbering of sections, and typos.
Failure to follow recommended format *Please follow departmental template for reports* *Order!*	If the department or school provides a template for the submission of dissertations and reports, then you must follow it. There are good reasons, such as the need to follow professional conventions, especially in sciences; you must conform. If you don't, then your grade may be reduced.

How often will my supervisor read my draft versions?

This is a thorny issue. Supervisors are busy people; they may be supervising students on programmes other than yours. The department may lay down a ruling that limits supervisors to surveying only one draft before submission. Other supervisors may choose to look at a number of versions. If there is a restriction in your department, then you should be sure to optimise the opportunity by submitting a version that is almost complete.

Practical tips for dealing with feedback

Be mentally prepared to learn from the views of your supervisor. You may initially feel that feedback is unfair, harsh or that it misunderstands the approach you were trying to take to the topic. A natural reaction might be to dismiss many of the comments. However, you should recognise that your supervisor probably has a much deeper understanding of the topic than you, and concede that if you want to do well in a subject then you need to gain a better understanding of what makes a good dissertation or project from the academic's point of view.

Always make sure you understand the feedback. Check with fellow students or your supervisor involved if you cannot read the comment or do not understand why it has been made.

Respond to feedback. Make a note of common or repeated errors, even in peripheral topics, so that you can avoid them in later drafts.

GO And now . . .

24.1 Check out your department's assessment criteria for dissertations and reports. As explained above, these may help you interpret feedback and understand how to reach the standard you want to achieve.

24.2 Decide what to do about feedback comments you frequently receive. For instance, does your supervisor always comment about your spelling or grammar; or suggest you should use more examples; or ask for more citations to be included? If so, look at relevant chapters in this book, to see if you can adjust appropriately, or seek assistance from the Academic Support Service in your institution.

24.3 Learn to criticise drafts of your own work. This is equivalent to giving feedback to yourself and is an essential academic skill. Annotate drafts of your own work - this is an important way to refine it and improve its quality. Stages you can adopt when reviewing your written work are discussed in **Ch 23**.

25 Presentation of dissertations and reports

How to follow the appropriate academic conventions

The presentation of your dissertation or report may be assessed directly and it may influence the way the content is marked. This chapter explains how to create a polished submission that follows the established standards of academic writing in your discipline.

Key topics:

→ Overall layout
→ Cover page
→ Main text
→ Citations and references
→ Quotes and formulae
→ Quoting numbers in text
→ Figures and tables

Key terms
Analogy Assignment Citation Legend Qualitative Quantitative Quotation

The quality of your dissertation or project report will be determined by a combination of factors, principally:

- activities that take place *before* you write, such as researching your sources, conducting experiments or analysing the literature;
- the way you express your ideas in writing.

However, directly or indirectly, presentation will make a statement about the overall care you have taken in conducting your analysis and preparing the content. Therefore, the final 'production' phase can influence your overall grading. This chapter provides reminders of what may seem to be the 'cosmetic' details of layout and visual elements, but which, in fact, reflect the professionalism you should attach to your work. If you follow the advice given here, you may be able to improve your grade.

Good presentation involves accuracy, consistency and attention to detail. For this reason it is often associated with editing and proof-reading (**Ch 23** and **Ch 24**). You'll need time to get these aspects right, so when you plan the writing-up process, you should allow for adding this final 'polish' to your work. For a longer assignment, such as a dissertation or project assignment, this could mean trying to complete the content phase at least a couple of days ahead of the submission date.

Why does good presentation matter?

- It may be an element of the assessment.
- It helps the marker understand what you have written.
- It shows you can adopt professional standards in your work.
- It demonstrates you have acquired important skills that will transfer to other subjects and, later, employment.

→ Overall layout

This will depend on the type of academic text you are producing. A dissertation like an essay could have a relatively simple structure: a cover page, the main text and a list of references (see **Ch 18** and **Ch 20**). A project report might be complex, with a title page, abstract, introduction and sections for materials and methods, results, discussion/conclusion and references (see **Ch 18** and **Ch 21**). Layouts for most types of assignment also vary slightly depending on discipline. You should research this carefully before you start to write up, by consulting the course handbook or other regulations.

→ Cover page

This is important to get right because it will create a good first impression. Your department may specify a cover-page design that is required for all submissions. If this is the case, then make sure that you follow the instructions closely, as the layout may have been constructed for a particular purpose. For example, it may aid anonymous marking or provide markers with a standard format for providing feedback (see Figure 25.1 for an example).

If detailed instructions for a cover page are not given, then ensure that you provide the title in the middle of the page. Some preferences are to put your personal details in the top right corner, as in Figure 25.1; other conventions favour a position below the title. The tutor's name is also helpful. The model layout in Figure 25.1 suggests one way to present the essential information neatly and clearly. Keep it simple: a cover sheet with fancy graphics is not generally the convention.

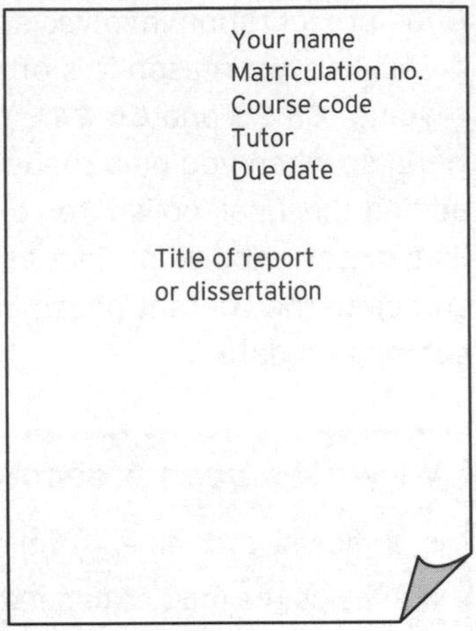

Figure 25.1 A model cover-page layout

→ Main text

Dissertations and project reports are normally word-processed. This gives a professional result and also makes the drafting and editing phases easier. Print on only one side of the paper - this makes it easier to read, and if you make a significant error you may only have to reprint a single sheet.

Font

There are two main choices: serif types, with extra strokes at the end of the main strokes of each letter, and sans serif types, without these strokes (see Figure 25.2). The type to use is usually left to personal preference, but a serif font is said to be easier to read. More likely to be specified is the point size (pt) of the font, which will probably be 11 or 12 point for ease of reading.

Serif font

Times roman 11 pt

Times roman 12 pt

Times roman 14 pt

Sans serif font

Arial 11 pt

Arial 12 pt

Arial 14 pt

Figure 25.2 Examples of the main types of font at different point sizes

You should avoid using elaborate font types as generally they will not help the reader to assimilate what you have written. For the same reason, you should not use too many forms of emphasis. Choose *italics* or **bold** and stick with one only. Symbols are often used in academic work and in Microsoft Word can be added using the 'Insert > Symbol' menu.

Margins

A typical convention is for left-hand margins to be 4 cm and the right-hand margins 2.5 cm. This allows space for the marker's comments and ensures that the text can be read if a left-hand binding is used.

Line spacing

It is easier to read text that is spaced at least at 1.5–2 lines apart. Some markers like to add comments as they read the text and this leaves them space to do so. The exception is where you wish to use long quotations. These should be indented and typed in single-line spacing.

Paragraphs

The key thing to remember about layout is to make good use of the 'white space'. This means that you should lay out your paragraphs clearly and consistently. Some people prefer the indentation method, where the paragraph begins on the fourth character space from the left-hand margin (Figure 25.3a). Others prefer the blocked paragraph

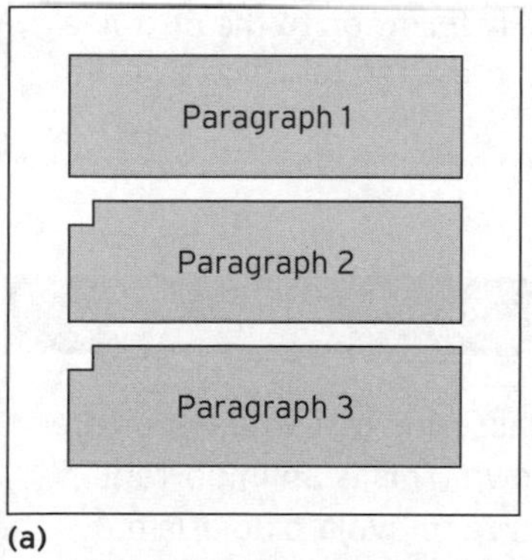

(a)

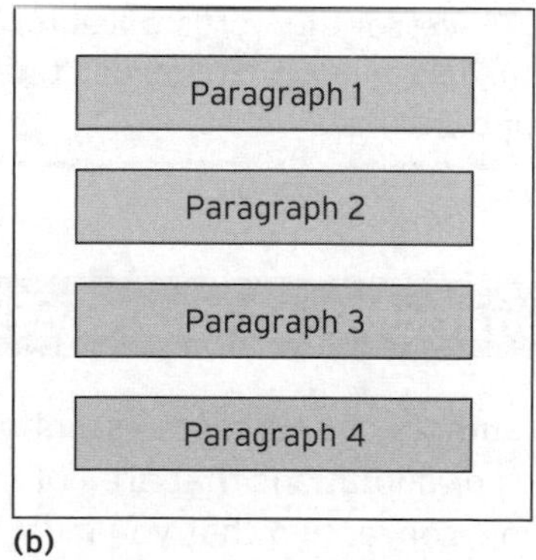

(b)

Figure 25.3 Types of paragraph layout. (a) indented and (b) blocked. Note that in the indented model, by convention the first paragraph in any section is *not* indented.

style, that is, where all paragraphs begin on the left-hand margin but are separated by a double-line space (Figure 25.3b). The space between paragraphs should be roughly equivalent to a missing line. In Microsoft Word these aspects can be controlled using the 'Format > Paragraph' menu.

Sub-headings

In some disciplines use of sub-headings is acceptable or even favoured, though in others these 'signpost' strategies are discouraged. It is best to consult your tutor or course handbook about this if you are uncertain. Sub-headings are usually in bold.

Punctuation

Standard punctuation applies to all types of academic writing (see **Ch 22**).

Word count

You may be asked to work to a word count and tips for doing this are provided in **Ch 25**. If you greatly exceed this limit, this will almost certainly impact on your presentation as you will confront the reader with too much information and will probably not be writing crisply and concisely (see p. 000).

smart tip

Automatic wrapping of text

A point to note for computing novices is that when typing text into a word processor the words will automatically follow on to the next line (wrap). This means that you don't need to press the return key at the end of every line.

→ Citations and references

Citing authors or sources is essential within your text when you refer to ideas or quotations that are not your own. This is an important academic convention that you must observe to avoid plagiarism. Providing a reference list is, therefore, standard practice (see **Ch 18**). A citation is mention of a source in the main body of your text – usually author surname(s) and date of publication and, in some styles, the relevant page(s). The associated reference consists of further details of the source that would, for example, allow the reader to find it in a library.

There are several ways in which citations can be presented, and one of the more common methods is outlined in **Ch 18**. References is usually listed at the end of your text in a separate section, although in some systems they may be positioned at the bottom of the page where the citation occurs. You must be consistent in the referencing style you adopt, and some disciplines impose strict subject-specific conventions. If in doubt, consult your course handbook, institutional regulations or library guidelines.

Examples:

The following is an example of a citation using the Harvard method (see pp. 200-1):

> 'According to Smith (2005), there are three reasons why aardvark tongues are long.'

The following is an example of a reference:

> Smith, J. V., 2005. Investigation of snout and tongue length in the African aardvark *(Orycteropus afer). Journal of Mammalian Research*, 34; 101-32.

→ Quotations and formulae

Quotations and formulae can be integrated into the text when short, but are usually presented as a 'special' type of paragraph when long. In both cases, the source and date of publication are provided after the quotation (see also **Ch 18**).

- **Short quotations** are integrated within the sentence and are placed within single inverted commas. Quotations within the quote are in double inverted commas (Figure 25.4).

> The cultural values identifiable in one minority group create what has been called the 'invisible clamour' (Henze, 1990) as they conflict with those of the dominant culture.

Figure 25.4 How to present a short quotation in text form

- **Long quotations** are usually 30 or more words of prose or more than two lines of poetry. They are indented by five character spaces from the left margin. No quotation marks are necessary unless there are quotation marks used in the text you are quoting (Figure 25.5 and p. 198).

Some disciplines, for example, English Literature and Law, have very specific rules for the way in which quotations are to be laid out and referenced. In such cases, consult your course handbook or ask for guidance from a tutor.

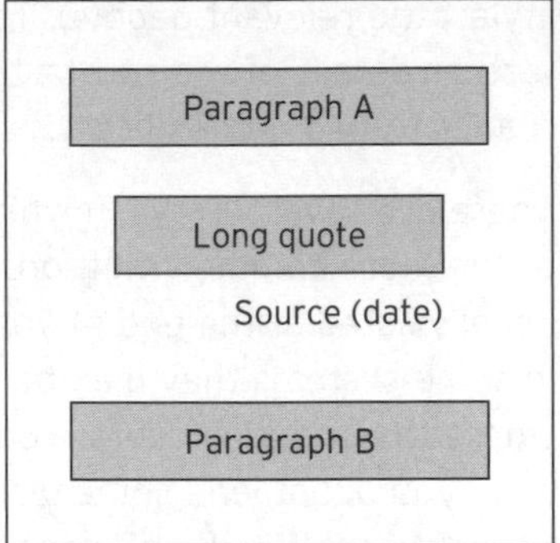

Figure 25.5 How to present a long quote, shown in outline form

Short formulae or equations can be included in text, but they are probably better presented on a separate line and indented, thus

$$\alpha + 4\beta / \eta^2 \pi = 0 \qquad \text{(Eqn. 46.1)}$$

Where a large number of formulae are included, they can be numbered for ease of cross-reference, as shown above.

→ Quoting numbers in text

Adopt the following rules:

- In general writing, spell out numbers from one to ten and use figures for 11 and above; in formal writing, spell out numbers from one to a hundred and use figures beyond this.
- Spell out high numbers that can be written in two words ('six hundred'). With a number like 4,200,000, you also have the choice of writing '4.2 million'.
- Always use figures for dates, times, currency or to give technical details ('5-amp fuse').
- Always spell out numbers that begin sentences, indefinite numbers ('hundreds of soldiers') or fractions ('seven-eighths').
- Hyphenate numbers and fractions appropriately.

→ Figures and tables

You may be expected to support your dissertation or project report with visual material or data, and it is important that you do so in a fashion that best helps the reader to assimilate the information. You must also follow any specific presentational rules that apply in your subject area (see **Ch 16**).

Inserting figures in text

Integrated suites of office-type software allow you to insert the graphs you produced using the spreadsheet program into text produced with the word-processing program. The two programs can even be linked so that changes on the spreadsheet data automatically appear in the graph within the word-processed file. Consult the manual or 'Help' facility to find out how to do this. In MS Word, digital photographs can be inserted using the 'Insert > Picture > From File' command.

Figures

The academic convention is to include a wide range of visual material under the term 'Figure' ('Fig.' for short). This includes graphs, diagrams, charts, sketches, pictures and photographs, although in some disciplines and contexts photographs may be referred to as plates. Here's a set of guidelines to follow when including figures in an assignment:

- All figures should be referred to in the text. There are 'standard' formulations for doing this, such as 'Figure 4 shows that . . .'; or '. . . results for one treatment were higher than for the other (see Fig. 2)'. Find what is appropriate from the literature or texts in your subject area.
- You should always number the figures in the order they are referred to in the text. If you are including the figures within the main body of text (usually more convenient for the reader) then they should appear at the next suitable position in the text after the first time of mention. At the very least this will be after the paragraph that includes the first citation, but more normally will be at the top of the following page.

- Try to position your figures at the top or bottom of a page, rather than sandwiched between blocks of text. This looks neater and makes the text easier to read.
- Each figure should have a legend, which will include the figure number, a title and some text (often a key to the symbols and line styles used). The convention is for figure legends to appear below each figure. Your aim should be to make each figure self-contained. That is, a reader who knows the general subject area should be able to work out what your figure shows, without reference to other material.

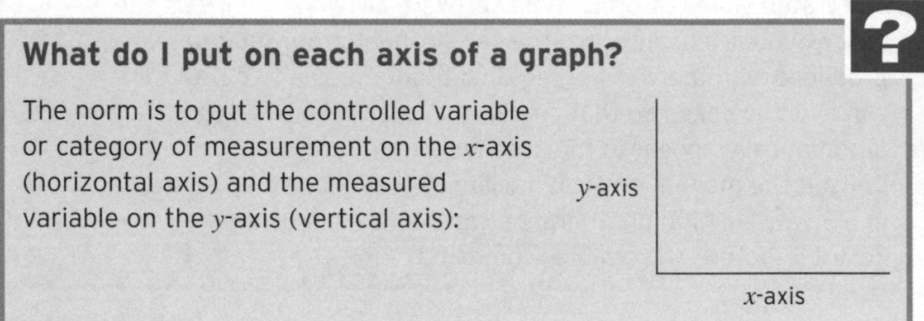

What do I put on each axis of a graph?
The norm is to put the controlled variable or category of measurement on the x-axis (horizontal axis) and the measured variable on the y-axis (vertical axis):
y-axis
x-axis

Choosing the right *type* of figure to display information is an art in itself (**Ch 16**). Although there are technical reasons why some forms of data should be presented in particular ways (for example, proportional data in a pie chart rather than a line chart), your main focus should always be on selecting a method that will best help the reader assimilate the information presented. Jones, Reed and Weyers (2003) or the 'Chart Wizard' in the Microsoft Office Excel spreadsheet program are possible starting points for exploring the range of possibilities.

When presenting individual figures, clarity should be your main aim – ensuring, for example, that the different slices of a pie chart or the lines and symbols in a graph are clearly distinguishable from one another. Consistency is also important, so you should use the same line or shading for the same entity in all your figures (for example, hollow symbols for 'controls'). The widespread availability of colour printers should help with this, but some departments may insist on the use of black and white, since this was the convention when colour printing was prohibitively expensive. If you are using colour, keep it 'tasteful' and remember that certain colour combinations are not easily differentiated by some readers. Take great care to ensure that the quantity plotted and its units are provided for all axes.

Tables

These are used to summarise large amounts of information, especially where a reader might be interested in some of the detail of the data (**Ch 16**). Tables are especially useful for qualitative information but numerical data can also be presented, especially if they relate to a discontinuous qualitative variable (for example, the population sizes and occupation breakdown of various geographical regions).

Tables generally include a number of columns (vertical) and rows (horizontal). By analogy with figures, the convention is to put the controlled or measured variable on the column headers (horizontal) and to place the measured variable or categories of measurement in the rows (vertical). Do not forget to include the units of the information listed if this is relevant.

The rules for presenting tables are very similar to those for figures, with the important exception that a table legend should appear above the table. It is quite common to note exceptions and other information as footnotes to tables.

Figure or table?

In certain cases it may be possible to present the same data set as a figure or as a table. The first rule in such cases is never do both - choose the method that best suits your data and the target reader. An important criterion is to decide which will best help the reader assimilate the information. If the take-home message is best shown visually, then a figure might be best; whereas, if details and numerical accuracy are important, then a table might be more suitable.

Practical tips for presenting your work

Don't let grammatical and stylistic errors spoil your work. It is a waste of effort to concentrate on presentation without also ensuring that you have ironed out minor errors at the review and proof-reading stages (**Ch 23**).

Adopt standard word-processing layout conventions. Adopting the following guidelines will ensure a neat, well-spaced presentation:

- one or two character spaces after the following punctuation – full stop, comma, colon, semicolon, closing inverted commas (double and single), question mark and exclamation mark;
- no character space after apostrophes in a 'medial' position e.g. it's, men's, monkey's;
- no indentation of paragraphs (that is, blocked style);
- one standard line space between paragraphs;
- left-justified text;
- italicised letters for foreign words and titles of books, journals and papers; and
- headings in same font size as text, but bold.

Adopt figure and table styles from the literature. If you have doubts about the precise style or arrangement of figures and tables, follow the model shown in texts or journal articles from your subject area. Also, check whether relevant instructions are published in the course handbook or your regulations.

Don't automatically accept the graphical output from spreadsheets and other programs. These are not always in the 'correct' style. For example, the default output for many charts produced by the Microsoft Office Excel spreadsheet includes a grey background and horizontal gridlines, neither of which is generally used. It is not difficult to alter these parts of the chart, however, and you should learn how to do this from manuals or the 'Help' facility.

GO And now . . .

25.1 Look at previously submitted work to gauge the overall standard or presentation expected. Ask a past student (perhaps someone in your supervisor's research group) whether you can look at their submission, or ask your supervisor whether he or she can show you a past example that was rated highly. Examine this carefully for elements of presentation mentioned in this chapter. Make a note of actions you will need to take to ensure that your submission meets or exceeds the standard you have seen.

25.2 Ensure the highest possible quality of printed output. One aspect of your submission that should under your control is the quality of the print-out that you submit. Choose a higher quality paper than you might otherwise select for drafting. Check printer settings so that the quality is high. If you do not think your own printer is of sufficiently high quality, ask to use a friend's or consider a professional printing service.

25.3 Think ahead regarding binding and other aspects of the 'final' presentation. There may be a requirement for you to bind your dissertation or project report – check this at an early stage. If this is the case, find out about local bindery services, ask how long they will take to complete the job, and make due allowances in your work plan. If binding is not necessary, you may be able to buy a high-quality folder that will enhance the presentation of your work. Visit a good stationery store to find out what the options are.

References and further reading

Bloom, B., Englehart, M., Furst, E., Hill, W. and Krathwohl, D. 1956. *Taxonomy of Educational Objectives: The Classification of Educational Goals. Handbook 1: Cognitive Domain*. New York: Longmans.

Chicago Manual of Style, 15th edn, 2003. Chicago: University of Chicago Press.

Foley, M. and Hall, D., 2003. *Longman Advanced Learner's Grammar*. Harlow: Longman.

Fowler, H. and Winchester, S., 2002. *Fowler's Modern English Usage*. Oxford: Oxford University Press.

Jones, A. M., Reed, R. and Weyers, J. D. B., 2003. *Practical Skills in Biology*, 3rd edn. London: Pearson Education.

Ritter, R. M., 2005. *New Hart's Rules: The Handbook of Style for Writers and Editors*. Oxford: Oxford University Press.

Robson, C., 1997. *Real World Research: A Resource for Social Scientists and Practitioner-researchers*. Oxford: Blackwell.

Sana, L., 2002. *Textbook of Research Ethics: Theory and Practice*. New York: Kluwer Academic.

Shamoo, A. E. and Resnik, D. B., 2003. *Responsible Conduct of Research*. Oxford: Oxford University Press.

Trask, R. L., 2004. *Penguin Guide to Punctuation*. London: Penguin Books.

UK Intellectual Property Office, 2007. Available from **www.ipo.gov.uk**. Last accessed 22/06/07.

University of Dundee, 2005. *Code of Practice on Plagiarism and Academic Dishonesty* [online]. Available from: **http://www.somis.dundee.ac.uk/academic/Plagiarism.htm**. Last accessed 22/06/07.

Glossary of key terms

Terms are defined as used in the higher education context; many will have other meanings elsewhere. A term in **colour** denotes a cross-reference within this list.

Abbreviations:

abbr. = abbreviation

gram. = grammatical term

Latin = a word or phrase expressed in the Latin language, but not 'adopted' into English

pl. = plural

sing. = singular

vb = verb

Abstract The summary of a paper that appears beneath the title and before the main text in a journal article. It provides an overview of the article's key findings.

Acronym (gram.) An abbreviation formed from the first letter of words to form a word in itself, e.g. radar, NATO.

Action research This mode of research involves the practitioner identifying a problem within their work, study or social situation and then setting out to plan and execute a fact-finding study for evaluation. The aim is to find solutions to practical problems.

Aims Statements of intent or purpose that are broad in nature, and hence defined in general terms perhaps relating to an overall outcome (compare with **objectives**).

Alphanumeric Using both letters and numerals in order to classify groups of items.

Analogy A comparison; a similar case from which parallels can be drawn.

Annotate To expand on given notes or text, e.g. to write extra notes on a printout of a PowerPoint presentation or a photocopied section of a book.

Antonym A word opposite in meaning to another.

Argue To make statements or introduce facts to establish or refute a proposition; to discuss and reason.

Assignment Coursework, usually completed in own (i.e. non-contact) time.

ATHENS The program that allows access to the institution's online subscriptions.

Bias A view or description of evidence that is not balanced, promoting one conclusion or viewpoint.

Bibliography A list of all the resources used in preparing for a piece of written work. The bibliography is usually placed at the end of a document. Compare with **Reference list**.

Blurb A piece of writing used as publicity, typically for a book, and appearing on the jacket or cover.

Brainstorm An intensive search for ideas, often carried out and recorded in a free-form or diagrammatic way.

Business report A report produced to provide information that helps decision-making in a commercial context. It often follows a formulaic or 'house' style.

Case study This is an in-depth examination of specific social groups, events, a process, individuals or institutions. Such studies can be quantitative or qualitative.

Causality The notion that one event causes another to occur. A high degree of **Correlation** does not imply causality.

Citation (1) The act of making reference to another source in one's own writing. (2) A passage or a quotation from another source provided word for word within a text. See **References**.

Citing Quoting a reference. See **Citation**.

Colloquial Informal words and phrases used in everyday speech (e.g. slang), and generally inappropriate for formal and academic writing.

Confounding variable An uncontrolled source of error that varies in step or opposition with some other controlled variable. This can give a 'spurious correlation' between the controlled variable and the measured variable, and hence which can lead to erroneous conclusions. See also **Control**.

Control In experiments, a treatment included to check whether a potential **confounding variable** appears to have an effect. For example, if examining the effects of an acidic drug on a response, it might be decided to check for the effects of pH on the response, to demonstrate that effects were due to the drug itself and not its effects on the acidity of the medium.

Copyright A legally enforceable restriction of the copying and publishing of original works, allowing the author(s) or assignee(s) or their agents alone to sell copies.

Correlation The strength and the direction of the relationship between two independent variables.

COSHH (abbr.) Control of Substances Hazardous to Health: UK regulations controlling the use and disposal of harmful substances.

Critical thinking The examination of facts, concepts and ideas in an objective manner. The ability to evaluate opinion and information systematically, clearly and with purpose.

Demographic information Data that relates to changes in population characteristics.

Denominator The lower part of a fraction.

Descriptive statistics Numerical descriptions of a data set, e.g. the average value (mean) of an array of numbers.

Dewey decimal system A library catalogue system that gives each book a numerical code. Compare with **Library of Congress system**.

Digit A single numeral, e.g. 5 in 24057.

Dispersion In statistics, a measure of the spread of values within a data set or frequency distribution, e.g. standard deviation.

Dissertation A formal written study of a specialised subject, usually submitted as part of the assessment for a university degree.

Ebrary Commercial software used to distribute and access electronic documents, such as e-books and e-journals.

Effectiveness Smart working, rather than putting in extra effort without significant impact. This means identifying SMART goals, that is, those that are **S**pecific, **M**easurable, **A**chievable, **R**ealistic and **T**angible.

Efficiency Cutting out wasteful or unproductive effort, and focussing on using your time to maximise productivity.

Ellipsis (gram.) The replacement of words deliberately omitted from the text by three dots, e.g. 'A range of online . . . methods of delivering materials and resources for learning'.

Engineering notation A form of writing numbers where numbers are expressed as powers of 10 divisible by 3, e.g. 10.4×10^3 rather than 1.04×10^4 or 10400.

Error Degree of deviation from a true value, which can be of two types, accuracy or precision. In practice, measurements are often assumed to be accurate (having a mean value close to the true value), and the more important thing to estimate is the precision (how much scatter there is among replicate values).

Error bars Lines extending from a symbol on a graph that indicate a (specified) error of a mean value (or other statistic of location).

Ethics The term 'ethics' in the research context refers to the moral principles, rules and standards of conduct that apply to investigations.

Ethics Committee Panel of academics within a university which considers research proposals in light of the institution's rules for clinical and non-clinical research. There may be at least one committee for each of these types of research.

Exemplify To provide an example of something.

Extrapolation In graphing, the act of creating an assumed line or relationship outside the limits of the available data points, assuming the line will follow trends identified using those points.

Fallacy A logically erroneous argument used in reasoning or debate.

Feedback Written comment on student submission, usually provided in a formative sense, so that improvements can be made.

Finger tracing The act of running your finger immediately below the line of text being read to follow your eyes' path across a page, starting and stopping a word or two from either side.

Focus group Small discussion group (4–6 members is considered ideal), where participants, often people who share a common experience, are asked to comment on an issue or, for business purposes, a product or marketing tool.

Gist The essence of something, e.g. a summary or a list of key ideas from a piece of writing or a talk.

Hypothesis A testable theory (pl. hypotheses).

Hypothesis testing In statistics, a form of analysis that allows a numerical probability to be assigned to the outcomes of a hypothesis.

***Ibid.* (abbr., Latin)** Short for *ibidem*, meaning 'in the same place'; especially used in some referencing systems, e.g. Chicago method, when referring to the immediately previous source mentioned.

Idiom (gram.) A form of language used in everyday speech and understood by native speakers, but whose meaning is not immediately apparent from the actual words used, e.g. to 'pull someone's leg' (make them believe something that is not true).

Indentation In text layout, the positioning of text (usually three to five character spaces in) from the margin to indicate a new paragraph.

Informants In research, this term is taken to mean a person who participates in the research activity by providing data in response to the enquiry method adopted by the researcher.

Information literacy A suite of skills that are required to find, access, analyse, create, evaluate and use information in all its formats, whether in print or online.

Informed consent Consent given based on the sound understanding of the research being undertaken.

Interpolation In graphing, the assumed trend or relationship between adjacent data points. Compare with **Extrapolation**.

Landscape orientation The positioning of paper so that the 'long' side is horizontal. See also **Portrait orientation**.

Learning objective What students should be able to accomplish having participated in a course or one of its elements, such as a lecture, and having carried out any other activities, such as further reading, that are specified. Often closely related to what students should be able to demonstrate under examination.

Learning outcome Similar to a learning objective, often focussing on some product that a student should be able to demonstrate, possibly under examination.

Legend The key to a diagram, chart or graph, e.g. showing which lines and symbols refer to which quantities.

Library of Congress system A library catalogue system that gives each book an alphanumeric code. Compare with **Dewey decimal system**.

Literature survey A report on the literature on a defined area, usually specified in the title. May include the author's independant conclusions based on the sources consulted.

Location In statistics, an estimate of the 'centre' of a data set or frequency distribution, e.g. the mean.

Matched samples In statistics, pairs of individuals chosen for comparison of a key **variable**, but sharing properties relative to known or potential confounding variables. As such, a mechanism for reducing the statistical effects of errors derived from such sources.

Mean In statistics, a measure of location of a **sample** or **population** calculated as the sum of all the data values divided by the number of values.

Median In statistics, a measure of location of a **sample** or **population** calculated as the mid-point of the data values when ranked in numerical order.

Mnemonic An aid to memory involving a sequence of letters or associations, e.g. 'Richard of York goes battling in vain', to remember the colours of the rainbow: red, orange, yellow, green, blue, indigo, violet.

Mode In statistics, a measure of location of a **sample** or **population** calculated as the most common value in a data set.

Moderator Acts as a facilitator in a **Focus Group** by instigating the discussion and ensuring that the conversation is maintained and remains on task.

Noun (gram.) A word denoting a person, place or thing.

Numerator The upper part of a fraction.

Objectives Goals outlined in specific terms and tending to relate to individual, achievable outcomes that are required to achieve the ultimate aim. Ideally objectives will state 'what', 'how', 'where' and 'when' (as appropriate). Some people favour SMART objectives that are **S**pecific, **M**easureable, **A**chievable, **R**ealistic and **T**angible.

Objectivity Having a view or approach based on a balanced consideration of the facts.

***Op. cit.* (abbr., Latin)** Short for *opus citatum*, meaning 'in the place cited'. In some forms of citation this term is used to refer to a previous citation of the same text or article.

Paraphrase To quote ideas indirectly by expressing them in other words.

Perfectionism The personal quality of wanting to produce the best possible product or outcome, sometimes regardless of other factors involved.

Phonetic Relating to the sounds made in speech.

Phrasal verb (gram.) An idiomatic verbal phrase consisting of a verb and adverb or a verb and preposition. See **Idiom**.

Plagiarism Copying the work of others and passing it off as one's own, without acknowledgement.

Population In statistics, the whole group of items that might be part of the study.

Portrait orientation The positioning of paper so that the 'short' side is horizontal. See also **Landscape orientation**.

Premise/premiss A statement or assertion that forms the basis for a position in thought, debate or argument.

Primary source The source in which ideas and data are first communicated.

Prioritising Ranking tasks in precedence, taking into account their urgency and importance.

Pronoun (gram.) A word that may replace a noun: I, you, he, she, it, we, they. For example, 'Traffic lights are red, green and amber. *They* light in a particular sequence.'

Proof In science, evidence that indicates a hypothesis is true. The word 'proof' should be used cautiously when applied to quantitative research – the term implies 100 per cent certainty, whereas this is very rarely justified owing to the ambiguity inherent in statistical analysis and experimental design.

Propaganda Skewed or biased reporting of the facts to favour a particular outcome or point of view.

Proposal For a dissertation or research project, a document outlining the scope and methods of the research you intend to carry out and, in some cases, indicating how you plan to organise your writing.

Provenance The history of a valued object or work of art or literature; a record of the ultimate derivation and passage of an item through its various owners.

Qualitative Data (information) that cannot be expressed in numbers, e.g. the colour of the lecturer's tie or the quality of life of elderly patients.

Quantitative Data (information) that can be expressed in numbers, e.g. the width of the lecturer's tie or the number of elderly patients included in a survey.

Question probes A style of question that encourages participants to develop the discussion further. For example, the researcher might ask, 'Could you expand on that point a little further?' or 'What do you mean by x?'.

Question prompts Prepared questions that are designed to direct the Focus Group's attention to the areas of discussion that are of interest to the researcher's purpose.

Quotation Words directly lifted from a source, e.g. a journal article or book, usually placed between inverted commas (quotation marks), i.e. '. . .' or '. . .'.

Reciprocal In mathematics, the inverse (i.e. one divided by the quantity in question). For example, the reciprocal of 2 is $^1/_2 = 0.5$.

Reference list A list of sources referred to in a piece of writing, usually provided at the end of the document. Compare with **Bibliography**.

Register (gram.) The style of language and grammar used in written or spoken form as appropriate to the context, often distinguishing formal from informal usage, for example.

Respondent An individual providing answers to a questionnaire or survey.

Rhetorical question A question asked as part of a talk or written work where an answer from the audience or reader is not required or expected, and indeed where the answer is usually subsequently provided by the speaker or author. Used as a device to direct the attention and thoughts of the audience or reader, e.g. 'Why is this important? I'll tell you why . . .'

Rounding The process of truncating a number to give the appropriate number of significant figures.

Sample In statistics, a sub-set of individuals from a specific **population**.

Scientific method The scientific approach to a problem, involving the creation of a hypothesis and testing it using evidence obtained in experiments or by observation.

Scientific notation A form of writing numbers where they are expressed as powers of 10, e.g. 1.04×10^4 rather than 10400.

Scientific report A report on a piece of scientific observation or experiment that follows a generic format, with subdivisions (e.g. abstract, introduction, materials and methods, etc.) in a particular order.

Secondary source A source that quotes, adapts, interprets, translates, develops or otherwise uses information drawn from **primary sources**.

Significant figure (s.f.) The number of digits in a number, counting from the first non-zero digit and including any final zeros.

SI system SI is the abbreviated form of **Système International d'Unités** - an internationally agreed metric system of units based on the metre (m), kilogram (kg) and second (s), and with specific conventions for denoting both the units (with symbols) and very large and small quantities (with **prefixes**).

Subjectivity Having a view or approach based on a personal opinion, not necessarily taking a balanced account of all the facts.

Summative assessment An exam or course assessment exercise that counts towards the final module or degree mark. Generally, no formal feedback is provided. See **Formative assessment**.

Superscript Text, including numerals, above the line of normal text, usually in a smaller font, e.g. ^{2}. Contrast with subscript, which is text or numerals below the line, thus $_a$.

Supervisor The academic who takes overall responsibility for a student as they conduct their research according to the agreed proposal outline.

Synonym (gram.) A word with the same meaning as another.

Syntax (gram.) The way words are used (in their appropriate grammatical forms), especially with respect to their connection and relationships within sentences.

Système International d'Unités (SI) The internationally agreed metre-kilogramme-second system of units used in most branches of the sciences.

Terminator paragraph (gram.) The paragraph that brings a piece or section of writing to an ending or conclusion.

Thesis (1) A written piece of work discussing a piece of research and submitted for assessment as part of a degree, often bound. (2) An intellectual proposition; a theory, concept or idea.

Tic (or tick) mark Graduation marks along a graph axis.

Topic An area within a study; the focus of a title in a written assignment.

Topic paragraph The paragraph, usually the first, that indicates or points to the topic of a section or piece of writing and how it can be expected to develop.

Topic sentence The sentence, usually the first, that indicates or points to the topic of a paragraph and how it can be expected to develop.

Typo (abbr.) Short for typographical error - a typing mistake or, less commonly, a typesetting error.

Value judgement A statement that reflects the views and values of the speaker or writer rather than the objective reality of what is being assessed or considered.

Variable A mathematical quantity that can take different values in different cases.

Verb (gram.) The 'doing' word(s) in a sentence. A part of speech by which action or state of being is indicated, serving to connect a subject with a predicate. A verb also shows, for example, time shifts by changes in tense, e.g. past, present or future.

Verbatim From Latin, meaning word for word, e.g. verbatim notes are word-for-word copies (transcriptions) of a lecture or text.

Wikipedia Said to be the world's biggest multilingual free-content encyclopaedia on the Internet; written collaboratively by volunteers. Most of the articles can be edited by anyone with access to the Internet. As such, the content is not regarded as being wholly reliable.

Work placement A period of study conducted in the workplace, carrying out work relevant to the course or degree programme and possibly assessed via reports and reflective summaries.

Writer's block The inability to structure thoughts; in particular, the inability to start the act of writing when this is required.